THE NEXUS OF ECONOMICS, SECURITY, AND INTERNATIONAL RELATIONS IN EAST ASIA

THE NEXUS OF ECONOMICS, SECURITY, AND INTERNATIONAL RELATIONS IN EAST ASIA

Edited by Avery Goldstein and Edward D. Mansfield

Stanford Security Studies
An Imprint of Stanford University Press
Stanford, California

Stanford University Press
Stanford, California

Printed in the United States of America on acid-free, archival-quality paper

Library of Congress Cataloging-in-Publication Data

The nexus of economics, security, and international relations in East Asia / edited by Avery Goldstein and Edward D. Mansfield.
    pages cm
Includes bibliographical references and index.
ISBN 978-0-8047-8273-9 (cloth : alk. paper)—ISBN 978-0-8047-8274-6 (pbk. : alk. paper)
    1. Security, International—Economic aspects—East Asia.   2. Security, International—East Asia.   3. East Asia—Foreign economic relations.   4. East Asia—Foreign relations.   I. Goldstein, Avery, editor of compilation.   II. Mansfield, Edward D., editor of compilation.
    JZ6009.E18N49 2012
    355′.033095—dc23

                                                                    2011052149

Special discounts for bulk quantities of Stanford Security Studies are available to corporations, professional associations, and other organizations. For details and discount information, contact the special sales department of Stanford University Press. Tel: (650) 736-1782, Fax: (650) 736-1784

Typeset by Newgen in 10/14 Minion

To the Memory of Christopher H. Browne

Contents

Illustrations

Tables

Figures

Acknowledgments

THE CHAPTERS IN THIS BOOK GREW OUT OF TWO CONFERENCES sponsored by the University of Pennsylvania's Christopher H. Browne Center for International Politics. The first was held in Philadelphia; the second was held in Beijing. We are very grateful to a distinguished set of discussants at these conferences whose insightful comments and suggestions were extremely valuable. These individuals include Liu Xuecheng, Michael Mastanduno, Patrick McDonald, Evan Medeiros, Robert Ross, Etel Solingen, Wang Yizhou, Zha Daojiong, and Zhang Qingmin. We are especially grateful to Etel Solingen for discussing the entire manuscript at the latter conference. We also wish to thank the other conference participants and two anonymous reviewers for helpful comments on the chapters. In Beijing, the China Foundation for International and Strategic Studies provided support for which we are grateful. We also owe a tremendous debt to Sarah Salwen, Munan Lü, Kaija Schilde, Ryan Grauer, and Matt Tubin for their extraordinary efforts in organizing these conferences and preparing this book. Sarah Salwen and Joseph Lin provided extensive editorial assistance.

Brief versions of the chapters included in this volume appeared in the summer 2011 issue of *Global Asia*. We are grateful to Chung-in Moon, the journal's editor in chief, and David Plott, the managing editor, for their interest in this project. The material included in Taylor Fravel's chapter also appears in *Asian Security*, volume 7, issue 3, and is reprinted here by permission of Taylor &

Francis Ltd. We are also very grateful to Geoffrey Burn, Jessica Walsh, and the other talented individuals at Stanford University Press, who have done a marvelous job preparing and producing this volume.

Contributors

Benjamin J. Cohen is Louis G. Lancaster Professor of International Political Economy at the University of California, Santa Barbara. He has held positions at the Federal Reserve Bank of New York, Princeton University, and the Fletcher School of Law and Diplomacy. His research focuses on international monetary and financial relations. His recent books include *International Political Economy: An Intellectual History* and *Global Monetary Governance.*

Danielle F. S. Cohen is a Ph.D. candidate in the Department of Government at Cornell University. Her research interests include East Asian strategic relations, Sino-Japanese relations, and international political economy.

M. Taylor Fravel is an associate professor of political science and member of the Security Studies Program at the Massachusetts Institute of Technology. His research focuses on international relations, with a particular emphasis on international security, China, and East Asia. He is the author of *Strong Borders, Secure Nation: Cooperation and Conflict in China's Territorial Disputes.*

Avery Goldstein is David M. Knott Professor of Global Politics and International Relations, professor of political science, director of the Center for the Study of Contemporary China, and associate director of the Christopher H. Browne Center for International Politics at the University of Pennsylvania, as well as a senior fellow at the Foreign Policy Research Institute in Philadelphia. He specializes in international relations, security studies, and Chinese politics. His publications include *Rising to the Challenge: China's Grand Strategy* *and International Security; Deterrence and Security in the 21st Century: China, Britain, France and the Enduring Legacy of the Nuclear Revolution;* and *From Bandwagon to Balance of Power Politics: Structural Constraints and Politics in China, 1949–1978.*

Michael C. Horowitz is an associate professor of political science at the University of Pennsylvania. His research interests include the intersection of religion and international relations, the role of leaders in international politics, and international security issues in East Asia. His publications include *The Spread of Military Power: Causes and Consequences for International Politics.*

Miles Kahler is Rohr Professor of Pacific International Relations at the School of International Relations and Pacific Studies and professor of political science at the University of California, San Diego. His research interests include international institutions and global governance, the evolution of the nation-state, multilateral strategies toward failed states, and the political economy of international finance. Among his recent publications are *Territoriality and Conflict in an Era of Globalization* and *Governance in a Global Economy.*

Jonathan Kirshner is a professor of government and director of the Reppy Institute for Peace and Conflict Studies, as well as coeditor of the book series Cornell Studies in Money. His research focuses on the political economy of national security and the politics of money. His recent publications include *Appeasing Bankers: Financial Caution on the Road to War* and *The Future of the Dollar.*

Edward D. Mansfield is Hum Rosen Professor of Political Science, chair of the Department of Political Science, and director of the Christopher H. Browne Center for International Politics at the University of Pennsylvania. His research focuses on international relations, international political economy, and international security. His publications include *Power, Trade, and War; Electing to Fight: Why Emerging Democracies Go to War* (with Jack Snyder); and *Votes, Vetoes, and the Political Economy of International Trade Agreements* (with Helen V. Milner).

Wu Xinbo is a professor, deputy director of the Center for American Studies, and associate dean for the School of International Relations and Public Affairs at Fudan University. His research interests include China's foreign and security policy, Sino-U.S. relations, and Asia-Pacific politics and security. He has published widely in both Chinese- and English-language journals and edited volumes, and he has been a visiting fellow at Stanford University's Asia-Pacific Research Center, the Henry Stimson Center, and the Brookings Institution in Washington, DC.

Yuan Peng is the director of the Institute of American Studies at the China Institutes of Contemporary International Relations. He conducts research on U.S. foreign policy, Sino-American relations, cross-strait relations, and East Asian and Pacific security studies. His latest books include *China-U.S. Relations: A Strategic Analysis* and *American Think Tanks and Their Attitudes Towards China*. Yuan was a visiting scholar at the Atlantic Council and a senior fellow at the Center for Northeast Asian Policy Studies of the Brookings Institution.

Zhang Tuosheng is the director of the Department of Research and a senior fellow at the China Foundation for International and Strategic Studies. Formerly an officer in the People's Liberation Army, Zhang was posted to the United Kingdom in the early 1990s as the deputy defense attaché. His main research interests are Sino-American relations, Sino-Japanese relations, Asia-Pacific security, and Chinese foreign policy.

THE NEXUS OF ECONOMICS, SECURITY, AND INTERNATIONAL RELATIONS IN EAST ASIA

1 The Political Economy of Regional Security in East Asia

Avery Goldstein and Edward D. Mansfield

EAST ASIA HAS EXPERIENCED MORE THAN THREE DECADES OF peace and prosperity, a sharp contrast with the recurrent wars and lagging development that plagued much of the region during earlier eras. The last major military conflict, the Sino-Vietnamese War, ended in 1979. Although skirmishes between the antagonists were not completely extinguished until the 1980s, the year 1979 marked the beginning of a clear secular decline in militarized conflict that has continued through the present (see Figures 1.1 and 1.2).[1] That year also marked the start of sweeping economic reforms initiated under Deng Xiaoping's leadership in China. China's reforms, however, were only the most widely publicized among various efforts at economic liberalization throughout the region since the late twentieth century. These policy shifts have enabled many East Asian countries to share in a newfound prosperity that had previously taken root in Japan and in the so-called four tigers. Yet this era of peace and growth has been punctuated by periodic reminders of enduring security problems in the region. Do these security problems pose a threat to East Asia's record of economic success? Or do economic success and the greater levels of international economic cooperation that have accompanied it provide a foundation for political cooperation and the management of security problems? The contributors to this volume shed new light on these important questions.

Three broad approaches to thinking about economics and security in East Asia can be identified. One approach views the region's growing economic

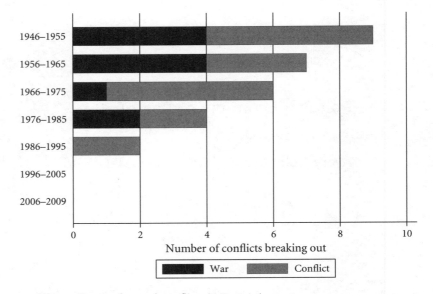

FIGURE 1.1 Onset of armed conflicts in East Asia, 1946–2009
SOURCE: Uppsala Conflict Data Program, Peace Research Institute Oslo, UCDP/PRIO Armed Conflict Dataset, available at http://www.prio.no/CSCW/Datasets/Armed-Conflict/ (accessed August 23, 2010).
NOTE: East Asia = ASEAN+5 (China, Hong Kong, Japan, South Korea, and Taiwan).

prosperity as a result of the peace that has prevailed. In an international setting fraught with fewer political tensions, nations could focus resources on domestic development and enjoy the fruits of international trade and investment with countries whose prosperity they no longer viewed through the prism of military rivalry. In this approach, what needs to be explained is the peaceful context that has provided the opportunity for economic activity to thrive. Explanations for this peace often point to the power and leadership of the United States. As the Soviet Union declined and then collapsed, the United States stood as the sole superpower. American preponderance not only mutes potential security rivalries among its allies but also serves as a hedge against future uncertainty over new military threats that might emerge. Consequently, East Asian countries can refrain from deploying the kinds of forces that they might otherwise need to cope with the possibility of conflicts with a resurgent Russia or an increasingly powerful China.

America's relationship with China has also contributed to peace in the region. During the 1980s, Sino-American cooperation rested on a common

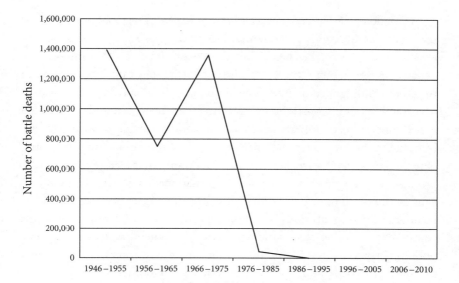

FIGURE 1.2 Battle deaths from armed conflicts in East Asia, 1946–2009

SOURCE: Uppsala Conflict Data Program, Peace Research Institute Oslo, UCDP/PRIO Armed Conflict Dataset, available at http://www.prio.no/CSCW/Datasets/Armed-Conflict/ (accessed August 23, 2010).

NOTE: East Asia = ASEAN+5 (China, Hong Kong, Japan, South Korea, and Taiwan).

interest in counterbalancing the Soviet Union's assertive foreign policy. But even following the collapse of the Soviet Union, and despite the outbreak of some serious political and economic disagreements between China and the United States, the latter two countries managed to sustain a largely cooperative working relationship. Absent a common adversary, their overlapping interests in coping with problems of proliferation, terrorism, and the dangers of instability on the Korean Peninsula helped prolong a constructive U.S.-China relationship initiated during the closing decades of the Cold War. Although some analysts suggested that China's rise would undermine Sino-American cooperation and perhaps jeopardize regional peace, the yawning disparity between Chinese and U.S. capabilities minimized concerns about the countries' shifting power and enabled both states to focus mainly on the absolute, rather than the relative, gains they derived from bilateral cooperation. In short, one approach is to suggest that American power and the ability of the United States and China to avoid an adversarial relationship have sustained a peaceful international context conducive to regional economic prosperity.

A second approach views peace as stemming from regional prosperity, or more accurately, from the economic activity that generates prosperity. The logic is discussed further below, but centers on the claim that interdependence between trade partners establishes benefits that would be scuttled in the event of military conflict. Participation in international economic institutions reinforces this constraint by clarifying these benefits and the associated opportunity costs of military conflict. Institutional participation also socializes elites to embrace transnational perspectives; in national policy debates, parochial perspectives are then less likely to prevail, thus facilitating the compromises that are necessary to sustain international cooperation and to prevent conflicts from escalating to the use of force. Aside from participation in international institutions, overseas commerce itself creates and sustains common interests between economic partners and encourages a more cosmopolitan perspective conducive to the peaceful adjudication of international disputes. Finally, economic exchange reshapes the domestic political landscape of the participating countries, thereby empowering those segments of society whose interests are served by a foreign policy that avoids disruptive military conflict.

A third approach is skeptical that peace in East Asia is linked to economic activity. As has often been noted, extensive economic interdependence and strong elite ties across the major European states in the early twentieth century failed to halt the slide to World War I. Other skeptics go further still and consider East Asia's current period of peace and prosperity a brief respite from the normal pattern of interstate rivalry or perhaps even a mirage misleading analysts who fail to appreciate the looming dangers of military conflict and economic disruption. Such views typically draw on the Western, mainly European, historical experience and suggest that Asia's future may well be Europe's bloody past.

Even analysts who had become optimistic about Europe's peaceful future in the immediate aftermath of the Cold War argued that the basis for such optimism was absent in East Asia. Multilateral institutions that evolved in Europe over the era since World War II had provided a trellis first for economic and then for security cooperation that had no parallel in East Asia. In the early 1990s, Aaron Friedberg (1993–1994: 22) famously drew a sharp contrast between the "rich 'alphabet soup'" of regional organizations in Europe and the "thin gruel" of such organizations in Asia. Moreover, Europe had forthrightly addressed many troubling historical legacies that had repeatedly generated conflict on the continent, as well as more recent sources of antagonism. By contrast, East Asia seemed a region still rife with such problems—competing territorial claims, divided states, and lingering historical grievances (especially toward Japan), all fueled by the heated nationalist sentiment of newly emerging, newly independent, or recently reviving states. For those subscribing to this dark vision, East Asia's story of economic prosperity was not just about rising living standards; it was equally about the accumulation of national resources that would sooner or later fuel military capabilities harnessed to competing national interests.

Such concerns notwithstanding, East Asia's peace and prosperity endures. If the existing evidence remains inconsistent with the pessimists' expectations, is that because their theories about the links between economics and security on which they base their predictions are flawed? Are there assessments of East Asia that are more solidly grounded in theories that identify connections between economics and security? More generally, how useful is the existing tool kit of international relations theories for explaining East Asia's recent peace and prosperity?

Any particular theory explains only a slice of reality by setting aside many of the details and some of the causes that produce observable outcomes. A more comprehensive understanding of historical or contemporary events requires tapping various theories and the partial insight that each offers. Consequently, when the authors of the chapters in this volume examine the nexus of economic and security relations in East Asia, they usefully draw on a rich variety of theoretical approaches that can illuminate important questions about a region whose significance for students of both international political economy and international security has grown dramatically over the past thirty years. Their work suggests, in various ways, that the interaction of economic and security concerns defies simply categorizing either as the independent variable (cause) and the other as the dependent variable (effect). To grasp the reasons for, and evaluate the durability of, East Asia's recent peace and prosperity, both economic and security fundamentals matter; the chapters here explore how they matter and, where possible, the extent to which existing theories explain why.

The remainder of this introduction provides some general background for the more focused chapters that follow. First, we set forth evidence that demonstrates the growth of economic regionalism in East Asia, comparing the current era with the recent past in the region and drawing some limited comparisons with evidence from the European experience. Second, we clarify the security issues whose links with regional economic developments our authors examine. Third, we briefly discuss leading theories that claim to offer explanations for the connection between economic and security affairs in international politics. Fourth, we discuss the prominence of China in many of the chapters, even as the volume addresses East Asia as a region. We conclude by describing the organization of the volume and by offering a preview of the perspectives in the chapters that follow.

The Growth of Economic Activity in East Asia

Over the course of the past thirty years, there has been a substantial rise in the amount of cross-border economic activity in East Asia. To illustrate this growth, we present some data drawn from the economies in East Asia: the ten Association of Southeast Asian Nations (ASEAN) states (Brunei Darussalam, Cambodia, Indonesia, Laos, Malaysia, Myanmar, the Philippines, Singapore, Thailand, and Vietnam), China, Hong Kong, Japan, South Korea, and Taiwan. Figure 1.3 shows the ratio of international trade among these countries to the total trade that they conducted for each year from 1979, when economic reform started gaining traction throughout the region, until 2009.[2] In 1979, roughly one-third of the trade these states conducted was intraregional, a value that spiked to about one-half by 2009. China has played a leading role in this rise. In 1979, about 10 percent of intra–East Asian trade stemmed from foreign commerce involving China; by 2009, the value exceeded 30 percent.

Figure 1.3 also reports the annual flow of trade from East Asian countries to the United States, the European Union, and Latin America, respectively, as a percentage of the total overseas commerce conducted by East Asian states. Clearly, the surge in intra–East Asian trade is not matched by East Asian trade with other key partners. States in the region have experienced no noticeable change in the amount of foreign commerce with the European Union and Latin America. Over the past decade, they have experienced a rather pronounced dip in trade with the United States.

In addition to trade, foreign direct investment (FDI) within East Asia has risen precipitously. Figure 1.4 shows the yearly stock of FDI emanating from East Asian home countries and located in host countries in the region as a percentage of total outward FDI by East Asian states. There is ample evidence that, over the past three decades, these states have located an increasing

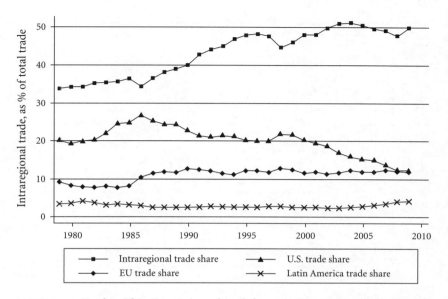

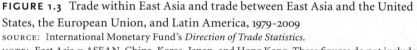

FIGURE 1.3 Trade within East Asia and trade between East Asia and the United States, the European Union, and Latin America, 1979-2009

SOURCE: International Monetary Fund's *Direction of Trade Statistics*.

NOTE: East Asia = ASEAN, China, Korea, Japan, and Hong Kong. These figures do not include Taiwan because it is not possible to obtain reliable data on Taiwanese trade before 1990.

amount of their foreign investment within East Asia. Indeed, the percentage of total outward East Asian FDI located in the region tripled, rising from about 20 percent in 1980 to roughly 60 percent by 2005.

Over the past thirty years, there has also been a dramatic increase in the number of economic institutions designed to promote and regulate trade, investment, and finance in East Asia. Only a few such institutions existed in 1980; currently, there are a few dozen. Moreover, plans are afoot to launch even more. China, Japan, and South Korea have each explored the possibility of forming a free-trade area (FTA) with members of ASEAN, the region's most important institution. Various East Asian countries have expressed interest in concluding a regionwide free-trade zone that would encompass not only China, Japan, South Korea, and ASEAN, but also Hong Kong, and Taiwan. More generally, policy makers throughout East Asia have commented on the desirability of forming additional economic institutions in the region. In 2005, for example, Indonesian Finance Minister Jusuf Anwar commented that

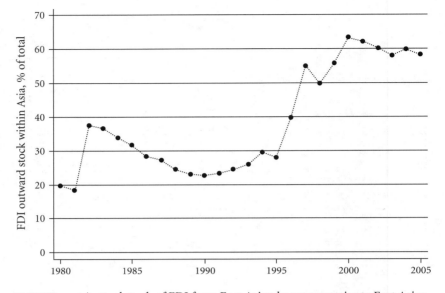

FIGURE 1.4 Annual stock of FDI from East Asian home countries to East Asian host countries as a percentage of total East Asian FDI, 1980–2005
SOURCE: Collected and compiled by Witold Henisz at the Wharton School of the University of Pennsylvania, from the UN Conference on Trade and Development and the Organisation for Economic Co-operation and Development.

East Asian integration should be promoted by "weaving a web of bilateral and multilateral FTAs" (*Nikkei Weekly* 2005).

The growth in economic activity within East Asia is impressive, even when compared to Western Europe, which sets the standard for regional economic integration. As shown in Table 1.1, both East Asia and the European Community (EC/EU) doubled the amount of intraregional trade as a percentage of total trade between 1960 and 2009.[3] To be sure, in any given year, the ratio of intraregional trade to total trade was anywhere from 10 percent to 60 percent greater for the Western European countries than for the East Asian states. Moreover, the value of total trade and intraregional trade conducted by EC/EU members far outstrips that conducted by East Asian states. Nonetheless, trade within East Asian has grown very rapidly in recent decades. There has also been a rise in investment; efforts at financial cooperation; and the establishment of institutions designed to promote economic cooperation in the region, a trend vividly illustrated in the chapter by Wu Xinbo.

TABLE 1.1 Intraregional trade as a percentage of total trade in East Asia and Western Europe, 1960–2009

Year	ASEAN+4	EC/EU
1960	25.66	32.65
1970	30.30	46.36
1980	34.28	42.73
1990	40.14	51.63
2000	48.12	53.35
2009	49.99	60.47

SOURCE: International Monetary Fund's *Direction of Trade Statistics*.
NOTE: ASEAN+4 = ASEAN, China, Korea, Japan, and Hong Kong. These figures do not include Taiwan because it is not possible to obtain reliable data on Taiwanese trade before 1990.

Security Issues

Over the past thirty years, East Asia has experienced rapid growth in intra-regional economic activity. It has also experienced a marked reduction in political-military conflict. No regional wars have broken out since 1979, and although isolated incidents have occurred, until the early 2011 border clashes between Thailand and Cambodia, there had been a complete absence of serious interstate military conflicts since 1988. Figure 1.1 shows the frequency of wars and conflicts in the region since 1946, based on data collected by the Peace Research Institute Oslo (PRIO). Following PRIO, we define wars as interstate and extrasystemic hostilities (i.e., disputes between a nation-state and a nonstate actor located outside of the nation-state) that generate at least one thousand battle deaths annually.[4] Conflicts are defined as interstate and extrasystemic disputes that yield between 25 and 999 fatalities per year. Both wars and conflicts have steadily declined over the post–World War II era. And, as is shown in Figure 1.2, battle deaths in the region declined precipitously once the Sino-Vietnamese War concluded in 1979. Indeed, for nearly a quarter of a century, no one had perished in formal military combat.

Is the recent expansion of economic activity in East Asia causally related to the reduction in political-military hostilities, or is this relationship spurious? Alternative explanations are readily available. Perhaps disputes in the region have simply failed to rise to the level of intensity that prompts states to choose war over diplomacy. Perhaps the robustness of military capabilities (including the ominous presence of nuclear weapons) and alliances that tie the U.S. military to key states in East Asia have discouraged recourse to the large-scale use of force. In short, other causes may account for the durability of the East Asian peace or may reinforce the pacifying effects of economic causes. The chapters in this volume begin to sort out the relevance of economics for regional security. They also touch on related questions. To the extent that economic causes have been a force for peace, how likely is it that this salutary effect will continue? Do current economic developments in the region, separately or in combination with other trends, provide grounds for optimism about an enduring peace? Or do those trends provide reasons for concern that the economic foundation for the thirty-year peace is weakening or that economic problems may even emerge instead as a source of conflict that could increase the likelihood of war in the future?

Although East Asia has been free of major war since 1979, it has not been free of interstate disputes, including conflicts marked by the use of military force. Peace, in other words, has not meant absolute security for the countries in the region, despite the remarkable diminution in the frequency and intensity of military conflict and crises. Most notably, although the Korean armistice has held, small-scale military incidents on the peninsula and in the nearby seas have occurred both before and after 1979. These, along with the tensions triggered by North Korea's nuclear weapons program since 1993, serve as reminders of the continuing potential for larger military conflict. The troubling security concerns on the Korean Peninsula, however, are not closely linked to the changes that have characterized the rest of East Asia over the past three decades. Pyongyang has stubbornly resisted suggestions that it follow the example of China and others to reform and open up its economy; in many ways it stands as a singular exception to the broader pattern. Perhaps most telling, security concerns on the Korean Peninsula have not served as a wedge in exacerbating conflicts of interest among the other East Asian states. On the contrary, the shared interest in preserving the peaceful regional environment conducive to international economic activity has led others to focus on containing instability in Korea and to work hard to minimize the risk of escalation to military action.[5]

Beyond Korea, however, there are other signs of continuing international insecurity, even as peace prevails and economic interactions deepen. One of the most prominent features of the region's security landscape is the presence of ongoing disputes about sovereignty claims, a topic addressed in the chapter by Zhang Tuosheng. Although most of the land-based territorial disputes in East Asia have been resolved, significant disagreements remain about a wide variety of maritime claims and claims to territories that lie across the sea from the principals. These disputes are not just about historical sovereignty but also about contemporary economic interests. China and Japan contest energy-rich patches of the East China Sea. Japan and Korea have not yet resolved their occasionally heated dispute about the islands known as Dokdo in Korea and Takeshima in Japan, which has implications for economic resource rights. Indonesia, Vietnam, Malaysia, Brunei, the Philippines, Taiwan, and China disagree about overlapping claims to territory, waters, and resource rights in the South China Sea, where some expect to find significant energy reserves. And because the United States is allied with Japan, Korea, and the Philippines, and has been cultivating a closer relationship with Vietnam, conflicts rooted in most of these East Asian maritime disputes carry the potential for escalation and for drawing in the world's most powerful states.[6] Thus far, the parties to these disputes have managed to contain the potential for military conflict by delaying the resolution of sovereignty claims and focusing instead on ways to permit ongoing economic activity.

The continuing tensions between China and Taiwan represent another East Asian conflict that has linked economic and security dimensions as well as the potential to involve the United States. China upholds a long-standing claim to sovereignty over Taiwan and the smaller islands administered by the government of the Republic of China (ROC) in Taipei. Although the United States no longer has a security treaty with (or even recognizes) the ROC, in 1979 the U.S. Congress passed the Taiwan Relations Act (TRA). The act asserted a continuing American interest in the island's fate, indicated that the United States might intervene in the event of military conflict in the Taiwan Strait, and established the basis for subsequent decisions to sell defensive weapons to the authorities in Taipei. Although the TRA's original assertion of a continuing American interest in Taiwan's fate reflected the history of political ties between Washington and the ruling party in Taipei, as Taiwan's economy soared after 1979, it became an important economic partner for the United States and its allies in East Asia. Perhaps more intriguing in light of this volume's theme, the interplay of economic and security interests has increasingly been reflected in the relationship between China and Taiwan. Despite their ongoing dispute about sovereignty and continued preparation for the possibility of military conflict in the strait separating them, Taiwan and China have experienced a boom in their economic relationship. The extensiveness and deepening of these ties has led them to sign the Economic Cooperation Framework Agreement, which institutionalizes their thickening network of economic relations and is likely to simplify Taiwan's ability manage economic activity, not only with the Chinese mainland but also with the vast majority of countries that no longer formally recognize the ROC government in Taipei (Richburg 2010).[7]

Intertwined with the varied territorial claims noted above are significant disagreements about the maritime rights defined by the international law of the sea. Most notably, China's decision to define its national security interests as extending to areas that other countries view as zones in which contiguous states have exclusive economic rights but not the right to exclude other countries' ships or aircraft has generated conflicts between China and the United States (Dutton 2010). Thus far, incidents growing out of these conflicts, especially disputes about the right of innocent passage by vessels that may be undertaking surveillance activities, have been contained. But the fundamentally different perspectives in Beijing and Washington make clear that, short of war, a crisis that develops from each side's insistence on its principled position and testing of the other party's resolve risks dangerous military escalation.[8]

Clearly, maritime disputes loom large in thinking about the way in which economics and security in East Asia condition each other. Economic interests in sustaining a peaceful regional context for development may dampen territorial and sovereignty disputes at sea before they escalate to the use of military force. Is it possible, however, that the economic costs of war fighting for the major states in East Asia are so high that some will believe that it is safe to press their maritime claims without fear of escalation? If so, then a corollary to the East Asian peace may be that it does not preclude the possibility of crises and perhaps even limited conflicts in which military power remains relevant.[9]

East Asian states have certainly demonstrated a keen interest in maintaining the military capabilities necessary to protect their political and economic interests. Some of these capabilities are familiar sorts of weapons systems necessary for power projection on, under, and above the seas to ensure national interests and territorial claims against potential threats. The ability of states in the region to invest in such military capabilities has grown along with the size and sophistication of the economies from which governments draw their revenues. But some military capabilities pursued in East Asia reflect new wrinkles in modern warfare that have resulted from the advance of, and reliance on, high technology. To the extent that such innovations alter the effectiveness of weapons systems, mastering new technologies and marrying them to military operations (or devising novel ways to disrupt the adversary's military operations dependent on such technology) assume an unprecedented significance. Because many of the relevant technologies are rooted in advances in electronics and computer systems that have civilian applications, and because the East Asian economies are home to some of the leaders in these fields, the increasing importance of high technology for military power indicates yet another way in which economic developments interact with the security environment and shape the prospects for conflict in East Asia—a consideration explored at length in Michael Horowitz's chapter.

A different connection between economic developments and political-military relations in East Asia pertains not to military capabilities but to strategy. As Taylor Fravel indicates in his chapter, aside from thinking about maritime disputes and the way these demand changes in the thinking of a military long focused on ground operations to defend China's borders, the People's Liberation Army (PLA) has begun to develop new strategies along with new capabilities to address nontraditional security concerns, especially disaster relief, counterterrorism, and peacekeeping operations. Though certainly not supplanting its ambitious program of military modernization designed to deal with the traditional contingency of interstate conflict, as China's economic involvements well beyond the mainland have increased, and as the regime has become more concerned about internal threats to the domestic stability necessary for economic progress, the PLA and especially its navy have begun to address the need to prepare for military operations other than war.

Although economic interests influence military-security relations, military-security interests also influence the region's economic relations. Concerns about vulnerability and domination inform the design of economic institutions and the choice of institutional venues for addressing economic problems, with enduring political considerations limiting their role and effectiveness, as the chapters by Miles Kahler and Benjamin Cohen make clear. Security concerns also condition the extent to which economic interests shape patterns of trade and investment in goods and services that may have military externalities, particularly technologies and systems for employing them that can affect the relative power that states can bring to bear in conflict. As the chapter by Horowitz indicates, this consideration can extend beyond the hardware and software to the education and training of personnel from which new technologies emerge and on which their military applications ultimately depend.

Yet security concerns can sometimes encourage the institutionalization of economic ties. To allay fears about its growing clout, during the mid-1990s China turned to multilateral economic institutions as part of an effort to cultivate its image as a responsible international actor rather than a potential threat. These efforts—including participation in regional financial arrangements; the conclusion of a free-trade agreement with ASEAN; and exploration of greater economic coordination among China, Japan, and South Korea—have had mixed results and have been tested by the strains of the global recession of 2008–2009. But from the perspective of our examination of the nexus of economics and security in East Asia, the point is that economic developments not only shape but also are shaped by security concerns.

Theoretical Perspectives on the Political Economy of National Security

Various theoretical perspectives exist on the relationship between international economic relations and security relations. One view is advanced by liberals, who argue that extensive economic interdependence discourages interstate conflict and reduces the likelihood that those disputes that do occur will escalate (Stein 1993; Doyle 1997; Mansfield and Pollins 2001). In advancing this claim, liberals have emphasized several causal mechanisms that could explain political-military relations in East Asia. For example, liberals frequently argue that economic exchange promotes greater contact and communication between governments and between private actors located in different countries, thereby fostering cooperative political relations (Doyle 1997: chap. 8; Hirschman 1977: 61; Stein 1993; Viner 1951: 261). Indeed, there is ample reason to believe that heightened economic activity in the region has increased such contact, although it is far less clear whether this has made any substantial contribution to political cooperation.

Furthermore, liberals stress that open international trade and FDI generate efficiency gains that contribute to growth and prosperity. Both individuals and firms benefit from these gains. As openness rises, private actors become increasingly dependent on foreign markets. Military conflict risks undermining openness and rupturing economic relations among the antagonists, thereby scuttling the gains from overseas economic exchange. Consequently, private actors have reason to press their governments to avoid becoming embroiled in hostilities with key economic partners. Government officials, in turn, have reason to attend to these societal pressures because they depend for political support on groups that would be adversely affected by conflict. As Montesquieu famously put it centuries ago, "the natural effect of commerce is to lead to peace. Two nations that trade together become mutually dependent: if one has an interest in buying, the other has an interest in selling; and all unions are based on mutual needs" (quoted in Hirschman 1977: 80).

However, liberal arguments about the political economy of national security have faced criticism. First, various observers have charged that open trade relations and extensive economic interdependence can adversely affect a state's security, as the efficiency gains from trade often do not accrue to states proportionately and the distribution of those gains can influence interstate power relations (Hirschman [1945] 1980; Gilpin 1981). In a particularly influential study, Albert Hirschman ([1945] 1980) concludes that trade relations can foster political dependence and domination. He argues that open trade affects power relations by generating efficiency gains that enhance the military capacity of the participating states and by increasing the costs associated with any disruption in the commercial relationship. States that would have trouble replacing economic exchange with a given trade partner are dependent on that partner. The more costly it is to shift trade from this partner to other markets, the greater this trade partner's influence. Consequently, states can use foreign trade to bolster their power by shifting trade to smaller and poorer partners, which have a particular need for commerce and the income that it yields. One source of concern in East Asia is that the rapid rise of China's trade with other countries in the region has increased their dependence on Beijing, thus providing it with leverage that could adversely affect their national security.

Second, some studies charge that liberals are insufficiently attentive to the institutional context in which trade is conducted. Robert Keohane (1990), for example, argues that economic openness can inhibit interstate conflict, but only if international institutions exist to promote openness and ensure that it will not falter in the future. Edward Mansfield and Jon Pevehouse (2000) make a related argument. They focus attention on preferential trading arrangements (PTAs), which are a set of interstate institutions that grant each member country preferential access to the market of every other participant.

Most states enter PTAs expecting to derive economic benefits. Sometimes these expected benefits are realized; sometimes they are not. Nonetheless, conflict between member states threatens to scuttle these anticipated gains by damaging economic relations between participants and the arrangement itself. As trade flows within a PTA rise, so do these anticipated gains and the economic costs of conflict. Consequently, heightened trade is most likely to discourage conflict among members of the same PTA.

Whereas these arguments stress the interactive effects of economic flows and institutions on conflict, other researchers stress that institutions promote both interdependence and cooperation among participants (Nye 1971; Keohane 1984). Institutions facilitate mutual policy adjustments, which can foster interdependence. They also establish focal points, create a forum for negotiation and conflict resolution, reduce transaction costs, and monitor and disseminate information about the actions of member states, all of which contribute to cooperation. Some observers have argued that institutions can also spur cooperation by altering the preferences and the identities of member states (Hopf 1998; Johnston 2001).

These claims are examined in a number of the following chapters. Consistent with the liberal argument, Wu Xinbo focuses on the ASEAN plus three (i.e., ASEAN plus China, Japan, and South Korea) and argues that heightened economic interdependence has stimulated political cooperation and dampened conflict in East Asia. Miles Kahler, however, offers a less sanguine assessment of economic institutions in East Asia, pointing out that although institutions in the region have promoted greater economic interdependence, this is unlikely to have the conflict-dampening effect that liberals would expect. Benjamin Cohen, focusing on regional finance rather than trade and FDI, emphasizes underlying security tensions among East Asian states as a reason to be skeptical that economic cooperation will inhibit military friction in East Asia. Although Cohen also maintains that, over the longer term, efforts to improve financial cooperation might help reduce political tensions in East Asia, to the extent he and Kahler underscore the importance of security concerns, they share much in common with realist critics of the liberal position. These critics charge that liberals privilege the effects of economic relations on political-military relations while giving short shrift to the tendency for political-military relations to drive economic relations.

This critique might suggest, for example, that we observe both heightened economic activity and a relative absence of conflict in East Asia because power relations in the region and globally have facilitated both peace and increasing economic exchange. During the last decade of the Cold War, when the international system was still bipolar, the United States, its allies, and China all shared an interest in resisting the Soviet Union. This encouraged their political cooperation and led them to welcome the positive security externalities that resulted from their economic interaction (Gowa and Mansfield 1993; Gowa 1994). After the Cold War, realists have argued that the international system became unipolar, dominated by the United States (Wohlforth 1999). The preponderance of U.S. power has helped ensure that existing rivalries in East Asia and elsewhere do not boil over, and it has restrained other powers in the region, most notably China. Moreover, there is a long tradition of realist thought that attributes the existence of a liberal international economy and heightened interdependence to the emergence of a single state that is powerful enough to manage the global system (Krasner 1976; Gilpin 1981, 1987). Global hegemony, in the view of such realists, underlies both the growth of economic exchange and political cooperation in East Asia and elsewhere.

The Prominence of China and U.S.-China Relations

This study illuminates links between the dramatic economic changes and enduring security concerns that have characterized East Asia since the late twentieth century. Some of the authors in this volume adopt a broad regional perspective. Others, however, focus most closely on China's role in the region, often with special attention to U.S.-China relations. That China looms so large in such a study is easy to explain, because of both its dramatic economic growth and its impressive military modernization. Since the 1980s, China has had the fastest-growing economy in the world's fastest-growing economic region (see Figures 1.5 and 1.6). In 2010, it surpassed Japan as the world's second-largest economy, trailing only the United States.[10] And at least since the early 1990s, China has been carrying out an impressive military modernization program during an era in which other major powers, with the noteworthy exception of the United States, have more often eschewed increases or even scaled back such investment (see Figures 1.7–1.9).[11] China's spending on military modernization has fueled speculation about its likely impact on East Asian security, and about its potential to end the era in which the United States remains the world's sole superpower and the preponderant power in East Asia. As noted above, some consider American power a bulwark for peace in the

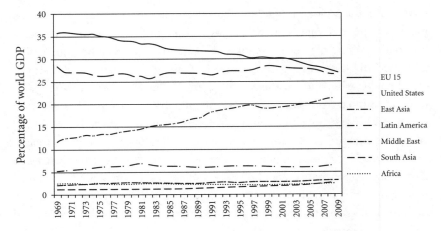

FIGURE 1.5 World shares of GDP, 1969–2009

SOURCE: *International Macroeconomic Data Set* (U.S. Department of Agriculture, Economic Research Service), available at http://www.ers.usda.gov/Data/Macroeconomics/Data/HistoricalGDPSharesValues.xls (USDA 2010).

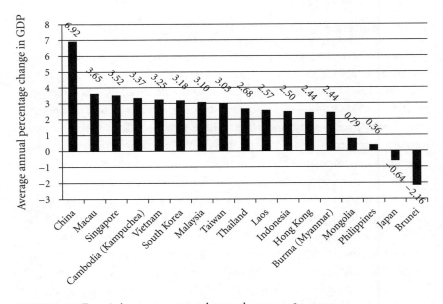

FIGURE 1.6 East Asia average annual growth rates, 1980–2009

SOURCE: *International Macroeconomic Data Set* (U.S. Department of Agriculture, Economic Research Service), available at http://www.ers.usda.gov/Data/Macroeconomics/Data/HistoricalGDPSharesValues.xls (USDA 2010).

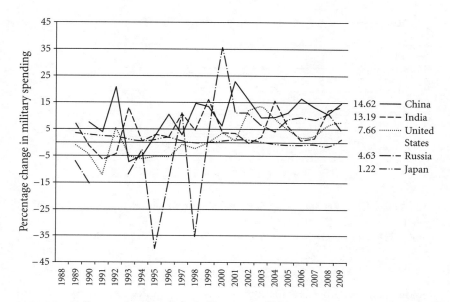

FIGURE 1.7 Percentage change in military spending, 1989–2009

SOURCE: *The SIPRI Military Expenditure Database* (Solna, Sweden: Stockholm International Peace Research Institute), available at http://milexdata.sipri.org/result.php4 (SIPRI 2009).

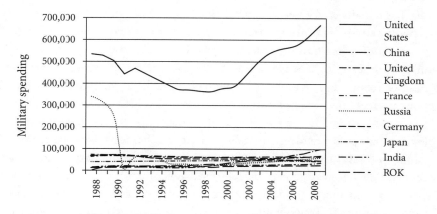

FIGURE 1.8 Military spending, 1989–2009 (millions of 2008 U.S. dollars)

SOURCE: *The SIPRI Military Expenditure Database* (Solna, Sweden: Stockholm International Peace Research Institute), available at http://milexdata.sipri.org/result.php4 (SIPRI 2009).

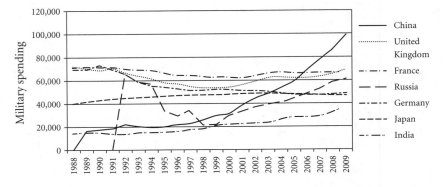

FIGURE 1.9 Military spending, 1989–2009, without United States (millions of 2008 U.S. dollars)

SOURCE: *The SIPRI Military Expenditure Database* (Solna, Sweden: Stockholm International Peace Research Institute), available at http://milexdata.sipri.org/result.php4 (SIPRI 2009).

region. Thus, whether one focuses on either economics or security, or, as we do in this volume, on the links between them, it is understandable that China and its relations with the United States are central to the assessment.

The United States remains by far the world's largest economy, representing slightly more than 25 percent of global gross domestic product (GDP), a share that has remained relatively consistent since 1970. Although the size of China's economy still pales in comparison with that of the United States, at roughly 7 percent of global GDP in 2009, it has experienced a remarkable sevenfold increase since 1980 (U.S. Department of Agriculture 2010). China's current position reflects annual economic growth rates that have averaged slightly less than 7 percent over the past thirty years (World Trade Organization [WTO] 2010a). This dramatic success since 1980 followed first from a round of major domestic policy reforms embracing market mechanisms that repaired the damage of a stultifying planned economy. Then, beginning in the 1990s and accelerating in the early 2000s, the reforms to revitalize the domestic economy were complemented by reforms to more effectively open China to the outside world and more thoroughly integrate it with the global economy. In contrast with its minor role in 1980, by 2009 China ranked second in the world in merchandise trade behind the United States, overtaking Germany as the world's top-ranked merchandise exporter and in position to surpass it as the world's second largest merchandise importer (behind the United States) (Central Intelligence Agency 2010a, 2010b; *Deutsche Welle* 2010; WTO 2010b).

As we mentioned earlier, China has also been a driving force behind the recent growth in East Asian trade and investment. Over the past decade, China became the largest trading partner for Japan, South Korea, and Taiwan, and the second largest for ASEAN. It became the largest export market for Japan, South Korea, and Taiwan, and the second largest for ASEAN. It became the largest source of imports for Japan and South Korea, and the second largest for Taiwan and ASEAN.[12] For some of its regional trade partners (especially Japan, South Korea, and Taiwan), trade with China has become an important engine of growth. Various East Asian firms have relocated factories to China to hold down the production costs of goods that face the increasingly intense competition that is characteristic of globalized markets, a pattern that helps explain why China has become one of the top destinations for FDI among emerging markets (EYGM Limited 2010).

As China's economy boomed, its demand for natural resources became a major factor in the regional and global economy. Most notably, to fuel its burgeoning industrial sector and to meet growing consumer demand for energy-intensive goods (especially automobiles and air-conditioning), China's need for imported oil and natural gas has been increasing steadily since the early 1990s. To ensure the availability of energy imports, China's leaders have crafted policies (including diversification of suppliers and encouraging Chinese participation in exploration, refining, and pipeline deals) that echo steps previously taken by Japan, South Korea, and Taiwan. Both because of its impact on world energy markets and because of potential competition among energy importers in East Asia and beyond who worry about the reliability of supplies and the predictability of prices, this aspect of China's economic rise commands special attention (Downs 2000; Ding 2005; Zha 2005). Its significance and the ramifications for international security are explored in the chapter by Danielle Cohen and Jonathan Kirshner.

Yet, as breathtaking as China's rise has been, the United States remains the world's leading economy and a major economic player in East Asia. The continuing importance of the United States and China's new stature are both reflected in regional trade volumes. China surpassed the United States as Japan's top trading partner in 2007, exceeding $214 billion total trade volume. But even in 2009 the United States remained a major trade partner for Japan, with a total of roughly $147 billion compared with China's total of $232 billion. China is also South Korea's largest trade partner, with trade totaling $156 billion in 2009, although U.S. trade still stood at an impressive $68 billion with the prospect of major increases once the United States–Korea (KORUS) Free Trade Agreement enters into force. In 2009 the volume of China's trade with Taiwan (for whom it became the largest trade partner in 2005) was $106 billion, as compared with $47 billion for the United States. And although China's trade with the ASEAN states in 2009 amounted to $160 billion, U.S. trade with ASEAN states totaled $147 billion (Census Bureau 2010).

In addition to their roles as two hubs for East Asian regional economic activity,[13] over the past three decades China and the United States have also developed a robust bilateral economic relationship. Since 1980, trade between the United States and China has blossomed. In 1980 China was the thirty-fifth largest source for American imports and the seventeenth largest destination for American exports. By 2009, China had become the United States' largest source of imports and third-largest destination for exports. In 1980, America was China's second-largest source of imports and the largest destination for exports, but the absolute amounts for each were comparatively small. By 2009, the United States had become the top destination for China's exports. Although the United States ranked fourth as a supplier of China's imports in 2009, compared with 1980, the dollar amount had increased more than fifteen-fold (from $3.8 billion to $77.4 billion) and ranked fourth only because of the even larger increases in imports from Japan, South Korea, and Taiwan. More telling, perhaps, bilateral annual trade volume between the United States and China grew from a meager $5 billion in 1980 to about $350 billion in 2009 (down from $400 billion just before the global recession), thus making China America's second-largest trade partner, just behind Canada (Census Bureau 2010).

The huge volumes and relative importance to each other as trade partners, however, has also generated friction between China and the United States. The bilateral trade balance, with growing Chinese surpluses and American deficits that rose from $84 billion in 2000 to more than $266 billion in 2008 became a hot political issue. Some Americans accused China of deliberately undervaluing its dollar-pegged currency to facilitate exports to the United States. More recently, some Americans have accused Beijing of devising policies that favor domestic over foreign business operations in China, thus hindering U.S. exports there in ways that some believe contravene the spirit and perhaps the letter of WTO rules (Wolff 2010). Whatever its cause, China's large trade surplus with the United States during the opening decade of the twenty-first century contributed to Beijing's rapid accumulation of the world's largest foreign-exchange reserves. Because a large fraction of these were held as U.S. Treasury securities, China's purchase of American debt thickened bilateral economic ties between the two countries and created the mutual vulnerabilities that define interdependence. On the one hand, China's T-bill purchases helped keep U.S. interest rates low, thereby sustaining an American economy fueled by credit-based consumption (including mortgage financing of the housing bubble). On the other hand, having invested so heavily in dollar-denominated notes, China acquired its own stake in the health of the U.S. economy and the strength of the American currency.[14]

In summary, by the end of the first decade of the twenty-first century, the United States and China displayed all the telltale signs of countries whose economies were becoming increasingly interdependent.[15] As the liberal theories that we discussed earlier suggest, such relationships provide benefits to both countries that raise the incentives for sustaining cooperation. But, as realist theories remind us, heightened interdependence can also generate points of conflict if one party perceives that the other is benefiting at its expense. The greater the degree of interdependence, the higher the stakes are for both sides and, potentially, the stronger their determination to see disagreements resolved in their favor. Whether, on balance, Sino-American economic interdependence contributes to cooperation or conflict is theoretically indeterminate; the impact of interdependence is affected by the institutional context in which the economic relationship takes place, the economic climate in each country, and domestic political concerns that reflect sectoral and regional interests. Theory aside, however, it is clear that rising Sino-American economic interdependence since the 1990s has increased both the mutual benefits that provide incentives for cooperation and the stakes when economic conflict occurs. Since the mid-1990s, the two sides in a string of American debates—about granting China permanent most-favored-nation (MFN) trade status, the terms for its accession to the WTO, Chinese exchange-rate policy, and the fairness of labor practices in its export sector—have been fueled by the two faces of economic interdependence. Consequently, a close focus not only on China but also on Sino-American relations is central to understanding economic factors that may affect security in East Asia where both play leading roles. Yuan Peng's chapter, in particular, makes clear the potential strategic significance of an erosion in the economic foundations of cooperation between China and the United States that have been in place since at least the 1990s.

The prominence of China in many of the following chapters, then, is partly a reflection of the dramatic increase in the country's international economic role over the previous three decades. At the same time, China draws increased attention because of its concerted effort to tap expanding resources to modernize the country's large, but in many respects still lagging, military. And as in the economic sphere, in the sphere of regional security, as China's salience has increased, so has the importance of its bilateral relationship with the United States.

The expectation that China's increasing military power will permit, or perhaps tempt, its leaders to press harder in pursuing their interests in East Asia has raised concerns about the potential for conflict with regional neighbors or the United States, which maintains a strong military presence throughout the western Pacific. To be sure, China is not the only East Asian country investing economic resources in military modernization. But China's vast territory, its large population that is both proudly nationalist and increasingly well educated, its huge and rapidly growing economy, and its strong central leadership in Beijing all have combined to shape the belief that a bigger, more modern Chinese military will have a significant impact on regional security that overshadows concerns about military modernization by others in the region. Belief that Beijing's ambitious military modernization program will be sustainable rests in part on the recognition that China's economic boom has enabled it to increase military spending since the mid-1990s without significantly increasing the fraction of national resources devoted to the military (see Figure 1.10). Regional concern about a militarily stronger China also reflects the fact that, although Beijing has resolved most of its territorial and sovereignty disputes with its neighbors, as noted above, those that remain put it at odds with key East Asian countries (Japan, the Philippines, and Vietnam) and, perhaps most notably, with Taiwan.

Aside from tensions in the Korean Peninsula, the most prominent East Asian security concerns on the early twenty-first century almost all center on scenarios that involve China, its neighbors, and potentially the United States. Beyond the unusual American relationship with Taiwan, the United States is an ally of many states worried about China's growing military capabilities and possible intentions.[16] Should conflicts emerge between China and these East Asian neighbors, the possibility of American involvement is clearly understood. Moreover, aside from the interests of allies, the United States has professed its own interest in sustaining the region's security architecture

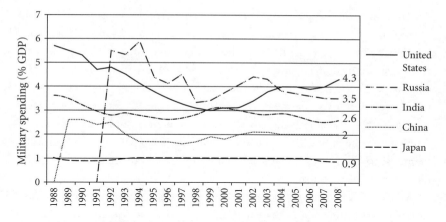

FIGURE 1.10 Military spending as a percentage of GDP, 1989–2009
SOURCE: *The SIPRI Military Expenditure Database* (Solna, Sweden: Stockholm International Peace Research Institute), available at http://milexdata.sipri.org/result.php4 (SIPRI 2009).

(a large-scale American military presence and its hub-and-spokes network of alliances) that it established in the aftermath of World War II and that it believes helps preserve East Asian peace and provides the collective good of freedom of navigation on the high seas.[17] Thus, regional doubts about the effects of China's rise reverberate in Washington. China's changing military profile, its consequences for regional security, and the American response to it are obviously central to any assessment of the nexus between economic and security relations in East Asia.

• • •

The contributors to this volume not only address a diverse set of topics that bear on the interaction of economics and security in East Asia; they also offer diverse assessments of the consequences of deepening economic activity and evolving security concerns in the region. Although there is no fundamental disagreement about the basic facts—increases in international economic exchanges, participation in a growing roster of regional institutions, and personal contacts among elites both in organizations and in less formal dialogues and side meetings—the authors disagree about whether and to what extent these trends are affecting regional security.

Benjamin Cohen's chapter argues that the relationship between cooperation in regional finance and in security matters is mutually endogenous.

Progress in promoting regional financial cooperation, especially since the Asian financial crisis of the late 1990s, has been noteworthy. But Cohen notes that it has also been constrained by the participants' underlying security concerns, especially states' concerns about maintaining control over their own destiny. Cohen is agnostic about the possibility for closer monetary and financial relations to moderate regional security tensions, and he acknowledges their potential for lubricating government interactions and altering national interests. Yet he emphasizes that such positive effects will depend on fundamental shifts in political relations among the East Asian states that seem unlikely for the near future.

Miles Kahler expresses skepticism about the positive effects on regional security that follow from the growth of regional economic interdependence and institutions. Kahler emphasizes both the weakness of East Asian institutional structures and their tendency to segregate economic and security issues. Although he does not rule out the possibility of future economic and institutional developments (especially the negotiation of new preferential trade agreements among key economies and a deepening of regional economic integration) that might significantly affect regional security, he views the current level of institutionalization as insufficient to have a major role in mitigating East Asia's potential for interstate conflict.

Wu Xinbo offers yet a third perspective on the interaction between trends in regional economics and security. As noted above, he considers economic regionalism manifest in the ASEAN plus three as having positive spillover effects on regional security. His chapter emphasizes the way institutionalized economic cooperation has facilitated cooperation on nontraditional security problems, has begun to foster regional consciousness among participants, and has generated common security interests that may give rise to a regional security architecture less dependent on the role of the United States.

Zhang Tuosheng examines territorial disputes in East Asia to determine the relative weight of economic and security interests that affect their intensity and intractability. In his survey of many of the disputes involving China, Japan, and their neighbors in the region, Zhang finds substantial variation in the ability of the parties to contain their disagreements and to finally resolve their disputes. He links these variations to the origins of the conflicts, the extent to which economic or political-security interests are at stake, and the differences between land-border disputes and disputes over maritime claims. Although Zhang expects that many of the disputes, especially those offshore, will not easily be resolved, he is relatively sanguine that the economic and political interests of the relevant parties will continue to foster dialogue that limits their potential for generating military conflict and that peaceful dialogue should eventually permit negotiated settlements. Thus, for Zhang economic and security interests are linked—both as a source of conflict and as an incentive for cooperation.

The chapter by Danielle Cohen and Jonathan Kirshner examines energy security, a topic that by definition combines the two principal interests in this volume. Discussing the increasing dependence of China, Japan, and the United States on foreign sources of oil and gas, Cohen and Kirshner acknowledge the widespread view that concern about reliable access to reasonably priced energy provides incentives for states to take steps, including preparation for the need to rely on military force, which could trigger interstate conflict. In this one area, the predominant view among analysts and government leaders tends to be pessimistic about the security consequences of economic expansion and interdependence. Cohen and Kirshner are concerned as well, but not because they agree with the conventional wisdom that military forces can provide a solution to the problem of energy security. Instead, they argue that the very real dangers that arise from concerns about energy security are in fact the result of a myth, a consequence of beliefs that are not supported by the facts. They assert that there are few real threats to the energy supplies of the great powers and that military means cannot solve the actual energy problems the great powers may face. For Cohen and Kirshner, it is the "cult of energy insecurity" based on a myth, rather than a real condition of insecurity, that is dangerously and needlessly aggravating political conflict among the three biggest powers interacting in East Asia.

Chapters by Taylor Fravel and Michael Horowitz both examine changes in the nature of military power in East Asia that are linked to the dramatic economic transformation sweeping the region. Fravel's focuses on the way China's rapid economic growth and rising international economic role are reflected in its program of military modernization. He explains that economic expansion and military modernization go hand in hand, although not simply in the sense that greater resources are funding larger and more sophisticated capabilities. Instead, Fravel describes the ways in which China's integration with the regional and global economy has altered the goals and content of the military strategy that modernization is to serve. Beyond traditional missions associated with interstate conflict, Fravel identifies a changed pattern of investment that aims to serve a Chinese military strategy that includes new goals: ensuring domestic stability and the ability to undertake nontraditional security missions abroad, such as disaster relief, counterterrorism, and peacekeeping.

Horowitz cautions against extrapolating from the apparently pacifying effects in East Asia of growing economic interdependence, which has characterized the past few decades. Instead, Horowitz warns, the globalization of advanced industrial production and information technologies may provide an increasing number of East Asian states with military capabilities that could well exacerbate security dilemmas, encourage arms races, and transform a strategic environment in which disruptive new technologies have made conquest harder into an unsettling strategic environment in which new technologies facilitate offensive power projection. Thus, for Horowitz, it is precisely because of the economic success of East Asia's leading states that they are likely to be among the first with the resources (human and material) necessary to exploit new military technologies with potentially dangerous consequences.

Yuan Peng's chapter examines the relationship between the two leading powers in East Asia: China and the United States. In the chapter, he describes the challenges to, and opportunities for, cooperation in this bilateral relationship, whose profound significance is reflected in the volume's preceding chapters. Yuan identifies four Chinese perspectives or schools of thought about the strategic situation in the region. These schools of thought reflect a dynamic that is clearly being driven by the interaction of economic and security concerns. He asserts that Sino-American economic relations have evolved from a basis for cooperation to a new and growing source of conflict between competitors. As mutually beneficial economic relations no longer so clearly help offset other areas of disagreement between Beijing and Washington, keeping bilateral ties on track becomes ever more complicated and demands greater efforts. Yuan then identifies Northeast Asia as a key area in which the potential for serious military conflicts involving the United States and China can be addressed by more concerted efforts at Sino-American cooperation. Because this part of the region lacks the sorts of multilateral institutions that have grown up around ASEAN, Yuan views Northeast Asia as providing a fresh slate for the United States and China to design a new mechanism for cooperation. While acknowledging the difficulties such a project faces, Yuan also argues that such cooperation in the most contentious area of Northeast

Asia could provide the basis for Sino-American cooperation in the rest of the Asia-Pacific.

In recent years, both social scientists and policy makers have expressed a growing interest in East Asia. In part, this reflects the tremendous economic strides that have been made throughout the region. It is also due to the rise of China, ongoing concerns about the Korean Peninsula, and Western interests in promoting regional stability. How the rapid expansion of cross-border economic activity in East Asia is linked to political-military relations is a crucial topic that has not been studied in sufficient depth. As the different perspectives of our contributors suggest, however, recent events provide evidence that the interaction of economic and security considerations in East Asia is not just a complex process. The thickening of economic ties amid remaining security concerns and the flowering of institutional arrangements among the countries of the region can be a double-edged sword.

In July 2010, for example, the ASEAN Regional Forum (ARF) served as a venue in which differences of opinion about competing maritime and territorial claims in the South China Sea, motivated partly by economic interests, led to increased tensions and security concerns among some of the region's key countries. Yet at the July 2011 ARF these same countries worked to defuse those tensions, thus furthering a trend that had begun outside of the multilateral setting earlier in the year. This suggests that East Asian regional institutions, like their counterparts elsewhere, do not in and of themselves forestall conflict or ensure cooperation, but instead they establish a pattern of regular interaction and a focal point for addressing vital issues. Such regular interaction can provide an opportunity for member states to clarify conflicting economic or security interests. However, it also establishes a predictable rhythm for attention to such issues that can facilitate attempts to mitigate conflicts if and when the member states see such efforts as useful for repairing relations damaged by disputes.

Outside of multilateral regional institutions, the complex implications of economic and security concerns have also been apparent. In September 2010, a sharp dispute erupted between China and Japan over the arrest of a Chinese fishing-boat captain whose ship collided with a Japanese Coast Guard vessel after he refused to comply with calls to leave disputed waters in the East China Sea. While a disturbing diplomatic standoff between Beijing and Tokyo played out, reports surfaced that China's exports of economically crucial rare-earth minerals to Japan had been halted. Although these reports proved difficult to confirm, the perception that China was using economic leverage to exert political pressure on Japan fed broader security concerns about potentially worrisome aspects of China's growing clout in the region. At the same time, however, China and Japan's interest in sustaining their extensive, mutually beneficial economic ties provided powerful incentives to prevent the incident from escalating. Consequently, despite the incident's adverse effects on Japanese public opinion toward China and a surge of Chinese anger directed at Japan, once Tokyo decided to release the fishing-boat captain, official relations with Beijing were quickly normalized.

The nexus of economics and security affairs may also be evident in a broader pattern that caught the attention of observers after the global economic crisis erupted in 2008, especially once it became clear that the crisis would cause relatively little damage to China. In 2009–2010, some observers began commenting on what they viewed as China's more assertive behavior in East Asia, focusing mainly on what they saw as Beijing's stepped-up efforts to back territorial claims in the South China Sea that were disputed by the Philippines and Vietnam and claims in the East China Sea that were disputed by Japan. To explain this apparent change in China's regional behavior, analysts suggested that America's economic difficulties during the financial crisis, together with its military burdens in Iraq and especially Afghanistan, had convinced leaders in Beijing that China's strength relative to that of the United States was growing more rapidly than previously anticipated (Glaser and Dooley 2009; Glaser and Morris 2009; Swaine 2011; Swaine and Fravel 2011). In this account, America's domestic and international preoccupations and a rising China's role as an indispensible global economic actor had created an opening for China to press harder on behalf of its regional interests than had been possible during the preceding decade. Whether such claims accurately described an objective change in China's policy and behavior or simply reflected others' subjective interpretation of regional events, the new perception was widespread and was having real consequences. Beijing apparently recognized the problems being created by the perception that it had become increasingly assertive. Those who considered China's greater regional activism a worrisome challenge to their own interests were beginning to cooperate in ways that could be inimical to China's security and jeopardize the benefits China derived from robust economic relations in the region. This reality led Beijing at the end of 2010 to reiterate its previous commitment to peaceful development. In doing so, China's leaders emphasized that a stable security environment was as essential for its own continued economic rise as for the prosperity of others in the region (Dai 2010).

The aforementioned examples do not constitute evidence conclusively confirming either optimism or pessimism about the security implications of burgeoning economic relations in East Asia. Instead, as is apparent in the varied perspectives contained in the following chapters, such examples illustrate that economic and security affairs in the region have become inextricably intertwined. The nexus of economics, security, and international relations in East Asia demands greater attention and a more concerted effort by students of international political economy and international security affairs to closely coordinate their research agendas. This book constitutes a modest step in that direction.

Notes

1. As reflected in Figures 1.1 and 1.2, whether one focuses on the incidence of military conflicts or on battle deaths, the major data sets on which international relations scholars rely provide clear evidence of this trend. In retrospect, the 1980s marked the beginning of this trend in East Asia, although the trend became most pronounced with the end of the Cold War. In this respect the Uppsala Conflict Data Program and Peace Research Institute Oslo (UCDP/PRIO 2010) data are consistent with the updated list of wars from the Correlates of War project; see http://www.correlatesof war.org/COW2%20Data/WarData_NEW/WarList_NEW.pdf (Sarkees and Wayman 2010).

2. These figures do not include Taiwan because it is not possible to obtain reliable data on Taiwanese trade before 1990.

3. The members of the EC/EU (with years of accession in parentheses) are as follows: Austria (1995), Belgium (1957), Bulgaria (2007), Cyprus (2004), Czech Republic (2004), Denmark (1973), Estonia (2004), Finland (1995), France (1957), Germany (1957), Greece (1981), Hungary (2004), Ireland (1973), Italy (1957), Latvia (2004), Lithuania (2004), Luxembourg (1957), Malta (2004), Netherlands (1957), Poland (2004), Portugal (1986), Romania (2007), Slovakia (2004), Slovenia (2004), Spain (1986), Sweden (1995), and United Kingdom (1973).

4. We also include two internationalized civil wars in our list of wars. One was fought by Laos and Vietnam; the other was waged by Cambodia and Vietnam. These are included because, in both cases, the insurgency was being actively supported by Vietnam.

5. China's preferences about the future of Korea differ from those of the United States, Japan, and South Korea. All four, however, share an interest in minimizing the risks generated by North Korea's nuclear weapons program; this has sustained

multilateral negotiations seeking a diplomatic resolution of the issue. Similarly, although China (unlike the United States) did not embrace the findings of the official South Korean report citing the North Koreans for the sinking of the *Cheonan* in March 2010, the official Chinese response focused on preventing escalation of North-South tensions and on the need to preserve stability and peace on the peninsula. Beijing's stance on both the nuclear standoff and the Cheonan sinking are consistent with its broader Korea policy since the 1990s: (1) placing top priority on stability to avoid potentially catastrophic turmoil along its northeastern border, (2) refusing to publicly take sides against the North (with whom it still has a treaty of alliance), and (3) engaging in quiet diplomacy and pressure behind the scenes to send the message to Pyongyang that it cannot count on China to rescue it from the consequences its military provocations may trigger.

6. The potential for American entanglement, intended or not, was reflected in the sharp Chinese reaction to U.S. Secretary of State Hillary Rodham Clinton's July 2010 remarks about territorial disputes and maritime rights in the South China Sea. Some interpreted the venue (the ASEAN Regional Forum held in Hanoi) and the American call for multilateral negotiations, as an indication that the United States was taking sides and opposing China's preference for bilateral negotiations to resolve the disputes. Others viewed Clinton's remarks as merely a restatement of long-standing American policy urging the noncoercive resolution of East Asia's territorial disputes and supporting the principle of freedom of navigation on the high seas, along with an offer to play a role in regional diplomacy if the principals should find that helpful (Landler 2010).

7. For a comprehensive discussion of cross-strait economic relations and their relevance for China-Taiwan political developments, see Kastner (2009).

8. In addition to the disagreements about naval rights in the South China Sea, the United States and China sharply disagreed about military exercises that the United States and South Korea conducted in reaction to the sinking of the *Cheonan*. Although not claiming the waters as China's territorial seas, Beijing objected to military operations in the Yellow Sea by the U.S. Navy, especially including the *George Washington* aircraft carrier, arguing that proximity to China's coast gave it special security interests in those waters. The United States dismissed the concern and reasserted its right to conduct military exercises in international waters, although the initial joint exercise with South Korea was actually held in the Sea of Japan off Korea's eastern coast.

9. Confidence that war is unattractive for all concerned may encourage intransigence and diplomacy backed by military force held in reserve. During the Cold War, military analysts spoke about the stability-instability paradox, arguing that the clear irrationality of general nuclear war made limited conventional wars more likely; states allegedly would believe that they could safely fight small wars because escalation to a major war was so unlikely.

10. This ranking refers to GDP calculated at the market exchange rates for currencies. An alternative approach to calculating GDP is to rely on purchasing power parity (PPP), a methodology that Alan Heston and Robert Summers developed to

adjust for variations in the prices of goods in different countries. The PPP figures depend on local surveys of baskets of representative goods to determine how much nominal GDP figures must be adjusted. In the 1990s, the World Bank adopted the PPP estimates, a change that dramatically increased the reported size of China's (and some other countries') GDP. Using PPP, some estimated that China's GDP was the world's second largest economy more than a decade ago. The PPP methodology has been contested, however, and difficulty in evaluating the validity and reliability of PPP estimates led the World Bank in 2007 to recalculate its PPP estimates, which resulted in a 40 percent downward revision for its figures on China's GDP. China's economy, however, has grown to the point that even by the more conservative exchange rate method, it was larger than Japan's in 2010 (Summers and Heston 1991; Davis 2007; Keidel 2007).

11. Estimates about China's military spending are even more hotly contested than estimates of the country's GDP. In the case of military spending, however, the controversy reflects disagreements about the comprehensiveness of data. China's official military budget is at the low end of the available estimates, with others estimating totals that range as high as twice China's reported total. For the purposes of this volume, however, two facts about which there is little controversy are most important. First, the rate of increase in China's military spending since 1990 has been very large (averaging well more than 10 percent per year). Second, whatever the actual size of China's military budget, since 1990, and especially since 1996, there has been a marked improvement in the quality and quantity of the most modern forces that the PLA deploys. See also Stockholm International Peace Research Institute (2009).

12. The rankings are for ASEAN trade with individual countries. Otherwise, the EU as an aggregate of countries ranks second behind Japan (ASEAN 2009). See also entries in *The World Factbook* (Central Intelligence Agency 2010a, 2010b); Blustein (2005); Kim and Buckley (2010); Ujikane (2010); Xinhua (2010).

13. Indeed, beyond the region, the central roles of the United States and China, and the importance of consultation between them to address international economic problems, were brought into stark relief during the economic crisis of 2008. Leaders and analysts around the world immediately looked to the United States and China to spearhead responses that would mitigate its worst effects and help spur recovery. The G-20 (which includes China) overshadowed the G-8 (which does not include China) and became the institutional focus for global economic consultation about the crisis. Some even argued for relying on a G-2 (United States and China) to manage the international economy, although this was quickly dismissed by most as at best premature. Along the same lines, Niall Ferguson coined the neologism *Chimerica* to represent the alleged global preponderance and thorough interdependence of these two economic giants. See Ferguson (2007); Clarke (2009); Bergsten (2009); Economy and Segal (2010).

14. "From June 2002 to June 2009, China's holdings of U.S. securities as a share of total foreign holdings of U.S. securities rose from 3.9% to 15.2%, increasing its

ranking of major foreign holders of U.S. securities from fifth to first. Over this period, China's holdings grew by nearly $1.28 trillion (or 707%), by far the largest increase in U.S. securities holdings of any other country. . . . The largest type of U.S. securities held by China are short-term and long-term U.S. Treasury securities, which are used to finance U.S. federal budget deficits. . . . China's holdings of U.S. Treasury securities rose from $118 billion (or 9.6% of total foreign holdings) at the end of 2002 to $895 billion in 2009 year-end. . . . As of April 2010, those holdings stood at $900 billion, which were 23.0% of total foreign holdings. China has been the largest foreign holder of U.S. Treasuries since September 2008" (Morrison 2010: 11).

15. Such interdependence reflects the high costs and difficulty of adjusting to any major disruption in their economic relationship that both sides face. In this sense, the relationship displays vulnerability interdependence rather than just sensitivity interdependence. See Hirschman ([1945] 1980); Keohane and Nye (1977); Baldwin (1980). Although the benefits each side derives from the relationship are not equal, the costs of a disruption for both (and given their global roles, the fallout for others, as well) would be severe—especially in terms of its impact on employment, inflation, and financial markets. The depth and breadth of the economic relationship also produces sensitivity interdependence. For example, adjustments in interest rates and stock indexes in one country reflect reactions to economic announcements and decisions in the other. Announcements by the U.S. Federal Reserve Board about interest rates or comments about the composition of China's foreign exchange reserves elicit quick reactions among investors in both countries.

16. As noted above, the Taiwan Relations Act, though not providing the kind of security guarantee embodied in a bilateral treaty between states, signals the possibility of U.S. intervention if conflict erupts between China and Taiwan. Since the late 1990s, U.S. policy has explicitly opposed any attempt to alter the status quo in the Taiwan Strait except by peaceful means that are acceptable to both sides. Other than the distinctive relationship with Taiwan, in East Asia the United States has treaties of alliance with the Republic of Korea, Japan, the Philippines, and Thailand, and it has increasingly close ties with Vietnam.

17. The United States maintains military bases in the Republic of Korea and Japan; has agreements facilitating military operations with Thailand, Singapore, and the Philippines; and maintains naval and air bases in the U.S. territory of Guam. The American view about the regional benefits of its military presence is articulated most clearly in reports issued in 1995 and 1998, see East Asian Strategy Report (1998).

Works Cited

Association of Southeast Asian Nations. 2009. *ASEAN Statistics*. http://www.aseansec .org/stat/Table19.pdf (accessed January 19, 2011).
Baldwin, David A. 1980. "Interdependence and Power: A Conceptual Analysis." *International Organization* 34 (4): 471–506.

Bergsten, C. Fred. 2009. "Two's Company." *Foreign Affairs* 88 (5): 169–170.

Blustein, Paul. 2005. "China Passes U.S. in Trade with Japan: 2004 Figures Show Asian Giant's Muscle." *Washington Post.* January 27.

Census Bureau. 2010. "Top Trading Partners—Total Trade, Exports, Imports: Year-to-Date December 2009." U.S. Census Bureau, Foreign Trade Statistics. http://www.census.gov/foreign-trade/statistics/highlights/top/top0912yr.html (accessed January 19, 2011).

Central Intelligence Agency. 2010a. "Country Comparisons: Exports." *World Factbook.* https://www.cia.gov/library/publications/the-world-factbook/rankorder/2078rank.html (accessed January 19, 2011).

———. 2010b. "Country Comparisons: Imports." *World Factbook.* https://www.cia.gov/library/publications/the-world-factbook/rankorder/2087rank.html (accessed January 19, 2011).

Clarke, Christopher M. 2009. "US-China Duopoly Is a Pipedream." *Yale Global Online.* August 6. http://yaleglobal.yale.edu/content/us-china-duopoly-pipedream (accessed January 19, 2011).

Dai, Bingguo. 2010. "Stick to the Path of Peaceful Development: Why Has China Chosen the Path of Peaceful Development?" *Beijing Review.* December 23. http://www.bjreview.com.cn/quotes/txt/2010-12/27/content_320120.htm.

Davis, Bob. 2007. "Politics & Economics: World Bank Offers New Take on GDP." *Wall Street Journal.* December 18.

Deutsche Welle. 2010. "Germany Loses Export Crown to China." February 9. http://www.dw-world.de/dw/article/0,,5233278,00.html (accessed January 19, 2011).

Ding, Arthur S. 2005. "China's Energy Security Demands and the East China Sea: A Growing Likelihood of Conflict in East Asia?" *China and Eurasia Forum Quarterly* 3 (3): 25–38.

Downs, Erica Strecker. 2000. *China's Quest for Energy Security.* Santa Monica, CA: RAND Corporation.

Doyle, Michael W. 1997. *Ways of War and Peace: Realism, Liberalism, and Socialism.* New York: Norton.

Dutton, Peter A. 2010. "Through a Chinese Lens." *Proceedings of the United States Naval Institute* 136 (4): 24–29.

East Asian Strategy Report. 1998. *The United States Security Strategy for the East Asia-Pacific Region 1998.* Washington, DC: U.S. Department of Defense. http://www.dod.gov/pubs/easr98/easr98.pdf (accessed January 19, 2011).

Economy, Elizabeth, and Adam Segal. 2010. "Time to Defriend China: The Quest for the Illusory 'G-2' Has Wasted Everyone's Time for Long Enough." *Foreign Policy.* May 24. http://www.foreignpolicy.com/articles/2010/05/24/time_to_defriend_china (accessed January 19, 2011).

EYGM Limited. 2010. "Waking Up to the New Economy." *Ernst & Young's 2010 European Attractiveness Survey.* http://www.ey.com/Publication/vwLUAssets/Attractiveness_survey_2010_EU/$FILE/Attractiveness_survey_2010_EU.pdf (accessed January 19, 2011).

Ferguson, Niall. 2007. "Not Two Countries, but One: Chimerica." *Telegraph*. March 4. http://www.telegraph.co.uk/comment/personal-view/3638174/Not-two-countries-but-one-Chimerica.html (accessed January 19, 2011).

Friedberg, Aaron L. 1993–1994. "Ripe for Rivalry: Prospects for Peace in a Multipolar Asia." *International Security* 18 (3): 5–33.

Gilpin, Robert. 1981. *War and Change in World Politics*. New York: Cambridge University Press.

———. 1987. *The Political Economy of International Relations*. Princeton, NJ: Princeton University Press.

Glaser, Bonnie S., and Benjamin Dooley. 2009. "China's 11th Ambassadorial Conference Signals Continuity and Change in Foreign Policy." *China Brief* 9 (22): 1–7.

Glaser, Bonnie S., and Lyle Morris. 2009. "Chinese Perceptions of U.S. Decline and Power." *China Brief* 9 (14): 1–6.

Gowa, Joanne. 1994. *Allies, Adversaries, and International Trade*. Princeton, NJ: Princeton University Press.

Gowa, Joanne, and Edward D. Mansfield. 1993. "Power Politics and International Trade." *American Political Science Review* 87 (2): 408–420.

Hirschman, Albert O. [1945] 1980. *National Power and the Structure of Foreign Trade*. Berkeley: University of California Press.

———. 1977. *The Passions and the Interests: Political Arguments for Capitalism Before Its Triumph*. Princeton, NJ: Princeton University Press.

Hopf, Ted. 1998. "The Promise of Constructivism in IR Theory." *International Security* 23 (1): 171–200.

Johnston, Alastair Ian. 2001. "Treating Transnational Institutions as Social Environments." *International Studies Quarterly* 45 (4): 487–515.

Kastner, Scott. 2009. *Political Conflict and Economic Interdependence Across the Taiwan Strait and Beyond*. Stanford, CA: Stanford University Press.

Keidel, Albert. 2007. "Comment: The Limits of a Smaller, Poorer China." *Financial Times*. November 14.

Keohane, Robert O. 1984. *After Hegemony: Cooperation and Discord in the World Political Economy*. Princeton, NJ: Princeton University Press.

———. 1990. "Economic Liberalism Reconsidered." In *The Economic Limits to Politics*, edited by John Dunn. Cambridge: Cambridge University Press, 165–194.

Keohane, Robert O., and Joseph S. Nye. 1977. *Power and Interdependence: World Politics in Transition*. Boston: Little, Brown.

Kim, Jack, and Chris Buckley. 2010. "China PM Seeks to Cool Korean Standoff." *Reuters*. May 28. http://www.reuters.com/article/idUSTRE64N0F520100528 (accessed January 19, 2011).

Krasner, Stephen D. 1976. "State Power and the Structure of International Trade." *World Politics* 28 (3): 317–347.

Landler, Mark. 2010. "Offering to Aid Talks, U.S. Challenges China on Disputed Islands." *New York Times*. July 23. http://www.nytimes.com/2010/07/24/world/

asia/24diplo.html?scp=3&sq=clinton%20vietnam&st=cse; http://www.state
.gov/secretary/rm/2010/07/145095.htm (accessed January 19, 2011).

Mansfield, Edward D., and Jon C. Pevehouse. 2000. "Trade Blocs, Trade Flows, and International Conflict." *International Organization* 54 (4): 775–808.

Mansfield, Edward D., and Brian M. Pollins. 2001. "The Study of Interdependence and Conflict: Recent Advances, Open Questions, and Directions for Future Research." *Journal of Conflict Resolution* 45 (6): 834–859.

Morrison, Wayne M. 2010. *China-U.S. Trade Issues.* June 21. Congressional Research Service 7-5700. http://fpc.state.gov/documents/organization/145605.pdf (accessed January 18, 2012).

Nikkei Weekly. 2005. "FTAs Binding East Asian Region." May 30. LexisNexis Academic. http://www.lexisnexis.com/hottopics/lnacademic (accessed January 25, 2012).

Nye, Joseph S. 1971. *Peace in Parts: Integration and Conflict in Regional Organization.* Boston: Little, Brown.

Richburg, Keith B. 2010. "China, Taiwan Sign Trade Pact." *Washington Post.* June 30.

Sarkees, Meredith Reid, and Frank Wayman. 2010. *Resort to War: 1816–2007.* Washington, DC: CQ Press.

Stein, Arthur A. 1993. "Governments, Economic Interdependence, and International Cooperation." In *Behavior, Society, and Nuclear War,* vol. 3, edited by Philip E. Tetlock, Jo L. Husbands, Robert Jervis, Paul C. Stern, and Charles Tilly. New York: Oxford University Press, 241–324.

Stockholm International Peace Research Institute. 2009. "The SIPRI Military Expenditure Database." Solna, Sweden: Stockholm International Peace Research Institute. http://milexdata.sipri.org/result.php4 (accessed January 19, 2011).

Summers, Robert, and Alan Heston. 1991. "The Penn World Table (Mark 5): An Expanded Set of International Comparisons, 1950–1988." *Quarterly Journal of Economics* 106 (2): 327–368.

Swaine, Michael D. 2011. "China's Assertive Behavior, Part One: On 'Core Interests.'" *China Leadership Monitor,* no. 34 (Winter): 1–25.

Swaine, Michael D., and M. Taylor Fravel. 2011. "China's Assertive Behavior, Part Two: The Maritime Periphery." *China Leadership Monitor,* no. 35 (Summer): 1–34.

Ujikane, Keiko. 2010. "Japan Exports Rise More-Than-Estimated 40.4% on Asia." May 26. *Bloomberg.com.* http://www.bloomberg.com/apps/news?pid=20601080&sid=anrSn6ylCgnw# (accessed January 19, 2011).

Uppsala Conflict Data Program and Peace Research Institute Oslo (UCDP/PRIO). 2010. "UCDP/PRIO Armed Conflict Dataset." Oslo: Peace Research Institute Oslo. http://www.prio.no/CSCW/Datasets/Armed-Conflict/ (accessed January 19, 2011).

U.S. Department of Agriculture. 2010. *International Macroeconomic Data Set.* Washington, DC: U.S. Department of Agriculture, Economic Research Service. http://www.ers.usda.gov/Data/Macroeconomics/Data/HistoricalGDPSharesValues.xls (accessed January 19, 2011).

Viner, Jacob. 1951. *International Economics*. Glencoe, IL: Free Press.

Wohlforth, William C. 1999. "The Stability of a Unipolar World." *International Security* 24 (1): 5–41.

Wolff, Alan Wm. 2010. China in the WTO: Testimony of Co-chair, International Trade Practice, Hearing on Evaluating China's Role in the World Trade Organization over the Past Decade before the U.S. China Economic and Security Review Commission. June 9. Washington, DC.

World Trade Organization. 2010a. "Trade Profiles: China." March. http://stat.wto.org/CountryProfiles/CN_e.htm (accessed January 19, 2011).

———. 2010b. "Trade to Expand by 9.5% in 2010 After a Dismal 2009, WTO Reports." Press Releases: International Trade Statistics. March 26. http://www.wto.org/english/news_e/pres10_e/pr598_e.htm (accessed January 19, 2011).

Xinhua. 2010. "China-ASEAN Free Trade Area." January 1. http://news.xinhuanet.com/english/2010-01/01/content_12740470.htm (accessed January 19, 2011).

Zha, Daojiong. 2005. "China's Energy Security and Its International Relations." *China and Eurasia Forum Quarterly* 3 (3): 39–54.

2   Finance and Security in East Asia

Benjamin J. Cohen

WHAT DRIVES THE RELATIONSHIP BETWEEN REGIONAL finance and security in East Asia? Overall, I suggest, the relationship may be regarded as mutually endogenous. Financial cooperation in the region, long promoted in principle, is constrained in practice by underlying security tensions. Yet over time, tentative steps toward financial cooperation could also have the effect of moderating regional strains, as governments become more accustomed to working with one another and as interests become more densely intertwined. Some form of financial regionalism, entailing closer monetary and financial relations, can almost certainly be expected. In the absence of a fundamental shift in regional politics, however, tangible achievements will most likely remain modest for a long time to come.

Proposals promoting financial regionalism have floated around East Asia for decades. But few in a position of authority ever took the idea seriously until the great banking and currency crisis of 1997–1998, which profoundly shook most of the region's economies. Seen today as a genuine watershed in Asian economic history, the upheaval triggered active consideration of all kinds of financial initiatives, from more formal coordination of monetary and exchange-rate policies to the possibility of reserve pooling or perhaps even a common currency. Eventually, agreement was reached on several proposals, including an Asian Bond Market Initiative (ABMI) and an Asian Bond Fund (ABF), both launched in 2003–2004 with the intention of promoting the development of local capital markets. Most notable was the so-called Chiang

Mai Initiative (CMI), dating from 2000, which established a basis for mutual liquidity assistance among central banks—now expanded under the label Chiang Mai Initiative Multilateralization (CMIM). All have been announced with great fanfare.

Yet despite the hype, it is clear that actual achievements so far have fallen far short of aspirations. Governments continue to operate more or less autonomously, tailoring their monetary and exchange-rate policies to their own particular needs, and the degree of integration of capital markets across the region remains low. Payments financing is still dependent, first and foremost, on hoards of national reserves. As one source delicately puts it: "The direction of regional financial policies remains contested" (Hamilton-Hart 2006: 108).

Why? The main reason, I contend, can be found in underlying security tensions across the region—anxieties over the risk of threat or conflict—which lead governments to seek to preserve for themselves as much room for maneuver as possible. East Asia is replete with historical animosities and festering border disputes, leaving little sense of community or enduring common interest. There are the sensitive unresolved issues of Taiwan and the divided Korean Peninsula. There is the continuing rivalry between China and Japan, both of which aspire to regional leadership. And hovering over it all is the complicating presence of the United States, with its own multiple interests in the area. With so much at stake, governments are understandably reluctant to commit to far-reaching financial reforms that might limit their autonomy.

But the relationship is not one way. I would contend that a reverse causation may also be at work, a process by which tentative steps toward financial regionalism could in time have the effect of moderating security tensions by socializing policy makers to the benefits of cooperation. A kind of self-reinforcing virtuous circle is possible, triggered by crises like that of 1997–1998 or today's global recession. Crises can raise the appeal of cooperation, at least temporarily, thus leading to the institutionalization of initiatives like Chiang Mai. Such initiatives cannot go beyond limits set by broad security concerns. But once some degree of cooperation is institutionalized, a basis for building mutual trust is established that, over time, can serve to ease historical suspicions, setting the stage for yet more financial initiatives down the road.

The Record to Date

For analytical purposes, financial regionalism is understood to encompass public policy initiatives intended to deepen monetary and financial cooperation among governments. Financial regionalism is typically distinguished from financial regionalization, by which is meant concentrations of internationally linked private-sector activities. The aim of financial regionalism is to create institutions at the state level and to institutionalize policy practices in support of market integration. Interest in financial regionalism in East Asia has been high since the crisis of 1997–1998.

That crisis was traumatic for the region. Confidence in the Asian development model, hitherto seemingly so successful, was severely shaken. Financial openness, it turned out, had left economies painfully vulnerable to the whims of international investors. Worse, the perception took hold that the region had been ill served by key outsiders, especially the United States and the International Monetary Fund (IMF). Henceforth, many concluded, regional players would have to cooperate more closely to better defend their collective interests in a global financial architecture that seemed biased against them—"to become *rule makers*," in the pithy phrase of one commentary, "rather than *rule takers*" (Sohn 2005: 488, italics in original).

The result was a flurry of discussions aiming to promote an effective counterweight strategy (Sohn 2007) for the region, stressing three issues in particular: (1) currency management, (2) development of regional capital markets, and (3) emergency liquidity assistance. In practice, however, accomplishments have been modest. As compared with the *status quo ante*, achievements have not been inconsiderable. But relative to the region's own loftier ambitions, the record to date must be rated as limited at best—no more than baby steps, according to the *Financial Times* (2009).

Currency Management

The least progress has been made in the area of currency management. The region has not lacked for proposals. To the contrary, ideas have been a dime a dozen, addressing every aspect of the complex relations among national monetary, fiscal, and exchange-rate policies, from closer coordination of interest rates and spending programs or various forms of mutual exchange-rate stabilization to the creation of an Asian currency unit or even a formal monetary union, complete with a joint central bank and common currency à la the euro.[1] It may be true, as one source suggests, that "a strong case for regional monetary integration tends to be taken for granted in Asia" (Chung and Eichengreen 2007a: 11). But between inspiration and implementation there still lies enormous resistance to change. In practice, as I have noted elsewhere (Cohen 2008), individual monetary regimes have changed little since the crisis and remain remarkably diverse, ranging from currency boards at one extreme to free floating at the other. Governments show little interest in anything that might force them to reconsider their policy preferences. Concludes one recent survey (Hamada, Reszat, and Volz 2009a: 1): "Deeper integration . . . is still a ways away."

Capital Markets

Progress in the development of regional capital markets has been little better. Two projects have been initiated—the Asian Bond Market Initiative and the Asian Bond Fund—both intended to correct for private-sector vulnerabilities that were thought to have contributed directly to the troubles of 1997–1998. The aim of the ABMI was to promote infrastructural improvements that might foster local financial development, aiming eventually to create one regional capital market for all of East Asia. In parallel, the purpose of the ABF was to increase liquidity in Asian capital markets, mainly through purchases of local government bonds by regional central banks. In practice, however, results have been anything but impressive. Although the volume of new debt issues has grown, markets remain thin and overly dependent on government bonds of relatively short maturity, and the amounts of money committed by regional governments to the ABF have been laughably small. "Market participants," reports one informed observer (Park 2007: 103), "believe that [the ABMI and ABF] may have had little effect." More than a decade later, capital market integration remains a distant dream.

Liquidity Assistance

Most progress has been made in the provision of emergency liquidity assistance via the Chiang Mai Initiative, now to be expanded under the label Chiang Mai Initiative Multilateralization. The impetus has come from the so-called ASEAN+3 group, which comprises the ten members of the Association of Southeast Asian nations (ASEAN) plus the three northeast Asian countries of China, Japan, and Korea. More or less by default, ASEAN+3 has become the principal forum for financial regionalism in East Asia.

Launched in May 2000 at a meeting in the Thai resort town of Chiang Mai, the CMI established the basis for a new network of bilateral swap arrangements (BSAs) between the Plus Three countries on the one hand and members of ASEAN on the other hand. The Plus Three countries promised to make dollar resources available to selected ASEAN members, when needed, in exchange for equivalent amounts of local currency. As BSAs were negotiated and concluded over subsequent years, their number grew to as many as nineteen.[2] Initially, the total amount of money that could be mobilized under the CMI came to some $33.5 billion. After the start of a stage 2 in 2005, the nominal size of the swaps was roughly doubled to a net total (after eliminating double counting) of about $60 billion (Henning 2009: 2).[3]

The roots of the CMI go back to Japan's failed proposal for an Asian Monetary Fund (AMF), first mooted in the midst of the region's crisis in September 1997. As nearly every economy in East Asia came under pressure from investor panic and capital flight, Tokyo urged the creation of a new $100 billion regional financing facility, quickly dubbed the AMF, to help protect local currencies against speculative attack. Although nothing came of the proposal at the time—owing to the determined opposition of the United States and IMF, backed tacitly by China—the idea of some kind of mutual safety net survived and eventually took shape at Chiang Mai. The projected network of BSAs, negotiators declared, would finally give East Asia a crisis management capacity it could call its own.

Great hopes have been placed in the CMI as the foundation for increasingly close financial and monetary relations in the region. Functions of the scheme would include monitoring; surveillance; and, if possible, coordination of exchange rates and other related policies. Here, too, however, tangible achievements have so far been modest at best.

For example, all the participating countries understand that if a BSA network is to function effectively, it must be supported by an independent surveillance system. Governments are naturally reluctant to lend to a neighbor in time of crisis unless they can have some degree of confidence that they will eventually be paid back. A firm surveillance mechanism is vital to ensure that borrowers undertake requisite policy adjustments. But nothing of the sort has yet been put into place, despite repeated discussions. Finance ministers regularly reiterate their commitment to enhancing the ASEAN+3's surveillance capacity and have sponsored multiple studies of the feasibility of constructing a regional monitoring institution. But to date their only accomplishment is a vague peer-review scheme known as the Economic Review and Policy Dialogue (ERPD), dating from 2000, which has no set format and lacks any sort of enforcement mechanism beyond nonbinding, informal cautions.

Similar timidity has also plagued the BSA network itself, which requires laborious and time-consuming negotiation (and renegotiation). Member countries agreed that participants would be authorized to draw funds only up to 10 percent of the contractual amount of a BSA (raised to 20 percent in 2005). Beyond that limit a government would have to agree to place itself under IMF tutelage, complete with a macroeconomic and structural adjustment program, thus effectively substituting IMF conditionality for a surveillance system of the region's own making. In part, it appears, this was to placate the United States and the IMF, which might otherwise have objected to a possible dilution of the IMF's authority. But mainly it was to avoid putting regional governments in the position of having to judge one another's policies. William Grimes (2009b: 12) describes the IMF link as an "elegant solution," as "it allows the lending governments to elide responsibility for imposing conditions by delegating conditionality to the IMF." In the absence of a regional surveillance mechanism, the link is obviously necessary to protect the credibility of the CMI. But it has also had a significant chilling effect on actual behavior, owing to memories of the 1997–1998 experience. No participating country has ever actually drawn on a BSA, not even during the global crisis in 2008–2009.

In an attempt to overcome some of these limitations, governments agreed as early as 2005 to seek to "multilateralize" the CMI, pooling funds together to enhance the amounts that any single country might draw when in need. Four years later, in December 2009, agreement was finally struck, transforming the CMI into a new common facility dubbed the CMIM. Beyond the existing BSAs, some of which were to be retained,[4] resources were effectively doubled to $120 billion. Of this total, 80 percent came from the Plus Three countries together with Hong Kong, a new participant, and 20 percent from the ten members of ASEAN, based on a carefully calibrated set of quotas. Japan and China each contributed 32 percent, with Hong Kong contributing 3.5 percent as part of China's share, and Korea put up 16 percent. Indonesia, Malaysia, Singapore, and Thailand contributed 4 percent each, and 4 percent came from the remaining six ASEAN members. Contributions were based on quotas that also determine voting rights and borrowing limits.[5] Formal launching was set for March 2010. In addition, building on the ERPD, a new surveillance unit is at last supposed to be created.

However, it remains to be seen how much further multilateralization will actually take the nations of East Asia. Some observers see the CMIM as a critical step toward realizing, at long last, Japan's original idea of an Asian Monetary Fund. Of particular importance, it is said, is the commitment to a joint decision-making process as BSAs are superseded by the common facility, with access to loans to be decided by majority voting. In practice, however, crucial details have yet to be negotiated, concerning especially issues of borrowing accessibility, lending terms, and how funds will be disbursed.

To date, ministers have described their latest initiative as a "self-managed reserve pooling arrangement" (SRPA), with each government doing no more than earmarking a portion of its own reserves for joint use. That is a far cry from a genuine common fund of the sort envisioned at the time of the Japanese proposal. An SRPA is no AMF. Moreover, the total amount of money involved, though representing a substantial increase from the existing BSA network, is still trivial in relation to potential need or the value of reserves currently hoarded away by the region's central banks (totaling more than $3.5 trillion overall for the thirteen ASEAN+3 countries and Hong Kong). And even less consequential is the proposed surveillance unit, which is expected to be very small (between ten and twenty individuals at most) and with responsibilities limited to no more than a sharing of information. Without a truly autonomous monitor with enforcement powers, it is clear that the IMF link will have to be retained, thus still discouraging potential borrowers. Moreover, broad governance of the system will continue to be based on consensus, minimizing any compromise of national sovereignty.

Overall, therefore, one has the impression that the value of the CMIM lies mainly in its symbolism, which signals little more than a minimal spirit of goodwill and comity. Its practical impact on actual behavior does not promise to be dramatic.

Explaining the Record

What explains the modesty of the record to date? Many factors are undoubtedly involved, both economic and political. Most discussions focus on the economic side, highlighting structural and institutional differences among the economies of the region. But none of these barriers is necessarily insurmountable, given a sufficient degree of commitment. The real problem lies on the political side, where security tensions dominate. For all the talk of financial regionalism in East Asia, little real progress is possible without a significant moderation of underlying rivalries and animosities.

Economics

On the economic side, the impediments are obvious. The nations of East Asia are a remarkably diverse lot in terms of economic structure and level of development, with little in common other than geographical proximity. A high degree of heterogeneity, not homogeneity, rules. In some cases, as Natasha Hamilton-Hart (2003) has emphasized, government capacity is simply inadequate to handle the demanding complexities of financial cooperation.

Moreover, financial ties among the economies of the region are generally weak, which reinforces centrifugal forces. In capital markets, little has changed despite the ABMI and ABF. Although a few governments have made progress in deregulating domestic monetary systems and opening up financial services to foreign competition, overall integration remains a distant dream. Apart from Japan, Hong Kong, and Singapore, most states still impose strict exchange controls and other barriers to limit the free flow of funds. Restrictions are particularly tight in China and the poorer members of ASEAN, where financial systems remain underdeveloped and shallow.

Likewise, at the macroeconomic level there are few signs yet of significant convergence in terms of either performance or policy. Business cycles across the region are far from synchronized, and little correlation exists in inflation or growth rates. Fiscal deficits and public debt burdens vary enormously, and monetary policy in most cases remains insular in orientation. Governments continue to look first to their own national resources for defense against external payments pressures.

Yet for all the challenges they pose, such impediments need not be prohibitive. Offsetting the many centrifugal forces in East Asia are also some powerful and growing economic connections. That is especially true in the area of trade, where the pace of activity in the region has grown exponentially over the past third of a century. Among the forces driving the expansion of intraregional trade are the many "invisible" linkages created by extensive ethnic business networks, which encompass overseas Chinese communities or other groups such as Koreans or Vietnamese (Peng 2002). Equally important are the much more visible linkages created by the direct investments of multinational corporations—initially coming mainly from Japan, Europe, and the United States, but followed increasingly from within the region itself. The result has been a bourgeoning of tightly organized production networks and supply chains across East Asia, promoting vertical intraindustry trade in capital equipment, parts and components, semifinished goods, and final products.

Among the ASEAN+3 countries, the share of intraregional exchanges in total trade has risen from some 30 percent in 1980 to close to 40 percent in 2007. If Hong Kong and Taiwan are added, the intraregional share has soared from 37 percent to nearly 55 percent (Kawai 2008). Even allowing for a certain amount of double counting due to the high proportion of trade in components and the special role of Hong Kong and Singapore as entrepôts, these numbers are impressive. Overall, trade shares match the scale of commercial integration found in North America today among Canada, Mexico, and the United States, and actually exceed the rate of intraregional trade within the European Union (Park and Shin 2009).

Among economists, it is common to judge prospects for financial regionalism on the basis of the well-known optimum-currency-area (OCA) theory, which highlights the salience to any integration project of such considerations as structural homogeneity, openness, and the degree of convergence among the countries involved. In many respects East Asia scores remarkably well, particularly when compared with the members of Europe's euro zone (Eichengreen and Bayoumi 1999; Zhang, Sato, and McAleer 2001; Kawai and Motonishi 2004; Kawai 2008). Econometric analyses, including some fourteen studies surveyed by the Bank of Japan (Watanabe and Ogura 2006), confirm that selected subgroups in the region, if not the region as a whole, meet the usual criteria of OCA theory at least as well as did European nations before their monetary union (Watanabe and Ogura 2006). One knowledgeable source (De Grauwe 2009: 115–117) summarizes: "The consensus emerging from that literature is that Asian countries do not experience more asymmetry than the members of the Euro area. . . . It would appear that East Asia comes at least as close as Europe to forming an optimum currency area."[6]

So if Europe could overcome the impediments to financial cooperation, going so far as to create a common currency, why have results been so limited in Asia? Why has the quite remarkable expansion of intraregional trade not inspired a parallel commitment to closer monetary and financial relations? The answer, I submit, must lie on the political side.

Politics

If history teaches us anything, it is that economic obstacles to cooperation among states—no matter how seemingly prohibitive—can be overcome if the political will is there. We need only remind ourselves of the successful negotiation a half century ago of a new common market in Europe, incorporating previously implacable enemies, not much more than a decade after the most destructive war that Europeans had ever seen. We know that the idea of financial regionalism has broad appeal in East Asia; otherwise, how could we explain all the time and effort that has gone into the construction of the CMI and CMIM? But we also know that, at least until now, the requisite political will has not yet been in evidence. In effect, governments have been unwilling to put their money where their mouth is—at least, not much money. The question is, Why?

Intuitively, the answer might seem obvious. At least in part, one might think, the problem could lie at the domestic level, in the perpetual tug-of-war among diverse political constituencies. No government, no matter how autocratic, can afford to ignore internal distributional considerations entirely. Perhaps policy makers who might otherwise be favorably disposed to cooperation abroad have been hamstrung by elements of opposition at home. In reality, however, there is scant evidence of any such influence at work, as acute observers such as Saori Katada (2008, 2009) have noted. Formal research has yet to demonstrate any significant mobilization by societal actors to influence regional financial negotiations.

The reason is evident. On issues of trade policy, where potential winners and losers are relatively easy to identify, interest cleavages can indeed make a real difference; in most economies, the risk is high that trade officials will find themselves being actively lobbied by enterprises or industries with a specific axe to grind. In matters of money and finance, by contrast, distributional implications of alternative policy choices tend to be more ambiguous, which reduces the likelihood of well-organized collective action for or against specific initiatives. The contrast was long ago highlighted by Joanne Gowa (1988) in an analysis of trade and monetary policy processes in the United States. The logic is equally applicable in East Asia. Regional authorities simply have a freer hand when it comes to finance. In Katada's (2009: 8) words, decision makers are "much more autonomous from pressure when it comes to financial and monetary policy making." If governments have been unwilling to put their money where their mouth is, it is not because of domestic politics.

In practice, the answer appears to lie more at the international level, where differences of perceived state interest dominate. For Asian governments, the dilemma is clear. Financial cooperation of any sort involves a degree of commitment that is naturally antithetical to the preferences of formally sovereign nations. Unlike trade agreements, which merely ask governments to step aside and let markets operate, initiatives like the CMI are proactive, mandating specific forms of behavior in specified circumstances. Involved is what one source (Litfin 1997) calls a sovereignty bargain: a voluntary agreement to accept certain limitations on national autonomy in exchange for anticipated benefits. In effect, sovereignty is pooled. The conditions generally conducive to such a commitment are, to say the least, demanding.

What are those conditions? Previously (Cohen 2001), I have used comparative historical analysis to identify the key conditions that appear to determine the sustainability of close financial cooperation among states. The same factors can be assumed to be instrumental in gaining the necessary commitment to regionalism in the first place. Two requisites stand out. One, suggested by traditional realist approaches to international relations theory, is the presence or absence of a powerful state or combination of powerful states committed to using their influence to keep the joint effort functioning effectively on terms agreeable to all. The other, suggested by more institutional approaches to world politics, is the presence or absence of a broad constellation of related ties and commitments sufficient to make the sacrifice of sovereignty, whatever the costs, basically acceptable to each partner. Judging from the historical record, I conclude that one or the other of these two types of linkage is necessary to sustain the necessary degree of commitment. Where both types have been present, they have been a sufficient condition for success. Where neither was present, cooperation has tended to erode or fail.

The first condition calls for one or more dominant countries—local leaders or hegemons—and is a direct reflection of the distribution of state power. Scholars have long recognized the critical role that the leadership of powerful states can play in preserving sovereignty bargains. At issue, as David Lake (1993) has emphasized, is the provision of a type of public good, an essential infrastructure that will support both short-term stabilization and longer-term growth. Leaders must be not only able but also willing to use their power, via side-payments or sanctions, to lower the costs or raise the benefits of commitment for their partners.

The second condition calls for a well-developed set of functional linkages and reflects, more amorphously, the degree to which a genuine sense of solidarity—of community—exists among the countries involved. Scholars have also long recognized the demanding cognitive dimension of sovereignty bargains. Participating states, at a quite fundamental level, must come to accept that individual interests can best be realized through joint undertakings—through what Robert Keohane and Stanley Hoffmann

(1991: 13) call a network form of organization "in which individual units are defined not by themselves but in relation to other units." Without such a sense of solidarity, governments will be more preoccupied with the costs of commitment than with any benefits.

The underlying logic goes to the heart of what we mean by "sovereignty." Governments need strong incentives to stick to bargains that might, at some point, turn out to be inconvenient. In practice, such incentives may derive either from the encouragement or discipline supplied by powerful states or else from the opportunities and constraints posed by a network of functional and cognitive linkages. The question of whether economic ties are weak or strong seems to be of secondary importance. What matters more is a convergence of state preferences, supported either by committed local hegemons or by a common sense of community.

The problem for East Asia is that neither of these critical conditions is presently much in evidence. Many in the region like to think that Asia is different; that unlike Europe, formal sovereignty bargains are unnecessary. They like to boast of the ASEAN way—the principle of noninterference in the internal affairs of member countries and a reliance on accommodation and consensus—which has long guided relations in ASEAN and has been extended to the ASEAN+3. The ASEAN way (or Asian way), it is said, combines cooperation with deference, allowing states sufficient autonomy to safeguard domestic priorities (Khong and Nesadurai 2007). But could this just be another way of avoiding real commitment? It is hard not to see celebration of the ASEAN way as simply an excuse for inaction. As the *Economist* (2010) has commented: "Prickly nation-states are loth to cede sovereignty to any regional body. The flip side of Asia's famous taste for consensus is an allergy to enforceable rules and obligations."

The reality is that prevailing circumstances give governments in the region little incentive to go beyond the most minimal sort of joint financial initiatives.

Leadership?

First, there is a dearth of coherent leadership. East Asia does not lack for plausible leaders. As everyone knows, there are in fact two of them, Japan and China, potentially not unlike the duopoly of France and Germany in post–World War II Europe that provided the decisive impetus for the early common market. But there is a distinct lack of comity between the Japanese and Chinese that makes it difficult for them to jointly lead the way.

In retrospect it is clear that Europe's common market, now the twenty-seven-member European Union, could never have come into being without the historic reconciliation of France and Germany after 1945—two longtime adversaries who decided to join together to promote a common regional project. Nothing comparable has emerged in relations between Japan and China, which still regard themselves more as rivals than partners. The lack of trust between East Asia's two giants is palpable, fraught with bitterness and mutual suspicion. Japan, once the dominant economic power of the region, fears falling under China's lengthening shadow—what the Japanese call the "China economic threat theory" (Samuels 2007: 144). The Chinese, meanwhile, continue to harbor acute resentments toward the Japanese for their military and colonial activities from 1895 to 1945—the so-called history problem (Grimes 2009a: 8). Neither country is willing to commit to any collective initiative that might cede a greater measure of influence or prestige to the other. Rather, as Kent Calder (2006) has suggested, "the stage is now set for a struggle between a mature power and a rising one." Moreover, in the background there is also the United States, still a major presence in the region, with lingering leadership aspirations of its own.

At the broadest geopolitical level East Asia is dominated by a strategic triangle involving Washington as well as Beijing and Tokyo, each with its own distinct interests and preferences that color every effort to promote financial cooperation in the region. For Japan, a once-dominant power fearful of losing its traditional preeminence, the key goal is to lock in as much influence as possible while not jeopardizing its close political and military ties with the United States—in the words of one observer, "to exist securely without being either too dependent on the United States or too vulnerable to China" (Samuels 2007: 9). Conversely, for China—the once and future Middle Kingdom—the objective must be to support institutional reforms that will allow it to continue to grow rapidly while avoiding commitments that could contain its anticipated world role. All the while the United States can be expected to seek to do what it can to preserve the historical role of the dollar and U.S. financial enterprises in the region. Washington has never been enthusiastic about the development of multilateral initiatives in the region, preferring instead to promote its own bilateral relationships with individual East Asian governments.

Even if Asians were prepared to accept U.S. leadership on any future financial project—a dubious premise, at best—it is doubtful that U.S. policy makers would see promotion of a nascent regional bloc including China as being in America's national interest.

The complex dynamics of what one source (Emmott 2008: 1) calls "Asia's new power game" were on vivid display as far back as 1997, when both China and the United States, each for its own reasons, resisted Tokyo's proposal for an Asian Monetary Fund. Apart from their concern about the possible dilution of IMF authority, the Americans evidently feared that the AMF might consolidate a dominant regional role for the yen, thus undermining U.S. interests and influence. Washington actively lobbied Beijing to join in opposition to the plan, emphasizing the threat of Japanese hegemony. The Chinese, meanwhile, always suspicious of Japanese motivations, were piqued by Tokyo's failure to consult with them before the plan was announced and agreed to maintain a passive stance, tacitly backing the United States. And behind both nations was the IMF, which had its own reasons for concern about the advent of a new institutional rival. Without Chinese support, Tokyo was unable to prevail over the combined forces of the United States and the Fund (Chey 2009).

Since then, the three governments have persistently jockeyed for position in a wary pas de trois. Aware of the lengthening shadow cast by China's peaceful rise, Tokyo has pushed one idea after another for new regional ventures, obviously hoping to consolidate whatever remains of Japan's position as a regional leader while there is still time. Tokyo played a key role as arbitrator in the negotiation of the CMI as countries in the region bargained over terms for the network of BSAs. Two years later came the ABMI, also a Japanese initiative. And since 2005 Tokyo has been an eager advocate of CMI multilateralization. Yet simultaneously, in a delicate balancing act, Tokyo has carefully sought to avoid any move that might jeopardize the broader security relationship that it has long enjoyed with the United States. By backing the CMI's IMF link, for example, Tokyo has sought to keep the IMF—and thus, indirectly, the United States, the IMF's most influential member—fully engaged in the region.

In turn, Beijing has gradually shifted toward a more proactive stance concerning financial regionalism, consistent with a broader embrace of multilateralism in Chinese grand strategy that has been evident since the 1990s (Goldstein 2005). The turn was first evident in the negotiation of the CMI in

2000. Though not the inspiration for the initiative, China was able quickly to join Japan in a leadership capacity because of the size of its foreign reserves. Japan and China were, at the time, the only two states whose role would clearly be limited to that of lender, should the BSA network be activated. Subsequently, China played a prominent part in CMI multilateralization. In part, Beijing's conversion to regionalism appears to have been motivated by a desire to calm concerns about the country's rapid development and incipient power—to signal, as Avery Goldstein (2005: 129) puts it, a "responsible internationalism." But there seems little doubt that paramount in the minds of policy makers was a desire to avoid ceding leadership in regional finance to their rivals, the Japanese.

The rivalry was perhaps best illustrated by the intense bargaining that took place in 2009 over the two countries' quotas in the CMIM. Tokyo was determined to gain the largest quota, to reflect its past dominance in regional finance. China, however, insisted that its own growth and size entitled it to an equal share of the total—an equal-firsts policy. The compromise that was finally reached, giving China (with 28.5 percent) together with Hong Kong (3.5 percent) a quota equal to Japan's 32 percent, would have been laughable had the stakes not been so serious. With this arcane formula, the Japanese could claim, truthfully, that they were the biggest single contributor. Yet the Chinese could make an equally valid claim that they had attained parity with Japan, as Hong Kong—though technically an autonomous region—is formally part of the People's Democratic Republic ("two systems, one country"). Both sides could go home as winners.

Significantly, in the period since the CMIM was announced, both Japan and China have been energetically negotiating or expanding their own bilateral local-currency swaps in the region even while planning to incorporate their existing bilateral dollar swaps into the CMIM. Each government, in effect, appears to be competing to line up as many regional clients as possible, offering access to the yen or yuan as bait.

All this is a far cry from the kind of historical reconciliation that enabled France and Germany to provide leadership for Europe after World War II. Some form of Sino-Japanese reconciliation is not impossible, of course, even though Asia's circumstances today are obviously quite different from those of postwar Europe. Once the Cold War began France and Germany, formerly enemies, soon became part of the same military alliance. In East Asia, by contrast, Japan and China find themselves in a more adversarial relationship—Japan still a partner of the United States, China a rising great-power competitor. Faced with the prospect of economic stagnation and long-term demographic decline, Tokyo could well be tempted at some point to bandwagon rather than balance with China, becoming in effect Beijing's junior partner—the equivalent of France to China's Germany. Concerns about the China economic-threat theory might simply be allowed to fade away. Conversely, the Chinese economic model could conceivably begin to falter, thus leading Beijing to turn to Tokyo as an ally in hard times. China's history problem with the Japanese might be conveniently forgotten. But what are the chances of either scenario materializing? The odds are long. Few specialists in Asian security anticipate a genuine easing of Asia's power game anytime soon.

Is it any wonder, then, that achievements to date have been so modest? The security tensions between East Asia's two giants cannot be denied. It is understandable, therefore, that others in the region might hesitate to commit to anything too demanding. Without coherent joint leadership, putative followers are naturally reluctant to take any steps that might, in effect, compel them to choose sides between mutually mistrustful rivals.

Solidarity?

There is also a dearth of genuine solidarity. Put simply, East Asia lacks any sense of common identity. As Grimes (2009a: 41) has noted, a "defining characteristic of East Asia has been regional fragmentation . . . a lack of centripetal forces." Other than geography, little binds the countries of the area together, whereas many factors work to keep them apart. These include deep differences of language, religion, ideology, and social organization, as well as stubborn legacies of World War II and the Cold War, such as Taiwan's contested status and the division of the Korean peninsula. As Zhang Tuosheng (Chapter 5) reminds us, the region is riven by numerous unresolved disputes over territorial and maritime rights and interests. Security tensions are not limited to Japan and China alone.

For all their protestations of amity, all the region's governments remain noticeably distrustful of one another and place a high premium on preservation of as much national sovereignty as possible. Unlike Europeans, East Asians are as yet unwilling to pay even lip service to the notion of an ever-closer union among their peoples. Most, having only recently emerged from colonial status, are more intent on individual state building than on promoting regional solidarity. Few demonstrate much inclination to define themselves in relation to one another rather than in their own terms. As one Asian observer (Kim 2009: 49) puts it, "one of the driving forces behind European integration was the desire for a united Europe. This idea of a common citizenship is lacking in East Asia."

Nor is there even any natural core of states on which to build a regional project, as there was in Europe's original inner six. The requisite like-mindedness is just not there. ASEAN+3 is a wholly artificial construct, in terms of both who is included (Myanmar?) and who is excluded (Taiwan?). The advantage of such a broad grouping is that it includes the two states, China and Japan, who separately or together could play the role of support-ive local hegemon. But even apart from the animosities that divide the two potential leaders, there is the problem that suspicions of both powers remain widespread throughout the region. Wariness about the Japanese goes back to Tokyo's attempts during the interwar period to create the Greater East Asia Co-Prosperity Sphere, which most Asians remember as an exploitative and demeaning relationship. Fears of future domination by a huge, rapidly grow-ing China are equally strong. Governments are not particularly eager to com-mit to the leadership of either of the two.

Should we be surprised, then, that the results of financial regionalism have until now been so unimpressive? The conditions needed to attain a successful sovereignty bargain have been most conspicuous by their absence. The lack of political will is by no means an accident.

Reverse Causation?

Political will is not written in stone, however. Attitudes can change. In par-ticular, we cannot dismiss the possibility of reverse causation—a relationship of mutual endogeneity. Although security tensions may cause East Asians to hesitate over a commitment to financial regionalism today, tomorrow could be different. Over time, tentative steps toward financial cooperation could actually have the effect of moderating those same regional strains. Govern-ments might be led to reconsider their security concerns, thus paving the way for additional cooperation on initiatives like the CMI and CMIM in a kind of self-reinforcing virtuous circle.

The idea is not new. The possibility of mutual endogeneity in situations like this has frequently been acknowledged in the general theoretical lit-erature. David Bearce (2003) and Yoram Haftel (2007), among others, have spoken of the way that frequent contacts through regional economic institutions may help create the trust needed to reduce security tensions and overcome commitment problems. Social psychologists call this the contact hypothesis. In Chapter 4, Wu Xinbo speaks specifically of the spillover effect of economic regionalism, which has led the ASEAN+3 nations to cooperate on such nontraditional security issues as piracy and drug trafficking. Likewise, in Chapter 3 Miles Kahler highlights the possible role of Asian regional organizations in promoting peace and security, although he cautions that the effect may be difficult to confirm empirically.

In none of these analyses, however, is an explanation provided for the precise mechanism that propels the process forward. A growth of trust may be a necessary condition for further cooperation, but it is hardly sufficient. What else is needed? In practice, I would argue, the dynamic of a self-reinforcing virtuous circle requires not one but two ingredients—not just regular contacts, to foster mutual confidence, but also a trigger of some kind, to overcome resistance to change. First comes a slow-moving process of socialization that works gradually to erode the foundations of prevailing attitudes. Then, at unpredictable intervals, come occasional fast-moving crises, sharp breaks in the economic environment that may alter incentives enough to overcome inertia and set off a new round of initiatives. Both ingredients are necessary to maintain the momentum of a virtuous circle. It is in the interaction of the two that we find the key to the prospect of any further progress in Asian financial cooperation.

Punctuated Equilibrium

I have spoken of the reasons a successful sovereignty bargain is so difficult to attain. For the same reasons sovereignty bargains, once struck, are also hard to change in any significant way. Typically, a certain degree of inertia sets in—an acceptance of the status quo and a resistance to fresh initiatives—that can be overcome only with considerable and determined effort. The progress of cooperation among states, therefore, tends to be subject to fits and starts: sustained periods of relative quiescence alternating with short bursts of reforming zeal.

A favored metaphor for the process is punctuated equilibrium, a concept borrowed from evolutionary biology and widely employed in various branches of social theory. First popularized by the paleontologist Stephen Jay Gould, *punctuated equilibrium* was defined as "a model for discontinuous tempos of change [in] the process of speciation and the deployment of species in geological time" (Eldredge and Gould 1972: 83). In social theory, the notion of punctuated equilibrium has been co-opted as a model to help explain discontinuities in public policy behavior, beginning with a seminal book by the political scientists Frank Baumgartner and Bryan Jones (1993). The model assumes that policy generally changes only incrementally because of a variety of constraints, such as the stickiness of institutional cultures, vested interests, and the bounded rationality of individual decision makers. The policy process, accordingly, tends to be characterized by long periods of stability, punctuated only on occasion by large, though less frequent, changes caused by major shifts in society or government. In recent years, the punctuated equilibrium model has been used to shed light on everything from the specifics of U.S. tobacco policy (Givel 2006) to the general incidence of war (Leventoğlu and Slantchev 2007).

In the East Asian context, a pattern of punctuated equilibrium does seem to have been in evidence since the 1990s. After decades of inaction in the region, the energy that suddenly went into negotiating the ABMI, ABF, and CMI at the start of the new century was striking. Then a renewed period of comparative stasis followed until interrupted by the much-celebrated multilateralization of the CMI in 2010. The stop-go quality of the pattern is unmistakable. What drives the pattern, I suggest, is the dynamic interaction of the two ingredients of socialization and crisis.

Socialization
Start with the first ingredient. In the absence of coherent leadership from Japan and China, a growing sense of solidarity in the region is essential to provide the political will needed to deepen monetary and financial ties. That is where socialization comes in, which has been defined as "a process of inducting actors into the norms and rules of a given community" (Checkel 2005: 804). Socialization occurs naturally when cooperation among states becomes institutionalized in initiatives like the CMI or CMIM. The more actors learn to work together, finding joint solutions to common problems, the less reason they may find to cling to ancient suspicions and animosities. Gradually, bitterness and fear can yield to an accumulation of the mutual trust needed for more far-reaching initiatives—"peaceful change through socialization," as one source describes it (Acharya 2009: 20).

The mechanics of the process were described long ago by Robert Keohane and Joseph Nye (1974), who stressed the development of what later came to be known as epistemic communities. From regularized cooperation over a period of time, they wrote, changes of attitude may result, creating "transgovernmental elite networks" linking decision makers to one another by ties of common interest, professional orientation, and even personal friendship. According to Keohane and Nye (1974: 45), "When the same officials meet recurrently, they sometimes develop a sense of collegiality, which may be reinforced by their membership in a common profession. . . . Regularized patterns of policy coordination can therefore create attitudes and relationships that will at least marginally change policy." Today, in the language of constructivism, that would be described as a reconstitution of actor identities and interests. Initiatives like the CMI and CMIM can create new social facts (intersubjective understandings) that, in turn, may lead to deeper forms of cooperation.

That some kind of socialization has been taking place in East Asia can hardly be questioned. Many have written specifically of the socializing role of Asian financial institutions (Acharya 2009). Indeed, how could attitudes not be affected, given the frequency of meetings across the region dealing with one financial issue or another? Some positive influence must be at work, quietly building a sense of common destiny. It is true, of course, that the actors most directly involved—central bankers, treasury officials, banking regulators, and the like—normally are not the same as the personnel responsible for security policy. The two issue areas are typically managed by different elite networks that only occasionally overlap in daily operation. But that caveat applies mostly to the lower levels of bureaucracy, which deal mainly with matters of a routine or technical nature. At higher levels of decision making, where grand strategy is involved, contacts among officials are bound to be broader and more intimate. It is hard to believe that finance and foreign ministers do not talk to one another on occasion, sharing their impressions on relations with regional neighbors.

On its own, however, socialization is unlikely to be decisive, precisely because it is such a gradual process. It takes time to shift intersubjective understandings. Peter Aykens (2005) distinguishes three stages in the process of trust development: (1) momentary trust, based on calculations of risk resting solely on immediately available information; (2) reputational trust, derived from growing familiarity and experience; and (3) affective trust, representing stable and unquestioned sets of expectations. Only when the final stage of affective trust is attained—the end product of a long process of social interaction and learning—can a really serious sovereignty bargain be struck as a result of socialization alone. Short of that stage, which could take decades to attain, some trigger is needed to overcome resistance to change. The most obvious candidate to play that role is an unexpected crisis of some kind.

Crisis

Enter the second ingredient: economic crisis. Scholars of international relations have long noted the potentially positive role of crises. The classical definition of a crisis is usually attributed to Charles Hermann (1972), who equated the phenomenon with three critical dimensions: high threat, short decision time, and an element of surprise. In such circumstances, it is not at all surprising that actors might be spurred to jump to a new level of cooperation—to use the well-worn analogy, much like a frog thrown into the proverbial pot of boiling water. The motivation for joining together may be fear, a defense against the unknown. But it could also be a matter of ambition, a determination to strike while the iron is hot. Crises represent a "critical juncture" (Calder and Ye 2004) that can create a tipping point or window of opportunity for strategic experimentation and policy adaptation.

Obviously, there is no certainty about the process. Much depends on what Jeffrey Chwieroth (2010) calls the four Cs of crisis resolution: carriers of new ideas, composition of advocacy groups, crossover appeal of innovative proposals, and credibility with external actors. Cooperation is most likely to be ratcheted up if it is promoted by a prominent and cohesive group of advocates and endorsed by other actors whose seal of approval is perceived as important.

For all the damage they may do, therefore, economic crises have frequently been cited favorably for their potentially powerful influence as a catalyst for new initiatives. Stephan Haggard and Sylvia Maxfield (1996), for example, have cited the key part played by balance-of-payments shocks in encouraging financial liberalization in developing countries. Although it might seem counterintuitive, they found that governments faced with the threat of a run on their currency have often found it expedient to increase rather than decrease financial openness, to cultivate credibility with market actors. Liberalization in the face of crisis, Haggard and Maxfield (1996: 211) write, "signals foreign investors that they will be able to liquidate their investments, indicates government intentions to maintain fiscal and monetary discipline, and thus ultimately increases capital inflows." Similarly, in an early analysis of my own (Cohen 1993), I have highlighted the effect that crises may have in easing, at least temporarily, resistance to new form of monetary cooperation. Major financial upheavals, I suggested, tend for a time to alter governments' calculations of the costs and benefits of cooperation. The perceived disadvantages of a commitment to common action are reduced when all parties seem threatened by a large systemic shock. As a result, cooperation may be ratcheted up a notch or two beyond what previously might have seemed possible. Equilibrium is punctuated.

The Dynamic in Action

The dynamic interaction of socialization and crisis has certainly seemed to be at work in East Asia—at least, so far. Crisis, we know, clearly played a role a decade ago in first stimulating East Asia's interest in financial regionalism. Observers overwhelmingly agree that the trauma of 1997–1998 was a "turning point" for the countries of the region (Chey 2009: 450); an "impetus for many financial cooperation initiatives" (Sussangkarn and Vichyanond 2007: 25); a shock that "opened the door to significant policy-led integration in East Asia" (Park 2007: 96). Many make use of the word *catalyst* (e.g., Amyx 2004: 98). Indeed, a recent major retrospective on the experience was entitled, simply, *Crisis as Catalyst* (MacIntyre, Pempel, and Ravenhill 2008). The burst of energy that followed the crisis, resulting in the ABMI, ABF, and CMI, is easy to understand.

Likewise, crisis plainly provided the impetus needed to complete multilateralization of the CMI. Here the shock was the global financial meltdown that started in 2007–2008, bringing with it the deepest downturn in the world economy since the Great Depression. Observers agree that in this instance, too, the perceived threat was serious enough to prod governments into action. In the words of the *China Daily* (2009): "Ever since the Asian financial turmoil of 1997–98, Asian countries have learned the importance of some kind of regional currency cooperative mechanism. . . . Now, with a second financial crisis in a decade and prospects still unclear as to when the global market would finally emerge from its shadow, it would be all the more crucial to build a collective protective mechanism." Skeptics may object, pointing out that the idea of multilateralization actually dates as far back as 2005. But it is clear that little of a practical nature was ever accomplished toward that goal, following agreement in principle, until crisis once more loomed. As Wheatley (2009) commented, "It took a global crisis to inject a sense of urgency into the project."

The question is, Can we expect the pattern to be repeated again? The shock in 1997–1998 was especially conducive to cooperation in East Asia because of two dominant features. First, just about every economy in the region was seriously affected, thus making it a collective experience. They all felt that they were in the same boat. Second, most found themselves especially vulnerable to external pressures because of their then-low levels of reserves. Few at the time were in a position to resist market speculators or the demands of the United States and IMF. The same two features were also in evidence during the more recent episode, owing to the breadth and gravity of the global recession. Despite higher reserve levels, most governments again felt vulnerable to events originating outside their region. There is no guarantee, however, that similar circumstances will ever arise again. The dynamic of punctuated equilibrium is real but by no means inevitable.

Conclusion

My conclusion, therefore, is positive but temperate. Though limited by security tensions, some form of financial regionalism is possible and could, with luck, help reduce barriers to further cooperation in the future. But the process, I suggest, will at best be both episodic and excruciatingly slow. The socializing effects of initiatives like the CMI and CMIM are by definition glacial in their velocity, unlikely in and of themselves to overcome resistance to a genuine sovereignty bargain; and crises, though potentially helpful, are inherently unpredictable in terms of timing as well as impact. In the absence of a truly fundamental transformation of East Asian politics, cumulative accomplishments in regional finance will most likely remain modest for a long time to come.

Notes

I have received helpful comments from the other contributors to this project and also from Dave Andrews, Michael Mastanduno, Evan Medeiros, Etel Solingen, and Tom Willett. The research assistance of Tabitha Benney is also gratefully acknowledged.

1. See, e.g., Asian Development Bank (2004); Chung and Eichengreen (2007b, 2009); Hamada, Reszat, and Volz 2009b; Volz (2010).

2. The number in effect at any one time has varied as arrangements have lapsed and been renegotiated and reinstated.

3. Formally, the CMI also included two other pillars in addition to the BSA network. One was a set of repurchase agreements totaling $1 billion. The other was an

agreement to expand an already-existing ASEAN swap arrangement (ASA), first established in 1977 by the five founding ASEAN members (Indonesia, Malaysia, Philippines, Singapore, and Thailand). The ASA was to include the Plus Three countries as well as other members of ASEAN, and the level of mutual commitments, originally set at $200 million, was raised to $1 billion (further increased to $2 billion in 2005). Because the amounts involved are so small, however, neither of the additional pillars is considered of particular importance.

4. At the time of writing, it was still not clear which BSAs would ultimately be retained and which would be effectively folded into the new common facility.

5. Formally, borrowing rights are defined by purchasing multipliers of 0.5, 1.0, 2.5, or 5.0, inversely related to the size of each country's quota (contribution).

6. For a notable dissent from this consensus, see Willett (2009: chap. 7).

Works Cited

Acharya, Amitav. 2009. "Asian Regional Institutions and the Possibilities for Socializing the Behavior of States." Background paper prepared for the Workshop on Institutions for Regionalism in Asia and the Pacific, Shanghai, December.

Amyx, Jennifer A. 2004. "Political Dynamics of Regional Financial Cooperation in East Asia." *Japanese Economy* 32 (2): 98–112.

Asian Development Bank. 2004. *Monetary and Financial Integration in East Asia: The Way Ahead.* 2 vols. New York: Palgrave Macmillan.

Aykens, Peter A. 2005. "(Mis)Trusting Authorities: A Social Theory of Currency Crises." *Review of International Political Economy* 12 (2): 310–333.

Baumgartner, Frank R., and Bryan D. Jones. 1993. *Agendas and Instability in American Politics.* Chicago: University of Chicago Press.

Bearce, David H. 2003. "Grasping the Commercial Institutional Peace." *International Studies Quarterly* 47 (3): 347–370.

Calder, Kent E. (2006), "China and Japan's Simmering Rivalry." *Foreign Affairs* 85 (2): 129–137.

Calder, Kent, and Min Ye (2004). "Regionalism and Critical Junctures: Explaining the 'Organization Gap' in Northeast Asia." *Journal of East Asian Studies* 4 (2): 191–226.

Checkel, Jeffrey. 2005. "International Institutions and Socialization in Europe: Introduction and Framework." *International Organization* 59 (4): 801–826.

Chey, Hyoung-kyu. 2009. "The Changing Political Dynamics of East Asian Financial Cooperation." *Asian Survey* 49 (3): 450–467.

China Daily. 2009. "Asia's IMF?" December 30.

Chung, Duck-Koo, and Barry Eichengreen. 2007a. "Exchange Rate Arrangements for Emerging East Asia." In *Toward an East Asian Exchange Rate Regime,* edited by Duck-Koo Chung and Barry Eichengreen. Washington, DC: Brookings Institution, 1–21.

———, eds. 2007b. *Toward an East Asian Exchange Rate Regime.* Washington, DC: Brookings Institution.

————, eds. 2009. *Fostering Monetary and Financial Cooperation in East Asia*. Singapore: World Scientific Publishing.

Chwieroth, Jeffrey M. 2010. "How Do Crises Lead to Change? Liberalizing Capital Controls in the Early Years of New Order Indonesia." *World Politics* 62 (3): 496–527.

Cohen, Benjamin J. 1993. "The Triad and the Unholy Trinity: Lessons for the Pacific Region." In *Pacific Economic Relations in the 1990s: Cooperation or Conflict?* edited by Richard Higgott, Richard Leaver, and John Ravenhill. Boulder, CO: Lynne Rienner, 133–158.

————. 2001. "Beyond EMU: The Problem of Sustainability." In *Political Economy of European Monetary Unification*, edited by Barry Eichengreen and Jeffry A. Frieden. 2nd ed. Boulder, CO: Westview Press, 179–204.

————. 2008. "After the Fall: East Asian Exchange Rates Since the Crisis." In *Crisis as Catalyst: Asia's Dynamic Political Economy*, edited by Andrew MacIntyre, T. J. Pempel, and John Ravenhill. Ithaca, NY: Cornell University Press, 25–44.

De Grauwe, Paul. 2009. "Asian Monetary Unification: Lessons from Europe." In *Fostering Monetary and Financial Cooperation in East Asia*, edited by Duck-Koo Chung and Barry Eichengreen. Singapore: World Scientific Publishing, 113–126.

Economist. 2010. "Asia's Never-Closer Union." February 6.

Eichengreen, Barry, and Tamim Bayoumi. 1999. "Is Asia an Optimum Currency Area? Can It Become One? Regional, Global, and Historical Perspectives on Asian Monetary Relations." In *Exchange Rate Policies in Emerging Asian Countries*, edited by Stefan Collignon, Jean Pisani-Ferry, and Yung Chul Park. London: Routledge, chap. 21.

Eldredge, Niles, and Stephen Jay Gould. 1972. "Punctuated Equilibria: An Alternative to Phyletic Gradualism." In *Models in Paleobiology*, edited by T. J. M. Schopf. San Francisco: Freeman, Cooper, 82–115.Emmott, Bill. 2008. *Rivals: How the Power Struggle Between China, India, and Japan Will Shape Our Next Decade*. New York: Harcourt.

Financial Times. 2009. "Asian Co-Operation Must Gain Currency." October 27.

Givel, Michael. 2006. "Punctuated Equilibrium in Limbo: The Tobacco Lobby and U.S. State Policymaking from 1990 to 2003." *Policy Studies Journal* 34 (3): 405–418.

Goldstein, Avery. 2005. *Rising to the Challenge: China's Grand Strategy and International Security*. Stanford, CA: Stanford University Press.

Gowa, Joanne. 1988. "Public Goods and Political Institutions: Trade and Monetary Policy Processes in the United States." *International Organization* 42 (1): 15–32.

Grimes, William W. 2009a. *Currency and Contest in East Asia: The Great Power Politics of Financial Regionalism*. Ithaca, NY: Cornell University Press.

————. 2009b. "The Global Financial Crisis and East Asia: Testing the Regional Financial Architecture." EAI Fellows Program Working Paper 20. Seoul: East Asia Institute.

Haftel, Yoram Z. 2007. "Designing for Peace: Regional Integration Agreements, Institutional Variation, and Militarized Interstate Disputes." *International Organization* 61 (1): 217–237.

Haggard, Stephan, and Sylvia Maxfield. 1996. "The Political Economy of Financial Internationalization in the Developing World." In *Internationalization and Domestic Politics*, edited by Robert O. Keohane and Helen V. Milner. New York: Cambridge University Press, 209–239.

Hamada, Koichi, Beate Reszat, and Ulrich Volz. 2009a. "Introduction: Prospects for Monetary and Financial Integration in East Asia—Dreams and Dilemmas." In *Towards Monetary and Financial Integration in East Asia*, edited by Koichi Hamada, Beate Reszat, and Ulrich Volz. Northampton, MA: Edward Elgar, 1–9.

———, eds. 2009b. *Towards Monetary and Financial Integration in East Asia*. Northampton, MA: Edward Elgar.

Hamilton-Hart, Natasha. 2003. "Asia's New Regionalism: Government Capacity and Cooperation in the Western Pacific." *Review of International Political Economy* 10 (2): 222–245.

———. 2006. "Creating a Regional Arena: Financial Sector Reconstruction, Globalization, and Region-Making." In *Beyond Japan: The Dynamics of East Asian Regionalism*, edited by Peter J. Katzenstein and Takashi Shiraishi. Ithaca, NY: Cornell University Press, 108–129.

Henning, C. Randall. 2009. *The Future of the Chiang Mai Initiative: An Asian Monetary Fund?* Policy Brief PB09-5. Washington, DC: Peterson Institute for International Economics.

Hermann, Charles F. 1972. "Threat, Time, and Surprise: A Simulation of International Crises." In *International Crises: Insights from Behavioral Research*, edited by Charles F. Hermann. New York: Free Press, 187–211.

Katada, Saori. 2008. "Fragmented Regionalism? Japan's Approach to East Asian Trade and Financial Architectures." University of Southern California, unpublished.

———. 2009. "Politics That Constrains: The Logic of Fragmented Regionalism in East Asia." EAI Fellows Program Working Paper 21. Seoul: East Asia Institute.

Kawai, Masahiro. 2008. "The Role of Asian Currencies in the International Monetary System." Paper prepared for the conference "The Global Monetary and Financial System and Its Governance," organized by the Tokyo Club Foundation for Global Studies. November 11–12.

Kawai, Masahiro, and Taizo Motonishi. 2004. "Is East Asia an Optimum Currency Area?" In *Financial Interdependence and Exchange Rates in East Asia*, edited by Masahiro Kawai. Tokyo: Policy Research Institute, Ministry of Finance, 157–203.

Keohane, Robert O., and Stanley Hoffmann. 1991. "Institutional Change in Europe in the 1980s." In *The New European Community: Decisionmaking and Institutional Change*, edited by Robert O. Keohane and Stanley Hoffmann. Boulder, CO: Westview Press, chap. 1.

Keohane, Robert O., and Joseph S. Nye. 1974. "Transgovernmental Relations and International Organizations." *World Politics* 27 (1): 39–62.

Khong, Yuen Foong, and Helen E. S. Nesadurai. 2007. "Hanging Together, Institutional Design, and Cooperation in Southeast Asia: AFTA and the ARF." In *Crafting Cooperation: Regional International Institutions in Comparative Perspective*, edited by Amitav Acharya and Alastair Iain Johnston. New York: Cambridge University Press, 32–82.

Kim, Heungchong. 2009. "The Political Economy of European Economic and Monetary Union Negotiations and Implications for East Asia." In *Towards Monetary and Financial Integration in East Asia*, edited by Koichi Hamada, Beate Reszat, and Ulrich Volz. Northampton, MA: Edward Elgar, 41–60.

Lake, David A. 1993. "Leadership, Hegemony, and the International Economy: Naked Emperor or Tattered Monarch with Potential?" *International Studies Quarterly* 37 (4): 459–489.

Leventoğlu, Bahar, and Branislav L. Slantchev. 2007. "The Armed Peace: A Punctuated Equilibrium Theory of War." *American Journal of Political Science* 51 (4): 755–771.

Litfin, Karen T. 1997. "Sovereignty in World Ecopolitics." *Mershon International Studies Review* 41 (2): 167–204.

MacIntyre, Andrew, T. J. Pempel, and John Ravenhill, eds. 2008. *Crisis as Catalyst: Asia's Dynamic Political Economy*. Ithaca, NY: Cornell University Press.

Park, Yung Chul. 2007. "Whither Financial and Monetary Integration in East Asia?" *Asian Economic Papers* 6 (3): 95–128.

Park, Yung Chul, and Kwanho Shin. 2009. "Economic Integration and Changes in the Business Cycle in East Asia: Is the Region Decoupling from the Rest of the World?" *Asian Economic Papers* 8 (1): 107–140.

Peng, Dajin. 2002. "Invisible Linkages: A Regional Perspective of East Asian Political Economy." *International Studies Quarterly* 46 (3): 423–447.

Samuels, Richard J. 2007. *Securing Japan: Tokyo's Grand Strategy and the Future of East Asia*. Ithaca, NY: Cornell University Press.

Sohn, Injoo. 2005. "Asian Financial Cooperation: The Problem of Legitimacy in Global Financial Governance." *Global Governance* 11 (4): 487–504.

———. 2007. *East Asia's Counterweight Strategy: Asian Financial Cooperation and Evolving International Monetary Order*. G-24 Discussion Paper No. 44 Geneva: UN Conference on Trade and Development.

Sussangkarn, Chalongphob, and Pakorn Vichyanond. 2007. "Directions of East Asian Regional Financial Cooperation." *Asian Economic Papers* 5 (3): 25–55.

Volz, Ulrich. 2010. *Prospects for Monetary Cooperation and Integration in East Asia*. Cambridge, MA: MIT Press.

Watanabe, Shingo, and Masanobu Ogura. 2006. "How Far Apart Are Two ACUs from Each Other? Asian Currency Unit and Asian Currency Union." Working Paper 06-E-20. Tokyo: Bank of Japan.

Wheatley, Alan. 2009. "Crisis Spurs Asia to Hasten Cooperation, a Little." Reuters. October 12.

Willett, Thomas D. 2009. *The Global Crisis and Korea's International Financial Policies*. Washington, DC: Korea Economic Institute.

Zhang, Zhaoyong, Kiyotaka Sato, and Michael McAleer. 2001. "Is East Asia an Optimum Currency Area?" Working Paper No. 2001-37. Perth, Australia: International Centre for the Study of East Asian Development, University of Western Australia.

3 Regional Economic Institutions and East Asian Security

Miles Kahler

THE CONTRIBUTION OF REGIONAL ECONOMIC INSTITUTIONS to enhanced national and international security is too often an easy, if unexamined, assumption in debates over the value of those institutions. A prominent regional exemplar, the European Union, seems to support a central role for regional institutions in the Kantian tripod of democracy, international organization, and economic interdependence. After a half century of increasingly deadly conflict, the European Union has presided over the longest period of peace in Europe's recent history. Not only has it presided over those pacific decades; it seems deeply implicated in the construction of peace—and the security of member states and populations—in a region that had earlier been beset by long-lasting rivalries.

If a proliferation of regional economic institutions adds to both economic integration and regional security, the prospects for Asian security would appear bright: the 1990s witnessed a wave of regional institution building in Asia, in which new economic institutions, such as Asia-Pacific Economic Cooperation (APEC) were created, and older institutions, such as the Association of Southeast Asian Nations (ASEAN) assumed new economic roles. Three new features were added to this trend in the new century: regionwide economic arrangements, such as ASEAN Plus Three (APT), that were limited to Asian members; a new prominence for monetary and financial cooperation (APT's Chiang Mai Initiative and Asian Bond Market Initiative); and perhaps the locus of greatest activity, a rapid expansion of bilateral and plurilateral preferential trade agreements (PTAs).[1] Given the rarity of interstate war globally and in East Asia, where the last interstate war was fought between China and Vietnam in 1979, one cannot conclusively associate three decades of reduced military conflict with a concomitant development of regional economic institutions. If regional economic institutions encourage pacific relations, however, Asia's future security trajectory should match its peaceful recent past.

If one probes below the surface of Asia's contemporary security environment, however, the evolution of the region's politics seems more puzzling and less supportive of a simple association among interdependence, regional institutions, and enhanced security. North Korea, an actor that presents a significant security threat to others in the region, remains largely outside the pattern of growing regional economic interdependence and institution building. Growing levels of interdependence continue to produce lower levels of formal, regionwide institutionalization than might be predicted on the basis of institutionalization in other regions. This institutional gap has "stubbornly refused to close, despite the recent proliferation of bilateral and minilateral PTAs and security dialogues" (Aggarwal and Koo 2008b: 288). For example, high levels of economic interdependence in Northeast Asia have not been coupled with new regional institutions among the three major economies and military powers: Japan, China, and South Korea.

Economic interdependence and regional institutions have also failed to produce a security community in any part of the region. Certainly, ASEAN comes closer to this goal than Northeast Asia, but recent territorial conflict between Cambodia and Thailand over Preah Vihear suggests that lingering territorial disputes can easily become militarized. Maritime territorial disputes continue throughout the region, despite their economic costs: in the South China Sea, in the East China Sea (between China and Japan), and in the Sea of Japan (East Sea) between South Korea and Japan. These conflicts have flared again recently. In September 2010, a collision between Japanese coast-guard vessels and a Chinese fishing trawler in a disputed area of the East China Sea, followed by the arrest of the trawler's captain by Japan, led to weeks of tension between China and Japan. China imposed retaliatory measures such as cancelation of cultural exchange programs and suspension of rare-earth exports to Japan. Recent amelioration of the relations between Taiwan and China cannot disguise the limited influence that burgeoning trade and investment have had on levels of conflict under the previous presidency of Chen Shui-bian (Kastner 2006). Not only do the interdependence and institutional legs of the Kantian tripod seem to have limited spillover effects on political conflict and militarized disputes in the region; policy makers appear to accept that economics and conventional security should not have spillover effects on one another—in particular, that political conflict should not be allowed to affect investment and trade.[2]

Given this regional experience, any easy equation of building regional economic institutions with greater security must be examined carefully in the Asian context. The next section of this chapter reviews for their Asian implications research results that reflect on the association of economic interdependence, regional economic institutions, and security (defined conventionally as a reduced risk of militarized conflict or war). This research also illuminates causal pathways and their relative importance: are regional institutions important primarily for deepening economic interdependence, or are organizational effects on their members of greater significance?

Following this initial consideration of models linking economic interdependence, regional institutions, and security, the following section applies the research findings to Asia and evaluates the contribution of regional economic institutions to the security environment. One aspect of variation—institutional design—is of particular importance in determining whether Asian regional institutions, as currently configured, are likely to produce positive effects. A subsequent comparison of regional economic institutions in Asia with those in other regions further illuminates the diverse linkages of economics and security. A final section contrasts the skeptical view presented in this chapter with more optimistic alternatives offered in chapters authored by Benjamin J. Cohen and Wu Xinbo. It concludes with a discussion of alternative institutional designs that might produce more significant security spillovers from growing economic exchange in the region.

Economic Interdependence, Regional Institutions, and Asian Security: Theoretical Arguments

Regional economic institutions may enhance or undermine security—defined as a reduction in the risk of military conflict—through direct institutional effects or a second-order effect: increasing economic interdependence beyond levels that would have occurred in their absence. I refer to these, respectively, as institutional and interdependence effects of regional economic institutions. Recent research regarding the Kantian tripod has been particularly useful for investigation of the effects of regional economic institutions on security and military conflict in Asia. Simple causal relations among interdependence, institutions, and conflict have been questioned through the addition of variation and contingency to the Kantian equation. For example, early studies of economic interdependence and conflict used trade data exclusively. A key driver of recent economic integration in Asia (and elsewhere), however, has been foreign direct investment. The asset specificity of foreign investment may have a larger effect on political behavior than exchange of goods and services. Portfolio investment flows and other forms of financial interdependence may have an additional range of consequences for foreign policy behavior. Variation in regional institutions is also of particular significance for Asia. The model that has dominated regional economic institutions does not resemble closely the institutional formulas in other regions, particularly Europe. Finally, on the other side of the causal equation, the meaning of *security* may also vary. Research has centered on standard measures of conflict and militarized disputes as a proxy for an improved or deteriorating security environment. Asia, however, has been at the forefront of new definitions of security, particularly economic security (Nesadurai 2006). Human security also figures in the evolving debate over the security environment in Asia. Although these new definitions are noted in the following analysis, a more conventional definition of security, centered on the risk of military conflict and its effects on territorial integrity and political autonomy, dominates the discussion.

Economic Interdependence and Regional Security

The second-order, interdependence effect of regional economic institutions is captured by scholarly investigation of the effects of international economic interdependence. Controversy continues to surround nearly all aspects of this leg of the Kantian tripod that connects economic exchange with enhanced security and peace: whether a positive effect exists; whether conflict affects interdependence (possible endogeneity); whether all forms of international economic exchange produce the same effects on conflict; and perhaps most elusive, the precise causal mechanisms through which economic interdependence influences levels of interstate conflict.[3]

Three causal avenues link economic interdependence and peace.[4] The first two highlight the costs of disrupting dense relationships of economic exchange and the influence that such costs have on foreign policy behavior and perceptions of resolve. Economic interdependence may simply constrain state behavior by raising the costs of military conflict. The economic consequences of conflict may influence the calculus of elites directly, or they may impose political costs, as domestic economic interests mobilize to prevent or sanction military action. These pacific effects of economic interdependence are qualified, however, when asymmetric trading patterns create perceptions of lowered resolve on the part of one state in a dispute (Morrow 1999: 486).

The second causal avenue also relies on costs, by linking economic interdependence to the prevention of bargaining failures that produce military conflict. Economic interdependence permits costly signaling of resolve that would not be possible in the absence of international economic exchange. Visible economic costs, such as the imposition of sanctions, allow bargainers to avoid costly (and risky) military actions that would serve the same purpose (Morrow 1999; Gartzke, Li, and Boehmer 2001). Although this route is theoretically appealing, there is little direct evidence that states employ economic ties in this way. In certain cases, such as the bargaining between China and Taiwan, China has explicitly attempted to avoid the use of economic relations in this way, insulating trade and investment from cross-strait political conflict and military threats (Kastner 2006: 336).

Economic interdependence may influence foreign policy in a third way, one with multiple (and often obscure) causal pathways: a transformation in state preferences that reduces the level of interstate conflict. Individual elite attitudes may change as the result of learning: the benefits of cross-border economic exchange lead to a reassessment or reordering of state goals away from territorial claims or conquest and toward economic development and openness. Even without evidence of such change in elite attitudes, however, more plausible political narratives can explain the transformational effects of international trade and investment. Public opinion may change because of economic exchange, and that shift in attitudes may be reflected—through electoral or other means—in state policy. Economic interests linked to the international economy or to exchange with particular partners may exert political influence on foreign and security policy; that influence may be amplified as cross-border economic exchange grows. Jonathan Kirshner (2007) argues, for example, that financial sectors have historically been averse to war and to policies that risk war. Extending this interest-based argument, Etel Solingen (1998) posits the existence of internationalist coalitions (favoring regional economic integration) and statist-nationalist coalitions that have clear preferences for divergent foreign and security policies. Policies of economic openness, if sustained, should strengthen internationalist coalitions and their more cooperative policies over time. In these interest-based variants of preference change, a state's apparent shift toward a more pacific orientation is attributable to change in the relative political influence of particular groups or factions.

The aggregate effects of economic interdependence on militarized disputes and conflict are contested, particularly given the ambiguous effects of interdependence on interstate bargaining. Recent investigations that have varied both the definition of interdependence and conflict, however, seem to confirm the positive effects of cross-border trade and investment in reducing military conflict. Gartzke (2007), using a measure of financial market integration rather than trade, discovers that economic liberalization and integration, on this measure, are more significant in reducing conflict between dyads than is democracy. Pevehouse (2004) describes more complex relationship between trade and conflict, expanding the dependent variable beyond militarized interstate disputes (MIDs) to include other measures of conflict. Interdependence produces more low-level interstate conflicts, but it retains its central role in the Kantian tripod by continuing to restrain the escalation and militarization of those conflicts.

Regional IGOs and the Security Environment

The direct, institutional effects of intergovernmental organizations (IGOs) on regional and global security are even more contested than the effects of economic interdependence. Researchers have discovered positive, negative, and no effects of IGO membership on militarized disputes and interstate conflict. In contrast to investigations of economic interdependence, however, investigators have moved more rapidly and successfully to disaggregate the universe of IGOs and their influence on military conflict. These disaggregated findings provide valuable suggestions for evaluating the influence of regional economic institutions in Asia. The causal mechanisms that are advanced to explain these organizational effects track closely those suggested for the conflict-reducing effect of economic interdependence: linkage between foreign policy behavior and the economic benefits of membership, influence on the informational and bargaining environment of member states, and preference change through socialization or institutional incentives. Unfortunately, existing research does not directly test the relative importance (or even the validity) of these candidate mechanisms. Findings may be consistent with their operation, but research has not conclusively confirmed their relative significance.

One category of IGO that is associated with reduced military conflict among its members (measured once again by MIDs) is preferential trading arrangements (Mansfield and Pevehouse 2000; Mansfield 2003). In explaining the pacific consequences of PTAs, the economic costs of militarized conflict for PTA members are emphasized: "By jeopardizing existing trade relations and the realization of potentially significant future economic benefits, military conflict threatens to exact a particularly heavy toll on states that have dense commercial ties and belong to the same PTA" (Mansfield and Pevehouse 2000: 780). Because PTAs are designed to ratchet up the growth of trade among their members (as compared to trade with outsiders), the constraining effects of prospective losses are likely to be more influential than the effects of economic interdependence outside such arrangements. Membership and membership benefits—either prospective or actual—may serve as an additional incentive to behavioral change, particularly if membership criteria are clear and credible. Judith Kelley (2004) has documented the importance of membership incentives in influencing the behavior of prospective members of European institutions, particularly the European Union. These incentive effects require clear membership benefits that are credibly linked to policy changes, ideally applied when "countries believe they have a fair chance of admission but cannot take it for granted" (Kelley 2004: 185).

Like other IGOs, PTAs are institutions, and institutional characteristics may add a second layer of conflict-inhibiting effects. Bargaining theory suggests contributions that some, but not all, IGOs may make to conflict reduction among their members. Informational arbitrage—the elimination of informational asymmetries that increase the risks of military conflict—may be one valuable function of IGOs. Institutions that incorporate intensive negotiations or other means of information exchange reduce the possibilities for miscalculating resolve in other bargaining arenas. As in the case of economic interdependence, membership in an IGO may also produce institutional substitutes for demonstrating resolve that are less costly than open conflict (Boehmer, Gartzke, and Nordstrom 2004). If membership is valuable, a threat of withdrawal or nonparticipation represents a costly signal that would otherwise be unavailable.

In more highly institutionalized settings, IGOs may also create institutional binding that resolves commitment problems and prevents conflict.

A rapidly growing and potentially threatening state may create incentives for preventive war among its neighbors and rivals. Embedding that power in international institutions may impose exit costs on the rising state that are sufficiently high to forestall fears that a shift in power in its favor will threaten other states in the organization (Eilstrup-Sangiovanni and Verdier 2005; Diez, Stetter, and Albert 2006). European institutions were instrumental in binding the region's most powerful state, Germany, after 1945. Finally, IGOs may simply offer an arena for negotiation and dispute resolution to their members, in which these functions and others can be fulfilled (Mansfield and Pevehouse 2000: 781).

A third, more ambitious role for IGOs, including regional economic institutions, is transformational, a change in core preferences or identities as the result of institutional membership and engagement. The precise mechanisms for transformation by economic interdependence remain poorly specified. In the case of IGOs, socialization and the internalization of institutional norms are often proposed as the principal mechanism for such transformation. Benjamin J. Cohen (Chapter 2) and Wu Xinbo (Chapter 4) emphasize the role of regional economic institutions in socialization: habits of cooperation developed in the settings of these institutions may then have spillover effects on security relations.

Assessing the significance of socialization is difficult, however. Sanctions and rewards associated with institutional membership may produce the same results, and discriminating between the two avenues of institutional influence requires careful research design.[5] Socialization may also operate on different levels: on individuals (both elite and nonelite) and on domestic organizations or even regimes that undergo shifts in their external orientations. Underlying socialization in international institutions are several distinct microprocesses, defined by Johnston (2008) as mimicking, persuasion, and social influence. These considerations call into question any easy transfer of behavior from regional economic institutions to other, more politically sensitive issue areas, such as territorial conflict or military competition. The individuals involved, apart from the top political leadership, are seldom subject to the same regional institutional environments; the microprocesses by which interests and behavior are transformed over time are seldom specified.

Selection effects plague any assessment of the influence of IGO membership on state behavior: do members join such institutions only when they intend to comply with institutional rules and norms (Downs, Rocke, and

Barsoom 1996)? Attentiveness to these effects has produced a renewed skepticism regarding the importance of institutions in changing the behavior of their members, even in the case of long-standing global institutions.[6] The methodological challenge in assessing the effects of regional economic institutions on conflict involves two steps: disentangling interdependence effects (promoted among their members by these organizations) from the institutional effects of membership on conflict in Asia. An assessment of the two effects on regional security and conflict requires the estimation of two difficult counterfactuals: the level of economic interdependence in the absence of these regional organizations and the likely conflict behavior of members in the absence of any institutional effects.

Alternative Definitions of Security

For each of these causal pathways linking economic interdependence or regional IGOs to conflict, war and the risk of war are assumed to define the security environment. That conventional, state-centric definition of security is employed throughout this analysis. As Wu Xinbo (Chapter 4) makes clear, however, nontraditional security domains, such as counterterrorism and cybersecurity, often demonstrate dynamics that differ from those in traditional military domains.

Alternative definitions of security—economic security and human security—may produce a different reading of the effects of both economic interdependence and regional economic institutions. Following the Asian financial crisis, for example, economic integration, particularly financial integration, was viewed as a source of national vulnerability, precipitating sharp (if short-lived) economic recessions in several Asian economies, spurring oppositional political movements, and (in the case of Indonesia) causing regime change.[7] Regional economic institutions, such as APEC, which were dedicated to an agenda of external liberalization, were judged ineffectual in dealing with a crisis that undermined economic security.

Regional IGOs may also influence economic security directly. Their contribution to greater policy transparency and reciprocity can reduce the ability of governments to exploit economic vulnerability on the part of their trading and investment partners. Regional and global institutions may also alleviate insecurity induced by economic integration. Institutions can provide insurance to national governments against financial crises and other unforeseen economic shocks. Institutional credibility can substitute for or add to national policy credibility, a valuable asset in the face of international economic volatility. Finally, IGOs can encourage adaptation of national policies in the face of environmental change (Kahler 2006).

Economic openness and integration—under the label of "globalization"— have been a target of those concerned with human security. Contested claims have been made that economic openness increases inequality in and between countries, and social safety nets are placed at risk by a regulatory race to the bottom on the part of governments. In contrast, global and regional institutions have been at the vanguard of those directing attention to definitions of security that are broader than the conventional state-centric variant. The United Nations and regional human rights organizations have directed attention to violent assaults on civilian populations and developed strategies to deal with human insecurity, from peacekeeping to the International Criminal Court to the evolving international norm of responsibility to protect. Economic security has been a core alternative security concept in Asia, promoted by Japan in particular. Human security, however, has received less attention than it has received in Europe and Latin America.

Regional Economic Institutions in Asia and International Security: A Skeptical View

Because of growing economic interdependence and a recent turn toward regional economic institutions in Asia, the region offers a promising field for testing theoretical propositions that link interdependence, institutions, and security. Despite this regional strengthening of two legs of the Kantian tripod, however, the sturdiness of both legs is doubtful. The interdependence effects of regional economic institutions have been limited, although the negotiation of additional PTAs may enhance those effects in the future. Apart from their second-order contribution to regional security through encouraging interdependence, the design of Asian regional institutions limits their direct institutional effects on levels of conflict in the region.

Asian Regional Institutions and Economic Interdependence
Economic interdependence in the Asia-Pacific region has increased in recent decades to rival levels in Europe and North America. The simplest measure of interdependence, intraregional shares of trade, indicates a region more integrated than North America but less integrated than Europe. More

demanding measures, such as intraregional trade intensities, point to declining levels as Asian economies have "gone global," with a recent (post–Asian financial crisis) increase (Asian Development Bank 2008: 40–42). The pattern of Asian economic integration demonstrates certain characteristics that have influenced its institutional development. Trade integration has been driven by foreign direct investment, which in turn is linked to global and regional production networks in particular sectors, such as electronics and automobiles. Central to these networks is China, whose trade with Asia represents half of the trade in the region, an increase from 29 percent in 1996 (Asian Development Bank 2008: 47). Those networks have also meant that an increase in regional economic interdependence has not produced a decline in dependence on European and North American markets, which supply a large share of final demand in many sectors.[8]

Although this market-driven growth in economic interdependence may have consequences for regional security, in line with theoretical predictions outlined earlier, the contribution of regional economic institutions has been minimal. Until 2000, the ASEAN Free Trade Area (AFTA) and Asia-Pacific Economic Cooperation were the sole regional economic organizations with trade and investment liberalization agendas. A transpacific organization, APEC has members in North and South America, as well as Asia. Although APEC promoted explicit commitments to trade and investment liberalization during the 1990s, reaching its peak at the Seattle and Bogor summits (1994 and 1995), the implementation of the liberalization agenda foundered later in the decade. The Early Voluntary Sectoral Liberalization (EVSL) initiative, begun in 1997, quickly collapsed over U.S. insistence on reciprocal liberalization and Japan's resistance to liberalization of its forestry and fisheries sectors. The end of EVSL signaled the end of any hope that APEC would become an alternative forum to the General Agreement on Tariffs and Trade (GATT) and World Trade Organization (WTO) for trade negotiations. Many of its Asian members were satisfied that their commitments to liberalization remained unilateral and voluntary. Apart from promoting a liberalization agenda in the WTO and encouraging trade facilitation measures, APEC's role as a vehicle for specific commitments to trade and investment liberalization had effectively ended.[9]

In 1992 AFTA was launched by ASEAN; it was successfully completed in 2002, after several renegotiations. Initially, ASEAN pursued an informal path in negotiating AFTA, avoiding institutions that would bind members to carry out agreed liberalization of tariffs and nontariff barriers. Competitive pressure from China, which presented a large, rapidly growing and unified site for trade and investment, eventually led ASEAN to construct a more formal and binding structure for liberalization, one with much clearer rules and procedures (Khong and Nesadurai 2007: 51–58). Despite the relative success of AFTA, its influence on trade and investment interdependence among its members is likely to emerge only over time. The share of trade among ASEAN economies as a percentage of their total trade has remained relatively stagnant for decades at about 20 percent.[10]

If APEC and AFTA cannot be viewed as major contributors to a primarily market-driven process of Asian economic integration, the proliferation of PTAs that have been negotiated or planned in this decade could make a larger contribution. Unfortunately, this prediction is undermined by PTA membership and provisions, which substantially weaken their likely interdependence effects on security relations in the region. First, any interdependence effects will be shared outside the region: the PTAs completed by Asian governments to date are not centered on the Asian region. Of 139 PTAs concluded, under negotiation, or proposed, 30 involve Asian partners; 109 involve partners outside Asia. A second weakness is the geographical coverage of the existing PTAs. Although the large economies of Northeast Asia—China, Japan, and Korea—have completed a substantial share of such agreements (sixty-five total), no agreement has been completed among those giants of the regional economy (or between any two of them).[11] A third shortcoming of Asian PTAs is their contents: as many critics have pointed out, they are trade-light agreements that are typically limited to tariff cuts, with few provisions that aim at deep integration through eliminating nontariff barriers or other behind-the-border barriers to trade and investment. Through divergent rules of origin, they have also contributed to a noodle bowl of agreements that raise transaction costs for firms and discourage use of the agreements (Sally 2010).

China has been particularly active in creating these "low-quality, politically motivated bilateral and regional arrangements," including the China-ASEAN Free Trade Agreement (CAFTA; Bergsten et al. 2008: 14). The agreement, which came into force on January 1, 2010, aims to affect the burgeoning trade between ASEAN and China largely through tariff cuts in sectors such as textiles and food in high-tariff ASEAN economies. The Economic Cooperation Framework Agreement (ECFA), concluded with Taiwan in 2010, is a partial exception to this pattern, because, in addition to tariff reductions, it also includes provisions on market access to service sectors and plans to negotiate investment protections and other measures to deepen economic cooperation. Although the beneficial effects of PTAs in reducing militarized conflict have been documented, this new wave of PTAs in Asia is too recent, too restricted in policy coverage, and too inclusive of non-Asian members to claim a significant role in deepening regional economic interdependence. The interdependence effects of these regional economic institutions are unlikely to shape Asia's security environment.

Institutional Effects on Security

Even though regional economic institutions have played a marginal role in promoting economic interdependence in Asia, their direct institutional effects on militarized conflict require a separate assessment. Asia is hardly lacking in regional institutions, even if the recent proliferation of PTAs is set aside. The institutional landscape can no longer be described as sparse: myriad functional institutions dot the region from the Tumen River to the Mekong. Their direct institutional effects on regional security are limited, however, by their design. The template for Asian PTAs, whether bilateral or plurilateral, is not dissimilar from those in other regions: most PTAs include some dispute settlement mechanisms; few are institutionalized beyond such limited and delegated authority. Other regional and subregional institutions, however, reveal Asia's particular institutional choices.

The most prominent Asian regional institutions share many design features with ASEAN, the oldest regional institution. The constituents of the ASEAN Way or the ASEAN institutional model have become an Asian way of institution building. Although regional economic institutions are hardly uniform, certain characteristics have become widespread across an otherwise diverse set of regional institutions. First, Asian governments have been reluctant to delegate substantial authority to regional institutions. The organizational core is slender: if any permanent staff has been designated, it is typically a minimal secretariat. The monitoring and enforcement powers of most regional institutions are, as a result, limited. Limited delegation to intergovernmental institutions is combined with low levels of legalization on two other dimensions: precise and binding obligations.[12]

Asian regional institutions are also exclusively intergovernmental: nonstate actors, whether individuals, corporations, or nongovernmental organizations are not directly enfranchised in regional courts or other institutions.

Rules for enfranchisement in regional courts, for example, are central to their effectiveness (Voeten 2009). Because governments are often reluctant to use regional dispute settlement mechanisms against other member states, action by private parties is often essential to the empowerment of regional courts. If regional institutions permit, these cooperators outside the cartel of governments are able to use courts and dispute settlement mechanisms to reactivate the process of economic integration and to prevent backsliding on the part of governments.

Finally, the decision rules and membership rules of Asian regional institutions are also relatively uniform. A key part of both the ASEAN and Asian way of decision making is consensus rather than majority voting, a process that emphasizes persuasion and deliberation over decisiveness. Membership regimes are very different from those adopted by the European Union and organizations in other regions. From the start, the European Union incorporated a club model of membership: prospective members are expected to adopt a wide range of policy changes before their accession (the *acquis communautaire*). The positive benefits of membership serve as a key incentive for these arduous and politically contentious changes in domestic policies and practices. Both ASEAN and other Asian regional organizations have promoted a different, convoy model of membership. Membership tends to be set by vague geographical criteria rather than policy stipulations. Rather than using membership to force policy changes in the desired direction, policy convergence is expected after accession through a process of socialization over time. Inclusive membership criteria imply permanent membership: ASEAN has no procedure for expelling a member from the organization (Khong and Nesadurai 2007: 48).[13] Rather than homogeneous clubs, Asian organizations are heterogeneous convoys. In all their characteristics, Asian regional institutions emphasize sovereignty preservation rather than pooling of sovereignty; regional institutions avoid intrusions into the sphere of domestic politics and policy.[14]

Asian institutional design is sometimes attributed to shared culture, but the extension of this model to regionwide institutions with culturally diverse memberships strains such an interpretation. Khong and Nesadurai (2007: 48) attribute the deployment of this institutional model to the domestic insecurity of authoritarian regimes that dominate the region; the ASEAN institutional model shields them from international pressure and scrutiny. Because Asian governments have participated in more formal and legalized institutions at the global level, regional power distribution may also play a role in this institutional preference. Asian governments rejected a more binding and formal set of arrangements for APEC in part to avoid giving the United States an additional lever with which to pressure them on trade liberalization (Kahler 2000). China's likely predominance in Asia-only organizations may serve to conserve the ASEAN model for the same reason.

That explanation is supported by the recent evolution of ASEAN itself. Paradoxically, the institutional model that has shaped other Asian regional organizations has begun to build more formal and binding structures. With the adoption of the ASEAN Charter, the regional group has moved in the direction of greater legalization and more powers delegated to the secretary-general.[15] The ASEAN Economic Community, an initiative begun in 2003, aims to create an integrated regional economic space by 2020. It incorporates a number of institutional changes that are designed to enhance compliance with collective decisions, including the ASEAN Consultation to Solve Trade and Investment Issues, the ASEAN Compliance Body (for mediation), and a strong dispute settlement mechanism that moves beyond the AFTA to resemble the WTO panel and appellate configuration (Khong and Nesadurai 2007: 56).

Other Asian regional institutions have not imitated ASEAN's recent formalization. Most notably, APT, the largest regional economic grouping, remains less an institution than a dialogue (Chu 2007: 156). The Chiang Mai Initiative, organized by the APT governments, remained a network of bilateral swap agreements until March 2010, when the Chiang Mai Initiative Multilateralization was launched. The creation of an APT Macroeconomic and Research Office in Singapore in early 2011 marked a modest initial delegation of Chiang Mai Initiative Multilateralization surveillance functions to a small regional secretariat.[16] Apart from this advance, however, APT, the East Asian Summit, and the ASEAN Regional Forum (ARF; a security forum also modeled on the ASEAN design) retain a minimal intergovernmental format, with little or no delegation to a permanent international staff or set of institutions.

Can Asian regional institutions of this design influence regional security by diminishing the risks of conflict? One quantitative study suggests that, among ASEAN, APEC, and the South Asian Association for Regional Cooperation, only ASEAN may have had a dampening effect on militarized conflict among its members (Goldsmith 2007). Those who have disaggregated institutional characteristics and their influence on militarized conflict suggest several features that appear to reduce conflict; these can be compared to the prevailing institutional design in Asia to estimate the likely effectiveness of those institutions.

The most convincing security-enhancing role for regional economic institutions is informational: providing a setting and a source for unbiased information regarding capabilities and resolve. The most effective institutional design for this function is unclear, however. Boehmer, Gartzke, and Nordstrom (2004) suggest that more elaborated institutions with "greater institutional structure" are more likely to allow informational arbitrage or costly signaling. Yoram Haftel (2007), using a sample of regional institutions already delimited by robust institutionalization, proposes the scope of issues considered by the institution and regular meetings of high-level officials as prime determinants of conflict reduction.[17] Although high-level summits are certainly characteristic of most Asian regional institutions, highly elaborated institutional structures that would promote continuous information exchange are not.

Member homogeneity and cohesion represent a second set of characteristics that have been associated with IGO contributions to lower levels of military conflict. The convoy model of membership undermines such homogeneity by including members that fail to converge on regime type or policy preferences. Moreover, IGOs that are democratic in their membership are more likely to promote peace—independent of the effects of domestic democratic regimes (Pevehouse and Russett 2006). Given the distribution of regime type in Asia, in which authoritarian regimes dominate the mainland and democratic regimes populate the periphery, few regional economic organizations are likely to demonstrate such democratic density. Asian regional institutions are also more heterogeneous in their members' levels of economic development. In the Americas and Europe, the gap (ratio) in regional institutions between members with the largest and smallest gross domestic product per capita is 10.9 and 7.0, respectively; in Asia, it is 48.8. Convoy membership strategies in ASEAN, for example, have included Singapore (US$50,304 per capita) and Myanmar (US$1,040 per capita) under the same organizational umbrella. Such divergence in economic status is unlikely to produce convergent policy preferences or institutional cohesion.

Institutional effects on regional security and interstate conflict are reduced by a final characteristic of Asian regional institutions: their typically sharp divide between the domains of economics and security. For example, IGOs with a security mandate are more likely to lower the probability of militarized conflict (Boehmer, Gartzke, and Nordstrom 2004: 16). Such institutions are rare in East and Southeast Asia. Only the ASEAN Regional Forum, a weakly institutionalized offshoot of ASEAN's dialogues with partner governments, qualifies. Regional economic institutions, however, rarely link economic agendas or negotiations with political and security issues. This distinctive Asian approach to economics and security becomes apparent when compared to the experience of other regions.

Economics and Security: Regional Comparisons

Regional economic institutions in Asia have often been subjected to misplaced comparisons with their counterparts in other regions.[18] Europe, in particular, has served, on the one hand, as a negative model for Asians who declaimed the advantages of the Asian way of institution building and, on the other hand, as a lodestar for future institutional development when Asia's own institutions appeared ineffective. This concentration on the European experience has tended to disguise more substantial similarities between Asia and other developing regions, where governments were equally protective of their sovereignty and suspicious of possible intrusion from regional overseers. With a broader sample of regions, Asia is no longer a distinctive outlier on all dimensions of institutional design. Nevertheless, other regions rarely demonstrate the same uniformity in institutional design represented by the ASEAN or Asian way. In Latin America or Africa, more institutional variation appears, even if the median institution converges on many of the characteristics of Asian regional institutions.

Regional variation is pronounced in the links between economics and security—and the regional institutions operating in those domains. Peace building and economic liberalization have reinforced each other in some regions; in others, political and military conflict has disrupted regional institutions and their agenda of economic opening. Europe exemplifies a region without a single, multipurpose pan-regional organization that nevertheless integrates economic and security issues. Early failures in constructing a regional security edifice with substantial delegated powers (the European Defense Community) produced a key regional security provider, the North Atlantic Treaty Organization (NATO), a highly institutionalized alliance led by an extraregional power. Only gradually has the dominant economic institution, the European Union, forged a collective foreign and security policy

(Hix 2005: 387–396; Hix 2009). Recent institutional changes, such as the appointment of the High Representative of the Union for Foreign Affairs and Security Policy and the European External Action Service, aim to give additional weight to the European Union's Common Foreign and Security Policy. Regional security is also encompassed by a wider network of regional institutions that frequently coordinate with the European Union, such as the Council of Europe and the Organization for Security and Cooperation in Europe (Kelley 2004).

The Americas display a second pattern in which peace building and economic integration have paralleled and reinforced each other. The most successful regional economic arrangements in the Americas, the Southern Common Market (MERCOSUR) and the North American Free Trade Agreement (NAFTA), were agreed to only after a resolution of long-standing security issues among the key parties (Dominguez 2009). At the same time, regional institutions clearly separated rules and forums governing intra- and interstate conflict and those dealing with regional economic integration. The Organization of American States had a recognized role in dispute mediation and settlement and later enforced the norm of democratic constitutionalism in the region. It played no role, however, in regional agreements to liberalize trade and investment. In contrast, until MERCOSUR limited membership to democracies through a treaty amendment in 1997, economic integration treaties had not included any clauses that reflected on the domestic political ordering or foreign policy behavior of their members (Dominguez 2007). Regional institutions dealt with both security and economic issues, but a clear division of labor existed.

A third pattern characterized subregions of Latin America, such as Central America, as well as the Middle East and Africa: conflict undermined or slowed regional institution building and integration. In some of these conflict zones militarized disputes and open conflict prevented a deepening of integration commitments in existing institutions, such as the Central American Common Market, but did not prevent trade liberalization and expansion (Dominguez 2009). In Africa, where the forces of regional economic integration were weaker, the costs of conflict rose, undermining regional institutions. For example, the Economic Community for Central African States became dormant during the 1990s because of internal conflicts in member states; despite recent efforts at revival, its agenda of regional economic integration and conflict resolution remains largely unfulfilled (Khadiagala 2009).

In East and Southeast Asia, a fourth model of linkage between economics and security has applied. The two domains run on distinct and separate tracks, neither disrupting nor reinforcing each other. Unlike the conflict zones of Africa and the Middle East, political conflict and militarized disputes are seldom allowed to obstruct the expansion of trade and investment. Particularly in Northeast Asia, an arena of territorial and political disputes, the economic benefits of this division are clear. At the level of national policies, economic sanctions are avoided. Regional economic institutions reflect this separation: few direct links exist between economic institutions and those, like the ARF, that address the security environment. One driver of this Asian two-track pattern may be a domestic political dilemma: nationalist resistance to resolution of long-standing disputes coupled with demands for high economic growth. The choice of outward-oriented development strategies has made economic performance—and political survival—dependent on regional stability.

Although some Asian regional institutions, such as ASEAN, have multiple mandates, the two-track approach to economics and security has not encouraged political reconciliation or military confidence building as a precursor or accompaniment to regional economic initiatives. Before AFTA was negotiated, ASEAN had developed norms for state behavior that were embodied in the Treaty of Amity and Cooperation (1976); ASEAN had also played a central role as a diplomatic community in mobilizing opposition to the Vietnamese invasion of Cambodia in 1978–1979. Among its members, however, ASEAN has played a distinctly minor role in resolving militarized disputes and territorial conflicts among its members. The organization's belated mediating role in the conflict between Cambodia and Thailand over Preah Vihear is only one recent example. Its response to new security issues such as terrorism has been criticized as hampered by the norm of state sovereignty and "hampered by mutual suspicion and domestic preoccupations" (Jones and Smith 2007:174).

Other economic institutions, such as APEC, have occasionally allowed very modest breaches in the divide between economics and security when member governments have argued for a direct connection between the two categories of issues. After September 11, for example, APEC recognized the economic dimensions of a security threat—terrorism—and explicitly included it on the institutional agenda. In addition, APEC created the Counter-Terrorism Task Force; it also issued a statement on North Korea, a more conventional security issue (Ravenhill 2007: 146–149). The sidelines of APEC summits have also served as a forum for diplomacy, even when the official agenda remained resolutely economic. The East Timor crisis, for example, was considered informally at the 1999 APEC Summit.

Asian regional economic institutions appear poorly equipped to dampen militarized conflicts, given their institutional design. They may provide diplomatic forums that supply credible information to potential adversaries, thus eliminating one cause of bargaining failures that lead to interstate conflict. However, their slender institutional structures and the bright line drawn between economic and security issues weigh against a central role in reducing conflict among members. As Wu Xinbo (Chapter 4) argues, that bright line may be less significant in nontraditional areas of security, which have much more direct economic consequences. Terrorist attacks, for example, can disrupt transportation and tourism; cybersecurity has clear implications for many sectors of the economy. Regional economic institutions have also been more active in promoting economic security, following the Asian financial crisis and the terrorist attacks of September 11. Even in this domain, however, the segregation of economic and security issues—in national policy processes and in regional organizations—has limited their usefulness. Despite irritation with global institutions in which Asian states are uniformly underrepresented, most Asian governments continue to prefer global institutions; bilateral alliances and defense arrangements; and especially national, unilateral measures as their primary insurance against threats to both conventional and economic security.

Conclusion: Regional Economic Institutions and a More Pacific Asia

The liberal intuition that deeper economic interdependence and engagement in IGOs will produce a more secure environment for states and their populations has found qualified support in scholarly research. Regional economic organizations can promote security (defined as reduction in the risk of militarized conflict) through first-order effects (the institutions themselves) and second-order effects (the promotion of deeper economic interdependence).

When applied to the Asian region, however, the independent role of regional organizations in promoting peace and security is difficult to confirm. First, the role of regional economic organizations in promoting economic interdependence has been limited: regional economic integration has surged on the basis of global trade and investment liberalization and market-driven processes, such as the creation of cross-border production networks. The appearance of significant liberalizing regional institutions occurred relatively recently; the increment of policy change that they are likely to contribute to future liberalization of cross-border exchange is slight. The proliferation of PTAs in this decade may increase the interdependence effect of these organizations, but many of the PTAs are centered on trading partners outside the Asian region and their provisions are often limited to tariff reduction rather than the nontariff and behind-the-border barriers that continue to restrict trade and investment flows.

The independent institutional effects of regional economic organizations are more likely to influence the probability of conflict and enhance regional security, but here as well, the specific characteristics of Asian regional institutions limits their positive benefits. The geographic concentration of key institutions on Southeast Asia is one drawback. Northeast Asia, the home of large, heavily armed powers with unresolved territorial disputes, is also the site of two locales that are more likely to result in significant military conflict: North Korea and Taiwan. North Korea, despite very limited economic liberalization, is not part of the web of interdependent economic relations in the regions, nor is it a member of any regional economic organization. Apart from its membership in APEC, Taiwan has been excluded from regional organizations and the expanding network of PTAs.[19] Northeast Asia is entirely lacking in subregional economic institutions (or, apart from the six-party talks, security institutions). The three major powers—China, Japan, and South Korea—have not negotiated any preferential trade or investment agreement.

Asian regional economic institutions have adopted an institutional model that limits their positive influence in dampening regional conflict. Institutions are spare and informal; legalization is limited. Only the region's reliance on high-level summit meetings matches the informational role that alleviates bargaining failures and heightens the risk of interstate conflict. In other respects, particularly their heterogeneous memberships, the institutions are imperfect instruments for enhancing regional security. The short-term benefits of separating economic and security relations—bilaterally and within regional arrangements—limits both the interdependence and institutional effects of regional economic institutions.

Those who adopt a more optimistic view of the effects of economic integration and institutions on security offer several counters to this skeptical view. Benjamin J. Cohen (Chapter 2) suggests that a combination of longer-run socialization in regional economic institutions and the shocks delivered by economic crisis will spur greater institutionalization in Asia. He argues that socialization in economic institutions will transfer to the domain of security at top levels of decision making, where "contacts among officials are bound to be broader and more intimate." He finds evidence of the acceleration induced by crisis in the recent (2009) agreement to multilateralize the Chiang Mai Initiative, a framework for financial cooperation that was nearly a decade old. This benign perspective is called into question, however, by the absence of any evidence for a transfer of trust from regional economic institutions to the realm of traditional security. The persistent territorial disputes in the East China and South China seas, described earlier, are only one prominent example: extensive and growing economic interdependence between Japan and China and their participation in a growing array of economic institutions, from APT to the new East Asian summits, did not prevent a rapid ratcheting up of tension and sanctions after a minor maritime confrontation. The acceleration in institutionalization provoked by the current economic crisis is also exaggerated: several of the largest emerging economies in Asia (China, India, Indonesia) have not experienced a recession; the interpretation of the crisis and its implications for deeper regional economic integration and institutionalization remain the subject of debate.

Wu Xinbo (Chapter 4) offers a more plausible reason for optimism: the transfer of cooperation from regional economic institutions and issues to emerging nontraditional security domains, such as infectious diseases, natural disasters, terrorism, and criminal networks. The prospects for building trust and collaboration in these areas, through a transfer of habits of cooperation from regional economic institutions, is probably greater than in traditional security issue areas. Wu documents the proliferation of negotiations, dialogues, and institutions that have developed in these nontraditional issue areas over the past decade. The mechanisms of socialization are not closely linked to these developments, however, and the evidence for further transfer to conventional security issue areas is slender. Given recent developments—the continuing arms buildup on either side of the Taiwan Strait, renewed tensions over maritime territorial claims, and the persistent and dangerous North Korean nuclear stalemate—more conclusive evidence is required for an emergence of trust and development of common security interests, as predicted by Wu.

The security environment of the Asian region presents a mixed picture. Military capabilities have grown with rapid industrialization. National policy transparency is limited, and many conflicts remain that could easily become militarized. Reliance on dispute resolution, rather than dispute management, is limited. The region is far from the status of a security community. In contrast, interstate warfare (though not militarized disputes) has not occurred for three decades, and in those crises that have occurred, governments have behaved prudently. In shaping this security environment in a more predictable and pacific direction, regional economic institutions could play a larger role as they continue to proliferate and develop. Only a future institutional model that reinforces both interdependence and institutional effects is likely to have a discernible and positive effect on regional security relations.

That institutional model need not resemble, even remotely, the trajectory followed by Europe, which is highly unlikely. Its sources are more likely to be found in the requirements of future economic liberalization and its promised gains for national economies than in any shift in the region's current, relatively benign security environment. Those who argue for either a modest or a more ambitious move forward in regional economic institutions confront a familiar conservatism: if the region has become the most dynamic economy in the world without elaborate regional institutions, why add them now? The response must include both the consolidation of existing economic gains— many based on purely unilateral measures—and the need for institutions of a new type for the next phase of deeper economic integration. In other words, regional institutionalization will help prevent backsliding by national governments and would also promote an agenda for removing behind-the-border barriers to trade and investment, barriers that are often politically sensitive and difficult to restrain in the absence of multilateral oversight.

To accomplish this regional economic agenda—and its necessary linkage to improvement in the regional security environment—two types of institutional innovations could occur. Groups of cooperating governments that agree on an agenda of deeper economic integration could opt for one or more of the following institutional alternatives: increasing the degree of precision and obligation in cooperative agreements, delegating more authority to regional institutions for monitoring and enforcing those agreements, or using initial membership conditionality to signal cooperative commitments. Each of these implies a break with the existing model of regional economic institutions. At the same time (or perhaps as an alternative), a large-membership, peak organization that combined economic, political, and foreign policy agendas would also permit programs of political reconciliation and possibly military confidence building that have been instrumental in furthering regional economic cooperation in other regions. The existing East Asian Summit (ASEAN Plus Six) incorporates all the major powers required for such an institution, although, at a minimum, its current shapeless agenda and informal organization would need to change.

Either or both of these institutional turns in the region's economic institutions would provide an opening for more substantial and positive effects on Asian security relations, effects much greater than those predicted for the existing web of PTAs, with their minimal institutionalization. First, movement toward formal institutional structures would allow regional economic organizations to reduce information asymmetries, allow costly signaling, and build trust that allows for credible commitments. Second, and more controversial, such institutionalization is more likely to deepen economic interdependence, particularly in issue areas beyond trade. Regional institutions that create greater interdependence effects are also likely to secure the regional environment. Third, although the political homogeneity of Asian regional institutions is unlikely to increase in the near term, membership criteria in new institutions and differentiated membership in existing ones could increase coherence and produce greater security effects. Finally, Asia has lagged in the creation of multilateral security institutions. Given the difficulty in building such institutions, regional institutions that link economics and security could play a more central role in shaping Asia's security environment. After September 11 APEC ventured into such issue areas: counterterrorism, energy security, cybersecurity, and measures to protect tourism and sea-lanes (Acharya 2007: 31; Ravenhill 2007). Since its foundation ASEAN has played a role in both security and economic issues. Paradoxically, the strong predisposition of Asian elites to insulate economic exchange from political and military disputes has decreased the leverage that regional economic institutions exercise in the realm of security.

What is the likelihood that such a new wave of regional institution building will take place? First, governments must calculate that the economic gains from the new agenda of deeper regional integration are worth the political costs of further constraining their national policy making and arousing the opposition of protectionist groups. Even after that calculation is made, a clear association between deeper economic integration and a different model of regional institutions must be accepted: another leap on the part of a political class that has long been suspicious of strengthening regional authority. For the largest economies—Japan, China, and India—accepting the value of binding their policies through regional institution building may be particularly difficult. For all these prerequisites to align, an external shock that underlines the fragility of either the region's current levels of economic integration or its tranquil security environment may also be required. Given the rapid recovery of the Asian economies from the current recession, it is difficult to imagine the conditions that could produce such a shock.

A final precondition concerns the role of those outside the region. Before the current economic crisis, Asia was highly dependent on North America and Europe as final markets for its manufactures; alliances and security relationships centered on the United States were critical constituents of the security portfolios of many states in the region. Any movement toward greater economic integration and regional institution building must occur with the cooperation of outsiders who have large stakes in the current regional status quo.

Asia demonstrates a contingent pacifism at the beginning of the second decade of the new century. Economic interdependence, a key source of its remarkable and resilient prosperity, is based on an intricate, cross-border production web based on large flows of trade and investment. Economic risks to that web of interdependent relationships are emphasized in an era of superficially placid security relationships. Regional economic institutions are primarily designed to ensure the growth and maintenance of those cross-border economic ties and to resolve economic disputes that threaten them. Political and military risks to those beneficial ties should not be underestimated. At the same time, the potential contribution of regional economic institutions to ameliorating the larger security environment—on which Asia's prosperity depends—should not be dismissed.

Notes

1. For a summary of East and Southeast Asian regional institutions, see Aggarwal and Koo 2008a, table 1.1; Ravenhill 2008, table 2.1. For an excellent analytic account of the new economic regionalism, see Munakata 2006.

2. The efforts by China to ensure that punitive measures against the Chen Shuibian government should not affect Taiwanese investment on the mainland exemplify this stance (Kastner 2006).

3. For recent contributions to a large literature, arguments that interdependence reduces conflict are presented in Oneal, Russett, and Berbaum (2003), Gartzke, Li, and Boehmer (2001), and Gartzke (2006, 2007); a recent argument claiming that trade does not reduce conflict is offered in Ward, Siversen, and Cao (2007).

4. These are summarized in Kastner (2006) and Kahler and Kastner (2006).

5. On this issue, see Kelley (2004), and the 2005 special issue (volume 59, number 4) of *International Organization*.

6. See, in particular, the debate over the effects of GATT and WTO membership on trade liberalization (Rose 2004; Goldstein, Rivers, and Tomz 2007).

7. On the redefinition of economic security in conditions of globalization, see Kahler (2006) and Nesadurai (2006).

8. The theoretical literature on economic interdependence has not explored the specific effects of production networks on foreign policy behavior and security relations. Although these networks include both trade and direct investment, they also include close supplier relationships that do not include cross-investment.

9. On the role of APEC and the EVSL episode, see Ravenhill (2001) and Munakata (2006: 86–89).

10. Intra-ASEAN trade rose from about 20 percent in 1992 to 22 percent in 2004, but ASEAN added four new members during that time period, a step that might have led to a greater intraregional share of trade.

11. A Japan-Korea FTA is under negotiation; a Japan-Korea-China FTA has been proposed.

12. Legalization is defined by three measures: precision of international commitments; the degree to which those commitments are legally binding; and the authority delegated to third parties, particularly global or regional institutions, for interpreting, monitoring, and enforcing those commitments. These dimensions need not covary; Asian regional institutions, however, tend to display low levels of legalization on all dimensions (Goldstein, Kahler, Keohane, and Slaughter 2001).

13. Khong and Nesadurai (2007: 48). As part of their recommendations for the new ASEAN charter, the Eminent Persons Group suggested that members might be suspended or expelled from ASEAN for "serious" breach of the charter. Their recommendation was not included by the high-level task force that drafted the charter (Severino 2009).

14. Accounts of the ASEAN model of regional institutions are given in Khong and Nesadurai (2007: 36, 41–42) and Johnston (2008: 161–163).

15. ASEAN's embrace of the ASEAN Way had always been less than uniform. Some agreements had entered into force without ratification by all members. Informal voting has also been used in decision making, even though the vote was later presented as a consensus (Severino 2009: 8).

16. See the account in Cohen, Chapter 2 of this volume.

17. Haftel excludes PTAs and APEC, which "lack a continuous institutional framework." (2007: 221–222) He therefore excludes the least institutionalized (and most abundant) of Asian regional economic institutions.

18. This section is adapted from the author's contribution to Asian Development Bank (2010, chap. 5).

19. Taiwan has one FTA in the wider Pacific region, with Panama. It is a member of the WTO, and in 2010 it negotiated the Economic Cooperation Framework Agreement (ECFA) with China, which may permit the negotiation of additional FTAs with Asian partners.

Works Cited

Acharya, Amitav. 2007. "Regional Institutions and Security in the Asia-Pacific: Evolution, Adaptation, and Prospects for Transformation." In *Reassessing Security Cooperation in the Asia-Pacific*, edited by Amitav Acharya and Evelyn Goh. Cambridge, MA: MIT Press, 19–40.

Aggarwal, Vinod K., and Min Gyo Koo. 2008a. "Asia's New Institutional Architecture: Evolving Structures for Managing Trade, Financial, and Security Realms." In *Asia's New Institutional Architecture*, edited by Vinod K. Aggarwal and Min Gyo Koo. Berlin: Springer Verlag, 1–34.

———. 2008b. "An Institutional Path: Community Building in Northeast Asia." In *The United States and Northeast Asia*, edited by G. John Ikenberry and Chung-in Moon. Lanham, MD: Rowman and Littlefield, 285–307.

Asian Development Bank. 2008. *Emerging Asian Regionalism: A Partnership for Shared Prosperity*. Manila: Asian Development Bank.

———. 2010. *Institutions for Regional Integration: Toward an Asian Economic Cooperation*. Manila: Asian Development Bank.

Bergsten, C. Fred, Charles Freeman, Nicholas R. Lardy, and Derek J. Mitchell. 2008. *China's Rise: Challenges and Opportunities*. Washington, DC: Peterson Institute for International Economics.

Boehmer, Charles, Erik Gartzke, and Timothy Nordstrom. 2004. "Do Intergovernmental Organizations Promote Peace?" *World Politics* 57 (1): 1–38.

Chu, Shulong. 2007. "The ASEAN Plus Three Process and East Asian Security Cooperation." In *Reassessing Security Cooperation in the Asia-Pacific*, edited by Amitav Acharya and Evelyn Goh. Cambridge, MA: MIT Press, 155–176.

Diez, Thomas, Stephan Stetter, and Mathias Albert. 2006. "The European Union and Border Conflicts: The Transformative Power of Integration." *International Organization* 60 (Summer): 563–593.

Dominguez, Jorge I. 2007. "International Cooperation in Latin America: The Design of Regional Institutions by Slow Accretion." In *Crafting Cooperation: Regional International Institutions in Comparative Perspective*, edited by Amitav Acharya and Alastair Iain Johnston. Cambridge: Cambridge University Press, 83–128.

———. 2009. "Regional Economic Institutions in Latin America: Politics, Profits, and Peace." Background paper prepared for the Asian Development Bank flagship study "Institutions for Regionalism: Enhancing Asia's Economic Cooperation and Integration."

Downs, George W., David M. Rocke, and Peter N. Barsoom. 1996. "Is the Good News About Compliance Good News About Cooperation?" *International Organization* 50 (3): 379–406.

Eilstrup-Sangiovanni, Mette, and Daniel Verdier. 2005. "European Integration as a Solution to War." *European Journal of International Relations* 11 (1): 99–135.

Gartzke, Erik. 2006. "Globalization, Economic Development, and Territorial Conflict." In *Territoriality and Conflict in an Era of Globalization*, edited by Miles Kahler and Barbara Walter. Cambridge: Cambridge University Press, 156–186.

———. 2007. "The Capitalist Peace." *American Journal of Political Science* 51 (1): 166–191.

Gartzke, Erik, Quan Li, and Charles Boehmer. 2001. "Investing in the Peace: Economic Interdependence and International Conflict." *International Organization* 55 (2): 391–438.

Goldsmith, Benjamin E. 2007. "A Liberal Peace in Asia?" *Journal of Peace Research* 44 (1): 5–27.

Goldstein, Judith L., Miles Kahler, Robert O. Keohane, and Anne-Marie Slaughter, eds. 2001. *Legalization in World Politics*. Cambridge, MA: MIT Press.

Goldstein, Judith L., Douglas Rivers, and Michael Tomz. 2007. "Institutions in International Relations: Understanding the Effects of the GATT and the WTO on World Trade." *International Organization* 61 (1): 37–67.

Haftel, Yoram Z. 2007. "Designing for Peace: Regional Integration Arrangements, Institutional Variation, and Militarized Interstate Disputes." *International Organization* 61 (1): 217–237.

Hix, Simon. 2005. *The Political System of the European Union*. New York: Palgrave Macmillan.

———. 2009. "Institutional Design of Regional Integration." Background paper prepared for the Asian Development Bank flagship study "Institutions for Regionalism: Enhancing Asia's Economic Cooperation and Integration."

Johnston, Alastair Iain. 2008. *Social States: China in International Institutions, 1980–2000*. Princeton, NJ: Princeton University Press.

Jones, David Martin, and Michael L. R. Smith. 2007. "Making Process, Not Progress: ASEAN and the Evolving East Asian Regional Order." *International Security* 32 (1): 143–184.

Kahler, Miles. 2000. "Legalization as Strategy: The Asia-Pacific Case." *International Organization* 54 (3): 549–571.

———. 2006. "Economic Security in an Era of Globalization: Definition and Provision." In *Globalisation and Economic Security in East Asia*, edited by Helen S. Nesadurai. New York: Routledge, 23–39.

Kahler, Miles, and Scott Kastner. 2006. "Strategic Uses of Economic Interdependence: Engagement Policies on the Korean Peninsula and Across the Taiwan Strait." *Journal of Peace Research* 43 (5): 523–541.

Kastner, Scott. 2006. "Does Economic Integration Across the Taiwan Strait Make Military Conflict Less Likely?" *Journal of East Asian Studies* 6: 319–346.

Kelley, Judith G. 2004. *Ethnic Politics in Europe: The Power of Norms and Incentives.* Princeton, NJ: Princeton University Press.

Khadiagala, Gilbert M. 2009. "Institution-Building for African Regionalism." Background paper prepared for the Asian Development Bank flagship study "Institutions for Regionalism: Enhancing Asia's Economic Cooperation and Integration."

Khong, Yuen Foong, and Helen E.S. Nesadurai. 2007. "Hanging Together, Institutional Design, and Cooperation in Southeast Asia: AFTA and the ARF." In *Crafting Cooperation: Regional Institutions in Comparative Perspective,* edited by Amitav Acharya and Alastair Iain Johnston. New York: Cambridge University Press, 32–82.

Kirshner, Jonathan. 2007. *Appeasing Bankers: Financial Caution on the Road to War.* Princeton, NJ: Princeton University Press.

Mansfield, Edward D. 2003. "Preferential Peace: Why Preferential Trading Arrangements Inhibit Interstate Conflict." In *Economic Interdependence and International Conflict,* edited by Edward D. Mansfield and Brian M. Pollins. Ann Arbor: University of Michigan Press, 222–253.

Mansfield, Edward D., and Jon C. Pevehouse. 2000. "Trade Blocs, Trade Flows, and International Conflict." *International Organization* 54 (4): 775–808.

Morrow, James. 1999. "How Could Trade Affect Conflict?" *Journal of Peace Research* 36 (4): 481–489.

Munakata, Naoko. 2006. *Transforming East Asia: The Evolution of Regional Economic Integration.* Washington, DC: Brookings Institution Press.

Nesadurai, Helen S. 2006. "Conceptualizing Economic Security in an Era of Globalisation: What Does the East Asian Experience Reveal?" In *Globalisation and Economic Security in East Asia,* edited by Helen S. Nesadurai. New York: Routledge, 3–22.

Oneal, John R., Bruce Russett, and Michael L. Berbaum. 2003. "Causes of Peace: Democracy, Interdependence, and International Organizations." *International Studies Quarterly* 47 (3): 371–393.

Pevehouse, Jon C. 2004. "Interdependence Theory and the Measurement of International Conflict." *Journal of Politics* 66 (1): 247–266.

Pevehouse, Jon, and Bruce Russett. 2006. "Democratic International Governmental Organizations Promote Peace." *International Organization* 60 (4): 969–1000.

Ravenhill, John. 2001. *APEC and the Construction of Pacific Rim Regionalism.* New York: Cambridge University Press.

———. 2007. "Mission Creep or Mission Impossible? APEC and Security." In *Reassessing Security Cooperation in the Asia-Pacific,* edited by Amitav Acharya and Evelyn Goh. Cambridge, MA: MIT Press, 135–154.

———. 2008. "Asia's New Economic Institutions." In *Asia's New Institutional Architecture,* edited by Vinod K. Aggarwal and Min Gyo Koo. Berlin: Springer Verlag, 35–58.

Rose, Andrew. 2004. "Do We Really Know That the WTO Increases Trade?" *American Economic Review* 94 (1): 98–114.

Sally, Razeen. 2010. "Regional Economic Integration in Asia: The Track Record and the Prospects." Occasional Paper No. 2/2010. Brussels: European Center for International Political Economy.

Severino, Rodolfo C. 2009. "Regional Institutions in Southeast Asia: The First Movers and Their Challenges." Background paper prepared for the Asian Development Bank flagship study "Institutions for Regionalism: Enhancing Asia's Economic Cooperation and Integration."

Solingen, Etel. 1998. *Regional Orders at Century's Dawn: Global and Domestic Influences on Grand Strategy.* Princeton, NJ: Princeton University Press.

Voeten, Erik. 2009. "Regional Judicial Institutions and Economic Cooperation: Lessons for Asia?" Background paper prepared for the Asian Development Bank flagship study "Institutions for Regionalism: Enhancing Asia's Economic Cooperation and Integration."

Ward, Michael D., Randolph M. Siversen, and Xun Cao. 2007. "Disputes, Democracies, and Dependencies: A Reexamination of the Kantian Peace." *American Journal of Political Science* 51 (3): 583–601.

4   The Spillover Effect of the ASEAN-Plus-Three Process on East Asian Security

Wu Xinbo

D OES ECONOMIC REGIONALISM ENHANCE SECURITY REGIONALISM in East Asia? Miles Kahler's chapter in this volume expresses skepticism, but I tend to be more optimistic. In this chapter, I explain why, adopting an approach that varies somewhat from Kahler's. First, instead of focusing on the deficiencies in the development of East Asian economic institutions relative to other regions, this chapter accepts those institutions as given and puts them in perspective. East Asian economic institutions are a new and encouraging development in the region's history; although relatively primitive at this stage, they will evolve and mature alongside regional trends toward economic cooperation and integration. Second, while considering the security implications of economic regionalism, this chapter adopts a broader definition of security, taking both traditional and nontraditional security concerns into account. Third, in probing the impact of economic regionalism on security regionalism, this chapter pays relatively more attention to effects achieved, although it also tries to explain why more has not been accomplished. Finally, a cross-paradigmatic approach, rather than reliance on a single paradigm, is used to examine the effects of economic institutions on regional security.

In contrast to Western Europe, where economic regionalism first emerged in the 1950s, regional integration did not appear in East Asia until more recently. It was only in the late 1970s and 1980s, with the emergence of production networks built by Japan and other newly industrialized economies and the adoption of export-oriented development strategies by China and other developing East Asian countries, that regionalism began to grow. A series of regional initiatives were advanced in the early 1990s, including the proposals of then prime minister of Malaysia Mahathir bin Mohamad for the East Asian Economic Group and the East Asian Economic Caucus. As is well known, these initiatives were unsuccessful largely because of opposition from the United States. It was the Asian Financial Crisis of 1997–1998 that finally ushered in East Asian economic regionalism. In December 1997, at the peak of the crisis, leaders from the nine member states of the Association for Southeast Asian Nations (ASEAN) and three Northeast Asian countries—China, Japan, and South Korea—gathered for the first time to discuss opportunities for cooperation. This meeting kicked off an arrangement that, after Cambodia joined ASEAN in 1998, became known as the ASEAN Plus Three (APT) process. In November 1999, the third APT summit released a joint statement outlining the orientation, principles, and areas for East Asian cooperation, marking a substantive step forward in the APT process. Specifically, the process includes cooperation at three different levels: APT, ASEAN Plus One (cooperation between ASEAN and one of the three Northeast Asian countries), and Plus Three (cooperation among China, Japan, and South Korea, without ASEAN).[1] The APT process has created cooperation in twenty areas and pays particular attention to financial and trade cooperation in East Asia, such as the Chiang Mai Initiative (bilateral currency-swap arrangements), a regional foreign-currency reserve pool, and free-trade agreements between ASEAN countries and China, Japan, and the Republic of Korea, respectively. An APT unit was also established in the ASEAN secretariat to provide institutional support to the cooperation process. Although the APT process is still young—it is not even two decades old—it is nonetheless the primary venue of East Asian cooperation and stands as the main symbol of East Asian regionalism. This chapter, therefore, examines the APT process to demonstrate how economic regionalism has affected security in East Asia.

Unlike in Western Europe, where regionalism was driven by politico-security concerns stemming from the two world wars and from the outset was intended to address traditional security concerns, the so-called new regionalism in East Asia was mainly motivated by economic considerations; initially, security cooperation was not a significant part of the agenda. Yet cooperation in East Asia gradually extended into the realm of security, particularly with regard to nontraditional security issues. Here, "nontraditional security" refers to "challenges to the survival and well-being of peoples and states that arise primarily out of nonmilitary sources, such as climate change, infectious diseases, natural disasters, irregular migration, food shortages, smuggling of persons, drug trafficking, and other forms of transnational crime" (Green and Gill 2009: 306). Nontraditional security challenges have three major features that set them apart from traditional security concerns: they are primarily nonmilitary; their origins, conception, and effects are usually transnational; and although they incorporate the state as a primary referent object, they also move beyond the state by including other referent objects like human collectivities (Emmers and Caballero-Anthony 2006: xiv). With the end of the Cold War, nontraditional security threats have become more salient in East Asia. They have received even more attention following the September 11 terrorist attacks.

Given the short history of economic regionalism in East Asia, as well as the lack of a security mandate in its initial stages, it is no surprise that the cooperation process has thus far produced much less of an impact on security matters than Western regional projects like the European Union. It is worth noting, however, that East Asian economic regionalism has spilled over into both the traditional and the nontraditional security domains. The questions to be answered, therefore, are how this spillover occurred and what factors either facilitated or hindered the phenomenon.

To answer these questions and to better understand the effects of East Asian economic institutions, it is necessary to adopt a cross-paradigmatic approach when examining the linkage between economic and security cooperation. Social and cultural differences between East Asia (or Asia more broadly) and the West give diverging meanings to institutions. Generally speaking, modern Western societies are legally oriented, based on rules and contracts, whereas East Asian societies remain largely socially oriented, with an emphasis on connections and implicit understandings. Thus, the values that they place on institutions and on their concepts of cooperation are also quite different. In the West, the purpose of institutions is to provide legally binding venues for actors to come to agreements with one another, whereas in East Asia their primary function is to enable actors to socialize with one another and to build connections. In the West, cooperation is understood in neoliberal terms as "the result of a process of policy coordination," which involves mutual adjustment for a common agenda (Keohane 1984: 52). In East Asia, however, cooperation has both political and sociological implications and is best understood through the perspective of social constructivism. It refers not only to the outcomes of coordination but also to the process of coordination itself, including such transnational interactions as meetings, dialogues, initiatives, and declarations that help bring about a mutually beneficial, stable pattern of behavior. Therefore, in examining the origin of institutions, neoliberal paradigms emphasizing how institutions increase opportunities for cooperation provide a useful framework. When assessing the effects of institutions, however, even though "both neoliberal institutionalism and constructivism suggest that institutions can shape preferences and ideas" (Solingen 2008: 266), social constructivist frameworks provide greater insight into the functions of regional institutions in the East Asian sociocultural context.

The Spillover Effect on Nontraditional Security Cooperation

Security cooperation was not intrinsic in the APT process by design; rather, it was a by-product of the APT process as a result of key events. Just as the Asian Financial Crisis served as a catalyst for East Asian cooperation, the eruption of a series of nontraditional security crises in the early twenty-first century triggered the spillover of cooperation from the economic to the security realm. Elsewhere in this volume, Benjamin J. Cohen explores the role of crisis as a catalyst for new initiatives and argues that the Asian Financial Crisis provided an impetus for East Asian financial cooperation. Similarly, the following empirical study details the role of crisis in causing East Asian cooperation to extend from the economic to the nontraditional security arena.

In November 1999, the third APT summit released a joint statement in which country leaders not only promised to strengthen efforts to accelerate economic cooperation but also agreed to continue dialogue, coordination, and cooperation in the political-security arena to increase mutual understanding and trust, as well as to strengthen cooperation in addressing common transnational concerns. Such claims conform to the neoliberal notion that institutions enhance information about mutual preferences and behavior as well as increase the opportunities for cooperation. The stated willingness to cooperate in the political-security arena, however, did not translate into immediately tangible outcomes.

It was September 11 that highlighted the urgency of regional cooperation in dealing with nontraditional security challenges. In November 2001, at the fifth APT summit, the Chinese premier Zhu Rongji suggested that, although the APT process should place particular emphasis on economic cooperation, it should also gradually be expanded to include dialogue and cooperation on political-security concerns beginning with nontraditional security issues. In July 2002, China proposed an APT ministerial meeting on transnational crime and the APT foreign ministers endorsed the idea. Then, in November 2002, the sixth APT summit meeting approved a final report submitted by the East Asia Study Group, a body established two years earlier by the APT summit in Singapore. The group explored the means by which cooperation in East Asia could be broadened and expanded, preparing concrete measures and action plans for closer cooperation in various areas. Among their recommendations was to "strengthen mechanisms for cooperation on non-traditional security issues, including, in particular, mechanisms to stem the tide of piracy, drug trafficking, and cyber crime" (APT Summit 2002: 37). The report argued that "the terrorist attacks on the United States on 11 September 2001 have increased peoples' awareness of the severity, pervasiveness, and the international linkage of terrorism and new kinds of threats to security. As transnational crime becomes more organized and threatening, it becomes more and more urgent for the governments of East Asian countries to establish mechanisms for coordination and cooperation on the new security challenges that we are facing in today's global arena" (APT Summit 2002: 37).

As a result of these efforts, the first APT Senior Officials Consultation on Transnational Crime (SOMTC+3 Consultations) was held in June 2003 in Hanoi; it has since become an annual gathering for senior law-enforcement officials from thirteen East Asian countries to exchange views on combating transnational crime in the region. In January 2004, the first "10+3" Ministerial Meeting on Transnational Crime (AMMTC+3) was held in Bangkok, where attendees endorsed the concept of cooperating in eight areas: terrorism, illicit drug trafficking, trafficking in persons, money laundering, arms smuggling, sea piracy, international economic crime, and cybercrime. Subsequently, the APT Work Plan to Combat Transnational Crime was developed and endorsed for implementation. Similar to the now-annual SOMTC+3 Consultations, AMMTC+3 has become a biennial gathering for ministers of public security, interior, and internal security to consult with one another on combating transnational crime in East Asia. The framework has facilitated concrete cooperation among APT countries on fighting transnational crime. For example, in August 2005, China hosted the Workshop on Policing Exchanges and Cooperation among the capital police agencies of ASEAN, China, Japan, and the Republic of Korea, aimed to enhance security in Beijing during the Beijing Olympics of 2008. Police chiefs from the capitals of the APT countries proposed in a declaration to set up a liaison mechanism among themselves to exchange intelligence and carry out close cooperation in unconventional security areas such as terrorism, drug trafficking, money laundering, organized crime, cross-border crimes, and computer crimes (Xinhua Agency 2005). Furthermore, in 2009 and 2010, China hosted a forum attended by military officials from APT countries to discuss broad nontraditional security issues, with the purpose of enhancing mutual trust and cooperation among APT countries (Xinhua Agency 2010).

The decision by the APT countries to begin collaborating on health-related issues was also event driven; namely, actors were driven to cooperate after the spring 2003 outbreak of severe acute respiratory syndrome (SARS) in China. During the SARS outbreak, health ministers from APT countries held two meetings. The first one, held in April 2003 in Malaysia, discussed how to fight the epidemic through transnational and international measures. The second one, held in June 2003 in Thailand, proposed an action plan for preventing and controlling SARS and other infectious diseases. Since then, two regional mechanisms have been established: the APT Senior Officials Meeting on Health and the APT Health Ministers Meeting. These meetings are intended to help promote collaborative responses to various health-related challenges, especially those concerning aging populations, emerging infectious diseases, and the impact of globalization and trade liberalization on health. Specifically, the APT countries have set up two frameworks on health cooperation, one on emerging infectious diseases and the other on traditional and complementary medicine.

In these frameworks, the APT countries have proposed concrete plans for action. For instance, the third APT Health Ministers Meeting endorsed the Year Two Action Plan of the APT Emerging Infectious Diseases Program in October 2008, which aims to both enhance regional preparedness and capacity through integrated approaches to prevention, surveillance, and timely response to emerging infectious diseases and to facilitate partnerships among existing regional networks and experts on public and animal health. The new Web site Information Center on Emerging Infectious Diseases in the ASEAN Plus Three Countries was established in 2008 with the objective of improving cooperation through communication and unified strategy. After the outbreak of Influenza A (H1N1) in the spring of 2009, the APT Health Ministers Meeting held a special session in May and agreed on regional collaboration measures, such as sharing data and information on epidemic situations.

The 2004 tsunami in the Indian Ocean, which inflicted heavy casualties on Southeast Asia, served to further regional cooperation efforts on nontraditional security threats and prompted the APT countries to work together on disaster relief. At the ninth APT summit held in December 2005, the Chinese premier Wen Jiabao proposed that APT cooperation should emphasize sudden public health incidents and serious natural disasters. In 2007, the first ASEAN Committee on Disaster Management Plus Three Senior Officials Meeting (ACDM+3) was held to explore possible areas of cooperation among the ACDM and the "plus three" countries, such as capacity building through training programs and information sharing. This has become an annual gathering of senior officials from the thirteen East Asian countries to discuss cooperation in the management of natural disasters. Other initiatives have also been adopted to promote regional cooperation in disaster relief. At the tenth APT summit held in January 2007, China offered to host an APT military workshop on international disaster relief, and in 2007 and 2008, two rounds of the APT Workshop on Disaster Relief by Armed Forces were held. At the workshop, officers from East Asia focused on practical measures for disaster relief cooperation among the APT nations, such as coordinating mechanisms and standard operating procedures (Xinhua Agency 2008). In May 2010, China hosted the APT Seminar on Urban Disaster Emergency Management in Beijing. Participants exchanged knowledge and expertise on disaster relief and explored how to expand cooperation in the APT framework. They specifically recommended the establishment of an expert pool for APT members in disaster relief. Later that the same year, Japan also held an APT conference on disaster management.

Though not originally part of the agenda, the pursuit of information sharing, capacity building, and coordination in the realm of nontraditional security cooperation has been a remarkable achievement during the first decade of the East Asian collaborative process. Such cooperation exhibits the features of soft regionalism in East Asia: It is not centrally orchestrated, lacks strong institutional support, and involves few substantive arrangements, yet it has achieved the widest possible participation from APT countries and allows for flexible reactions to common challenges. Encouraged by such accomplishments, the APT countries pledged in their Cooperation Work Plan for the second decade (2007–2017), which was adopted at the tenth APT summit in 2007, to engage in even more extensive security cooperation. According to the work plan, APT countries will further cooperate on efforts to counter the proliferation of weapons of mass destruction, terrorism, drug trafficking, human trafficking, and cybercrime, as well as efforts to improve maritime security, public health, and disaster management and relief (Ministry of Foreign Affairs of the People's Republic of China 2007). Building on the experience of its first decade, APT cooperation on nontraditional security is likely to accomplish even more during its second decade of development.

As demonstrated by the experiences of the APT countries in jointly coping with nontraditional security concerns, the path from economic to security cooperation lies in nurturing habits of cooperation, cultivating consciousness and an interest in extending cooperation into political and security realms, and providing institutional platforms for security cooperation. Economic regionalism is a learning process in the sense that it nurtures the habit of cooperation among regional members. As countries become accustomed to the idea and practice of cooperation, they seek to expand their efforts either to create a better environment for further economic cooperation or to gain benefits through the spillover of collaboration into other areas such as politics or security. In the case of the APT process, the spillover effect took place conceptually at the third summit when country leaders released a joint statement avowing their agreement to continue to dialogue, coordinate, and cooperate on political-security issues to increase mutual understanding and trust and to strengthen cooperation on transnational issues.

However, the spillover effect only occurred in practice after the September 11 terrorist attacks gave rise to beliefs about the immediate need for cooperation in nontraditional security matters. As the need for security cooperation arose, existing economic cooperation mechanisms provided a venue and thereby facilitated such a process. In the post–Cold War era, ASEAN sought to establish new regional mechanisms, such as the ASEAN Regional Forum (ARF), to promote security cooperation. However, the ARF's design as a forum has limited its ability to play this role. The APT framework, in contrast, provided a convenient platform for conducting security cooperation among its members that became more feasible as regional economic cooperation evolved. Because a preexisting process was available, the costs of creating new mechanisms and institutions were reduced. It is no surprise that when events such as the September 11 attacks, the SARS outbreak, and the tsunami disaster alerted regional members to the need for collaboration, they turned to the APT framework as a natural venue for regional coordination and cooperation.

Shaping Identity and Norms

Compared with cooperation on nontraditional security issues, cooperation on traditional security matters in East Asia appears to benefit less directly from improvements in economic regionalism. It would be incorrect, however, to conclude that economic regionalism does not have any effect on countries' behavior in this realm. The East Asian cooperation process is known for its regular and frequent meetings at various levels (summit, senior official, working), and socialization occurs amid these institutionalized interactions of policy makers and elites. Constructivists note that social interactions not only can shape identities and norms but also can affect the way a country defines and pursues its national interests (Acharya 2001: 3–4). For East Asian countries, the APT process has given rise to a regional consciousness and contributed to a willingness to cooperate on regional security affairs. It has also helped develop common security norms among regional members in part by shaping their security behavior.

In East Asia, economic cooperation introduced the concept of regionalism into the consciousness of participating countries while also supporting community-building efforts. This particular development was discussed at the fifth APT summit held in November 2001. In October 2001, the East Asia Vision Group, created in 1999 by the APT summit to provide a vision for East Asian cooperation, proposed the formation of an East Asian community, turning the region from a group of nations into a bona fide regional community. By building an East Asian community, the East Asia Vision Group hoped it would be possible to develop mechanisms for preventing conflict and promoting peace, achieving closer economic cooperation, advancing human security, bolstering common prosperity by enhancing cooperation in the development of education and human resources, and fostering a distinct communal identity (ASEAN 2001). The vision was endorsed by the East Asia Study Group and was positively received by leaders at the sixth APT summit in November 2002. Subsequently, the Second Joint Statement on East Asia Cooperation, released in November 2007, reaffirmed the long-term goal of building an East Asian community. The goal of community building in East Asia not only prompted broader and deeper regional cooperation but also created a sense of shared identity among regional members.

As countries pursue substantive economic cooperation, they begin to develop and observe common rules and norms in the political-security realm that shape their behavior and reduce the risk of conflict. This process is manifest in the APT's first joint statement, which highlights the countries' commitment to handling their mutual relations in accordance with the purposes and principles of the UN Charter, the Five Principles of Peaceful Coexistence, the Treaty of Amity and Cooperation in Southeast Asia (TAC), and the universally recognized principles of international law (ASEAN 1999). Collectively, this set of core norms includes mutual respect for the independence, sovereignty, equality, and territorial integrity of member countries, as well as the idea that the use of force to solve disputes among members should be prohibited.

It is worth noting that with the emergence of East Asian cooperation, TAC became the basis for common norms guiding relations among regional members. The treaty, established in 1976 when ASEAN was founded, embraces such fundamental principles as the "settlement of differences or disputes by peaceful means" and the "renunciation of the threat or use of force" (ASEAN 1976). China signed the TAC in October 2003, becoming the first non-ASEAN country to accept the treaty. ASEAN welcomed this significant step by stating, "China's accession to the TAC has contributed to the stature of the TAC as the code of conduct for inter-state relations in the region" (ASEAN 2009a). After China's accession, Japan, worried that it might lag behind Beijing in its relations with ASEAN, also signed the TAC in July 2004. ASEAN applauded Tokyo's decision by noting, "Japan's accession to the TAC added importance to the Treaty as a code of conduct governing relations among countries in the region and a diplomatic instrument for the promotion of peace and stability in the region" (ASEAN 2009b). All the APT countries have now signed on to the TAC. Thus, for the first time in history, most East Asian countries have agreed to observe a set of common norms in their relations with one another, which will have a profound impact on their external behavior.

To determine whether economic cooperation among states helps create new norms that constrain their behavior on security-related matters, it is worth considering the actions of the countries that are party to the South China Sea disputes. Sovereignty disputes in the South China Sea have long been a major obstacle in China-ASEAN relations.[2] As economic cooperation between China and ASEAN deepens in both bilateral and APT contexts, the two sides have made efforts to prevent the territorial disputes from interrupting and damaging their overall ties. In November 2002, China and ASEAN signed the Declaration on the Conduct of Parties in the South China Sea (DOC), pledging to resolve their territorial and jurisdictional disputes by peaceful means and friendly consultations and negotiations, without resorting to the threat or use of force. Similarly, these countries have agreed to exercise self-restraint in the conduct of activities that could complicate or escalate existing disputes and affect peace and stability in the region. Pending the peaceful settlement of the disputes, they also promised to make an effort to build trust and confidence among the concerned parties by holding dialogues between their defense and military officials and notifying other concerned parties of any impending military exercises. In the meantime, they have agreed to explore and undertake cooperative activities, such as marine environmental protection, marine scientific research, navigation safety and communication exercises, search-and-rescue operations, and counter-transnational crime operations (ASEAN 2002). Finally, as a follow-up, ASEAN and China established a joint working group in December 2004 tasked with formulating recommendations on guidelines and an action plan for the implementation of the DOC, as well as specific cooperative activities in the South China Sea (ASEAN 2004). They agreed to conduct six cooperation projects, including disaster prevention and mitigation, marine search and rescue, and marine scientific research in the South China Sea. In addition, in September 2004, the Philippine National Oil Company and the China National Offshore Oil Corporation agreed to conduct seismic soundings in the South China Sea. Vietnam joined the venture in March 2005, and the project was renamed the Joint Marine Seismic Undertaking.

However, the situation in the South China Sea deteriorated in 2009 because of a couple of factors. The registration with the United Nations of one's territorial sea baseline claims, as required by the UN Convention on the Law of Sea, caused quarrels among China, Vietnam, Malaysia, and the Philippines. The stepped-up efforts by relevant parties to consolidate their actual control of the disputed areas in support of their sovereignty claims also raised the temperature of the situation. Direct involvement of the United States, reflected in U.S. Secretary of State Hillary Clinton's speech at the annual ARF meeting in July 2009 (Ruwitch and Ahuja 2010) further complicated matters. As a result of emotionally charged quarrels, more fishing disputes, and military exercises (sometimes joined by the United States), the South China Sea disputes turned heated. In addition, the agreement among China, Vietnam, and the Philippines was not extended when it expired in mid-2008, as a result of changing domestic politics in the Philippines.

The effects of the aforementioned norms on the behavior of the disputants in the South China Sea disagreements are clear. In 1974 and 1988, military conflicts occurred around the Xisha (Paracel) Islands and Nansha (Spratly) Islands, respectively, between China and South Vietnam/Vietnam. In recent years, despite rising tensions, no serious military clashes have broken out. Since March 2009, in response to a growing number of fishing disputes in the South China Sea, China has intensified its deployment of patrol boats on administration missions to the areas around the Xisha (Paracel) Islands and Nansha (Spratly) Islands in an attempt to both assert its sovereignty claims and protect its maritime interests. The fact that Beijing deployed fishery patrol boats rather than navy ships reflects its desire to avoid military conflict and to rely on peaceful means to resolve the disputes. To reassure other parties to the South China Sea disputes regarding China's peaceful intentions, one senior Chinese military official emphasized at an important forum on regional security in 2009 that "China has always advocated a peaceful solution to the disputes over marine rights and interests" (Ma 2009). China's president Hu Jintao also promised at the Boao Forum of 2011 that China "will remain committed to seeking peaceful solutions to disputes with neighbors over territory and maritime rights and interests through friendly negotiation" (Hu 2011).

When military conflicts occurred between China and its Southeast Asian neighbors, such as South Vietnam (1974) and Vietnam (1988), the combatants were overt Cold War enemies. Today, China and the ASEAN states are close partners in regional political and economic affairs. Moreover, the TAC and DOC serve as common norms constraining the behaviors of states dealing with ongoing territorial disputes. In July 2009, the sixteenth ASEAN Regional Forum issued a statement indicating that "the Ministers reaffirmed the continuing importance of the Declaration on the Conduct of Parties in the South China Sea of 2002 (DOC) as a milestone document between the Member States of ASEAN and China, embodying their collective commitment to ensure the peaceful resolution of disputes in the area" (ASEAN Regional Forum 2009). In July 2011, after more than eight years of hard negotiation, China and ASEAN finally agreed on a set of guidelines for the implementation of possible joint cooperative activities, measures, and projects as stipulated in the

DOC (ASEAN 2011). The agreement, reached at the height of the South China Sea disputes, testified to the political willingness of relevant parties to avoid conflict and to solve the issue in a cooperative rather than a confrontational way. Although the guidelines do not signify the solution of the problem, they represent an important step in the right direction. As further evidence of the effects of behavior-constraining norms, the ASEAN countries and China are considering the adoption of the Regional Code of Conduct in the South China Sea, a legally binding document that would augment the nonbinding declarations in the DOC. To be sure, such norm-building efforts should not be expected to resolve sovereignty disputes in the South China Sea; however, they can still constrain the behaviors of the parties involved. Each state will likely continue to assert its claims of sovereignty and pursue its maritime interests in the disputed areas through economic, administrative, and security measures while avoiding the use of force to advance its goals. As a result, disputes and tensions may arise from time to time, but serious military conflicts are unlikely.

Changing Regional Security Dynamics

East Asian economic regionalism also contributes to the security of the region by changing regional security dynamics. The term *security dynamics*, as used here, refers to the key factors affecting regional security, such as the level of mutual trust among nations, the relative convergence or divergence of countries' national interests, security links, and regional security arrangements. When the Cold War ended in the early 1990s, the East Asian security landscape was highly complex. First, there was the preeminence of traditional security challenges. Because of the region's often-bellicose history, as well as the ideological divide stemming from the Cold War, strong animosity and distrust existed among states with diverging and conflicting security interests. Moreover, widespread territorial disputes strained relations. These problems were compounded by China's reemergence in the mid-1990s, which gave rise to concerns regarding a shift in the regional balance of power. Second, the United States played the role of "regional balancer, honest broker, and ultimate security guarantor" in East Asia (U.S. Department of Defense 1990: 5). Washington achieved this position during the Cold War through its forward military presence, hub-and-spoke alliance system, and provision of economic aid to countries in the region. As a result, regional members sought to enhance their security by strengthening ties with Washington rather than endeavoring to improve security relations with one another. It was not uncommon for East Asian countries to have stronger security connections with the United States than with their neighbors. Third, there was an absence of regional security cooperation mechanisms that were capable of addressing common security challenges. Even though ASEAN was founded in 1976 to cope with the perceived threat of communist expansion in Southeast Asia, there were no serious efforts in the organization to develop the norms and institutions required for security cooperation. Thus, although the end of Cold War helped improve the overall security environment in East Asia, the region lacked the foundations required for the institutionalization of peace.

The development of economic regionalism has altered East Asian security dynamics in several ways. First, institutionalized economic cooperation has helped build trust and reduce suspicion among regional members, thus improving the regional security atmosphere. The first joint statement on cooperation in East Asia, released in 1999, stated that the APT countries would "deepen and consolidate collective efforts with a view to advancing mutual understanding, trust, good neighborliness, and friendly relations, peace, stability and prosperity in East Asia and the world" (ASEAN 1999). This suggests that the APT process is not just aimed at economic cooperation but also geared toward political and security goals. Indeed, before the launch of the APT process, regular meetings exclusively for East Asian leaders did not exist; the ARF was a venue for the meeting of foreign ministers not just from East Asia but also from North America and Europe, whereas the Asia-Europe Meeting was a gathering for leaders from both Asia and Europe. The APT framework, which brings together East Asian leaders as well as senior and working-level officials on a regular basis, facilitates frequent interactions that help familiarize the individuals with one another. Such relationships advance "mutual understanding, trust, good neighborliness, and friendly relations," as envisioned by the first East Asian statement of cooperation. Moreover, socialization among policy makers in the region helps both constrain their options when dealing with either preexisting or newly emerging disputes and increase the likelihood that they will adopt conciliatory approaches. The turbulence that occurred in East Asia in 2010, including the escalation of the South China Sea disputes, sinking of the Korean warship *Cheonan*, and the sharpening dispute between China and Japan over the Diaoyu Islands, suggests that, in a region where Cold War antagonisms linger, mutual trust is fragile and peace and stability face periodic challenges. Under these circumstances, the moderating effect of economic regionalism on political and security ties is all the more important. Although it is hard to tell how much economic regionalism has helped reduce regional tensions, it is fair to say that, without a decade's institutionalized economic cooperation, mutual trust among regional members could be even lower, suspicions much deeper, and approaches to disputes less constrained.

Moreover, economic regionalism also helps to form common security interests. As Ming Wan put it, "Countries change their views and redefine national interests owing to interdependence and transnational connections" (Wan 2003: 290). Indeed, as the East Asian process of cooperation progressed, it introduced positive elements in relations among its members. Ten years after the process was initiated, APT leaders noted with satisfaction "that the ASEAN Plus Three process had brought about mutual benefits and closer linkages among the ASEAN Plus Three countries" (ASEAN 2007). Beneficial economic interactions cause countries to view one another more as useful partners than as malicious rivals, and relations with others are viewed more positively. Moreover, as cooperation improves the economic welfare of each country, economic factors become an increasingly important component of national security. With regional members placing economic growth and cooperation at the top of their national agendas, there emerges a common interest in securing and maintaining a stable environment in which economic gains are possible. This shared interest grows with the deepening of economic cooperation, thus pacifying the security policies of all member states.

Economic regionalism, in addition to creating economic interdependence and cooperation among member countries, also facilitates collaboration in traditional political-security fields. Wan suggests that economic interdependence and cooperation "facilitate countries' efforts to cooperate and reduce tensions in security matters by offering economic incentives and creating vested interests in continuous cooperation" (Wan 2003: 290–291). Furthermore, as economic regionalism causes countries to attach increasing importance to the economic benefits gained through cooperative action, cooperation becomes the preferred approach in relations with their regional partners and helps moderate the region's security environment. As evidence of just such a phenomenon at work, the APT process has helped promote military and defense exchanges among regional members. The first joint East Asian cooperation statement declared that member states "agreed to continuing dialogue, coordination, and cooperation to increase mutual understanding and trust towards forging lasting peace and stability in East Asia" (ASEAN 1999). The East Asian Study Group recommended in its final report to "nurture confidence-building among countries, especially exchanges, consultations, and other cooperative activities among military and defense officials," and to "establish and implement effective measures to prevent and avoid conflict, and manage tensions" (APT Summit 2002: 14–15).

The APT Cooperation Work Plan (2007–2017) also pledged that, to enhance mutual understanding and trust, APT countries aim to gradually increase their exchanges and cooperation among defense officials and to increase visits to one another's military academies. As a result, multilateral and bilateral military and defense exchanges among APT countries have increased in frequency. For instance, the ARF security policy conference has been held annually since 2004 to allow senior defense officials from all thirteen APT countries and other ARF members to discuss the regional security situation along with opportunities for defense and security cooperation. Although some participants at the gatherings come from non-APT countries, the conference was initiated and has been hosted by APT members as an effort to strengthen dialogue among themselves.

The APT countries view the ARF as a convenient platform through which to promote political and security cooperation in East Asia and have agreed to strengthen it (APT Summit 2002: 15). Moreover, the first China-ASEAN Defense and Security Dialogue was held in Beijing in March 2010. Defense officials and scholars from China and ASEAN member states explored the conditions for the development of a regional defense mechanism, China-ASEAN defense and security cooperation, and the national defense policies of China and ASEAN members. The dialogue aimed to enhance the mutual trust between China and ASEAN member states and to deepen China-ASEAN defense and security cooperation (Chinese Ministry of Defense 2010). Meanwhile, bilateral security dialogues; defense consultations; and military exchanges among China, Japan, and South Korea also have increased in recent years. In 2008, a military hotline was established between China and South Korea in an attempt to avoid incidents in the East China Sea. In 2007 and 2008, the first-ever port calls took place between China's People's Liberation Army Navy and Japan's Maritime Self-Defense Force. The visiting Japanese ship also conducted a joint telecommunication exercise with the Chinese Navy. After renewed contention over the Diaoyu Islands in 2010, Beijing and

Tokyo began contemplating the establishment of a military hotline to avoid similar future incidents. Overall, interactions among East Asian countries in the realm of traditional security reflect the features of a cooperative security approach, aimed to promote engagement and reassurance rather than resolving common security threats (Kay 2006: 64).

The impact of economic regionalism on security is reflected not only at the national but also at the international level. As noted by Muthiah Alagappa, "Concurrent with the emergence of Asia as a core economic region and the development of regional norms and organization, the security system in Asia has become more distinct and autonomous" (Alagappa 2008: 45). As a result of improvements in mutual trust, the emergence of shared security interests, and increases in positive and cooperative security interactions, countries in the region are more likely to develop security relations among themselves than to draw on ties with extraregional powers in their calculations of national security. As a result, interactions among regional members have taken on a weightier role in their security thinking, leading East Asia to become increasingly self-reliant in matters of security. This trend is gradually reducing both the degree to which regional members rely on the United States as a provider of security and the role of the United States as the "regional balancer, honest broker, and ultimate security guarantor" in East Asia. Although developments since 2010 may seem to have enhanced security ties between the United States and some East Asian countries, a closer examination would suggest that the U.S. role as a direct player in regional security affairs is actually declining. On the South China Sea issue, it is not a relevant party and cannot sit at the table along with other claimants to discuss management of the disputes. On the Diaoyu Islands issue, Washington did propose a China-Japan-U.S. trilateral dialogue, but Beijing rejected the suggestion, preferring to deal with Tokyo bilaterally. On the Korean Peninsula, China's influence has risen relative to that of the United States in recent years. In fact, as China's material power and influence grow, it is becoming a key player in regional security while the United States acts more and more as a background player. In the long term, this trend will give rise to a new security architecture in East Asia in which relations among regional members will play a more central role in regional security arrangements. Both existing economic cooperation mechanisms and newly created institutions for security cooperation will constitute the main means by which East Asian affairs are managed under this new regional architecture.

Is economic regionalism, aimed to build the envisioned East Asian Community, establishing the basis for a security community? Does it suggest that a regional security community is likely to emerge? As economic collaboration further enhances regional economic interdependence and contributes to institutional and normative frameworks of cooperation, East Asia is becoming more distinct and autonomous as a region (Alagappa 2008). Such developments help cultivate regional consciousness, foster a regional identity, and draw more attention to intraregional security relations. In addition, to varying degrees, security cooperation is already unfolding in both nontraditional and traditional areas. While nontraditional security cooperation contributes to the management of common security challenges, traditional security cooperation enhances reassurance and engagement. As deepening economic cooperation and integration drive the region toward an East Asian community, security cooperation also moves forward, increasing the possibility of transforming the region into a pluralistic security community. A constructivist and path-dependent approach suggests that the development of a security community has three stages: nascent, ascendant, and mature. The nascent stage is usually triggered by, among other factors, common threat perceptions, expectations of mutual trade benefits, and some degree of shared identity (Adler and Barnet 1998: 50–51). In the case of East Asia, all three factors exist: there exists a common threat perception among regional members regarding nontraditional security challenges, APT cooperation embodies the countries' expectations of mutual trade benefits, and the East Asian Community stands as a shared identity. The remaining challenges are the complicated relations among regional members on traditional security issues and the loose sense of regional identity. Thus, it is uncertain whether East Asia already possesses the push-or-pull factors necessary for the nascent stage of developing a security community. That stage requires the following: a dynamic and positive relationship among regional members, the emergence of social institutions and organization, an improvement in mutual trust, and the existence of a core state or coalition of states as a facilitator and stabilizer (Adler and Barnet 1998: 53). Over the past decade in East Asia, these conditions have been manifest in greater intraregional cooperation on nontraditional security matters; increases in interstate exchanges on traditional security; more bilateral and multilateral mechanisms for cooperation and exchanges; improved trust among regional members; and ASEAN's role as a facilitator of regional economic, political, and security cooperation. Given these positive indicators, it is not unreasonable to suggest that East Asia may be in the midst of the nascent stage of developing a pluralistic security community.

Concluding Observations

The recent history of the APT experience summarized in this chapter largely conforms to the logics of both neoliberalism and social constructivism. Economic regionalism has contributed to security regionalism by promoting and facilitating regional security cooperation, shaping identity and norms, enhancing socialization, improving mutual understanding and trust, and expanding security links among regional members. It is also apparent that in the case of East Asian security, the most tangible spillover effect of economic regionalism has been in the realm of nontraditional security; cooperation on traditional security remains underdeveloped and less substantive. Given the short history of East Asian economic regionalism, it is understandable that its spillover effect in regional security has not yet fully materialized. Those who tend to see the glass half full would view these developments as true achievements.

The flourishing of nontraditional security cooperation in East Asia as a by-product of economic regionalism is an understandable phenomenon. On the one hand, the acceleration of globalization in the twenty-first century has rendered nontraditional security challenges more salient in the region, and their transnational nature requires multilateral cooperation. Because nontraditional security challenges confront all the states in the region, their common interest in dealing with the challenges provides the political impetus for cooperation. The APT process provides an existing platform for cooperation and thus reduces the need to create entirely new mechanisms. Moreover, cooperation on nontraditional security matters tends to involve less sensitive issues, such as policy coordination and the sharing of data, information, and expertise, while leaving untouched more delicate matters, such as sovereignty and military security. In this sense, the relatively lower threshold for cooperation in the realm of nontraditional security, compared to that of traditional security, increases its likelihood.

In contrast, economic regionalism has had more limited spillover effects on political and security relations in East Asia, where, characterized by a lack of mutual trust, traditional security concerns continue to impede political-military cooperation. Nationalism and collective historical memories remain potent influences in East Asia, and from time to time, nationalist sentiment and disputes over historical issues strain political relations in the region. For instance the annual summit meeting of China, Japan, and South Korea, which began in 1999 as a result of the APT process, was canceled in 2005 after then Japanese prime minister Junichiro Koizumi's decision to once again visit the Yasukuni Shrine where Japanese class-A war criminals of World War II are enshrined. Moreover, divergent security interests also undermine incentives for cooperation on matters of traditional security. Enduring disputes on the Korean Peninsula, and with respect to Taiwan and the South China Sea, undermine the political willingness of regional states to cooperate on military and strategic matters. Furthermore, the fact that security cooperation touches on matters of state sovereignty complicates efforts for cooperation. The preeminent role of the United States in regional security also impedes the development of intraregional security relations. For East Asian countries, the United States stands as a security guarantor, a security broker, or a major security concern. To the extent that the road to security starts from Washington, East Asian countries still attach greater importance to their security relations with the United States than to coordinating security policies among themselves.

It is also worth repeating that an awareness of social and cultural factors is required to understand regional cooperation in East Asia. The concept of security cooperation is used loosely in this chapter. In the West, cooperation is usually measured in terms of material results achieved—that is, whether cooperation leads to mutual gains or building institutions. In East Asia, however, cooperation is understood in terms of not just tangible achievements but also the conduct of interstate social interactions. In his study of how ASEAN developed into a security community, Amitav Acharya notes that "without a constructive understanding, it would be difficult to explain the emergence of ASEAN" (Acharya 1998: 45). His research explores how "ASEAN regionalism developed as a highly deliberate process of elite socialization involving the creation of norms, principles, and symbols aimed at the management of diversity and the development of substantive regional cooperation" (Acharya 1998: 207). Acharya emphasizes that elite socialization, as a social constructivist variable, is crucial to the understanding of the evolution of ASEAN. According to him, the practice of multilateralism played an important role in the development of a collective identity in ASEAN. Its contribution to community building "lies not in providing a formal institutional mechanism for conflict resolution, but rather in encouraging the socialization of elites which facilitates problem-solving" (Acharya 1998: 208). Alexander Wendt, inspired by Kant, suggests the importance of "thinking systematically about the nature and consequences of friendship in international politics." He argues that "friendship is a role structure within which states expect each other to observe two simple rules: (1) disputes will be settled without war or the threat of war (the rule of non-violence); and (2) they will fight as a team if the security of anyone is threatened by a third party (the rule of mutual aid)" (Wendt 1999: 298–299).

It is with this in mind that the effects of institutions on security in East Asia should be gauged. This is a region with significant differences among its members, not only in material power but also in history, culture, and ideology. Nonetheless, East Asian countries have a general preference for socialization and connections. It is, therefore, all the more important and necessary to encourage interstate social interactions, especially those that facilitate elite socialization. Social interactions can increase mutual understanding and mutual trust, expand connections, and develop friendship and affinity among states. Although they may not automatically lead to a resolution of disputes, continued interaction can certainly help mitigate tension, avoid war, spread common norms, and increase the willingness for cooperation. With respect to Wendt's two rules of friendship as a role structure in international politics, the region's complicated political-strategic dynamics make it unlikely that the rule of mutual aid will be observed in East Asia in the foreseeable future; however, the rule of nonviolence has already been widely accepted with the introduction of the Treaty of Amity and Cooperation in the APT process. Disputes will surely continue to exist and remain difficult to solve. But the deliberate use of force to settle them may be less likely as a consequence of more frequent social interactions aimed to enhance economic and security cooperation. Even though East Asian cooperation appears to be more process oriented than results oriented and institutions have not yet delivered many tangible results in terms of traditional security cooperation, these institutions have fostered a significant improvement in the tone of regional discussions about security.

Notes

1. In November 1999, leaders from China, Japan, and South Korea held a breakfast meeting while attending the APT Summit, kicking off cooperation among the three

countries in the framework of APT. As cooperation among the three countries accumulated more momentum, they decided to hold their summit outside of the APT framework, thus signaling their greater devotion to trilateral cooperation. In December 2008, leaders from the three countries held their first summit outside of the framework of APT in Japan.

2. Parties involved in the disputes include China (including Taiwan), Vietnam, Brunei, Malaysia, and the Philippines.

Works Cited

Acharya, Amitav. 1998. "Collective Identity and Conflict Management in Southeast Asia." In *Security Communities*, edited by Emanuel Adler and Michael Barnett. Cambridge: Cambridge University Press, 198–227.

———. 2001. *Constructing a Security Community in Southeast Asia: ASEAN and the Problem of Regional Order*. London: Routledge.

Adler, Emanuel, and Michael Barnett. 1998. "A Framework for the Study of Security Communities." In *Security Communities*, edited by Emanuel Adler and Michael Barnett. Cambridge: Cambridge University Press, 29–66.

Alagappa, Muthiah. 2008. "Asia's Security Environment: From Subordinate to Region Dominant System." In *The Long Shadow: Nuclear Weapons and Security in 21st Century Asia*, edited by Muthiah Alagappa. Stanford, CA: Stanford University Press, 37–77.

ASEAN Plus Three (APT) Summit. 2002. "Final Report of the East Asian Study Group." http://www.aseansec.org/viewpdf.asp?file=/pdf/easg.pdf (accessed January 14, 2011).

ASEAN Regional Forum. 2009. "Chairman's Statement of 16th ASEAN Regional Forum." July 23. Phuket, Thailand. http://www.aseanregionalforum.org/LinkClick .aspx?fileticket=VM8ARIRAkXM%3d&tabid=66&mid=1072 (accessed January 14, 2011).

Association for Southeast Asian Nations. 1976. "Treaty of Amity and Cooperation in Southeast Asia." http://www.aseansec.org/1654.htm (accessed January 14, 2011).

———. 1999. "Joint Statement on East Asia Cooperation." November 28. http://www .aseansec.org/6337.htm (accessed January 14, 2011).

———. 2001. "Towards an East Asian Community." East Asia Vision Group Report. October 31. http://www.aseansec.org/pdf/east_asia_vision.pdf (accessed January 14, 2011).

———. 2002. "Declaration on the Conduct of Parties in the South China Sea." November 4. http://www.aseansec.org/13163.htm (accessed January 14, 2011).

———. 2004. "Terms of Reference of the ASEAN-China Joint Working Group on the Implementation of the Declaration on the Conduct of Parties in the South China Sea." http://www.aseansec.org/16886.htm (accessed January 14, 2011).

118   Wu Xinbo

———. 2007. "Second Joint Statement on East Asia Cooperation-Building on the Foundation of ASEAN Plus Three Cooperation." November 20. http://www.aseansec.org/21100.htm (accessed January 14, 2011).

———. 2009a. "ASEAN-China Dialogue Relations." August. http://www.aseansec.org/5874.htm (accessed January 14, 2011)

———. 2009b. "ASEAN-Japan Dialogue Relations." August. http://www.aseansec.org/5740.htm (accessed January 14, 2011).

———. 2011. "Guidelines for the Implementation of the DOC." July. http://www.aseansec.org/documents/20185-DOC.pdf (accessed September 1, 2011).

Chinese Ministry of Defense. 2010. "China-ASEAN Defense and Security Dialogue Held." http://eng.mod.gov.cn/DefenseNews/2010-03/30/content_4136154.htm (accessed January 14, 2011).

Emmers, Ralf, and Mely Caballero-Anthony. 2006. "Introduction." In *Studying Non-Traditional Security in Asia*, edited by Ralf Emmers, Mely Caballero-Anthony, and Amitav Acharya. Singapore: Marshall Cavendish Academic, xiii–xix.

Green, Michael J., and Bates Gill. 2009. *Asia's New Multilateralism: Cooperation, Competition, and the Search for Community.* New York: Columbia University Press.

Hu, Jintao. 2011. "Towards Common Development and a Harmonious Asia." Speech delivered at Boao Forum for Asia, Boao, China. April 15. http://www.fmprc.gov.cn/eng/wjdt/zyjh/t816535.htm (accessed August 31, 2011).

Kay, Sean. 2006. *Global Security in the Twenty-First Century.* New York: Rowman and Littlefield.

Keohane, Robert O. 1984. *After Hegemony: Cooperation and Discord in the World Political Economy.* Princeton, NJ: Princeton University Press.

Ma, Xiaotian. 2009. "Promote Security Cooperation for a Harmonious Asia Pacific Region." Speech delivered at the eighth International Institute for Strategic Studies' Asia Security Summit, Shangri-La Dialogue, Singapore. May 30. http://www.iiss.org/conferences/the-shangri-la-dialogue/shangri-la-dialogue-2009/plenary-session-speeches-2009/second-plenary-session/lieutenant-general-ma-xiaotian/ (accessed January 14, 2011).

Ministry of Foreign Affairs of the People's Republic of China. 2007. "APT Cooperation Work Plan (2007-2017)." November 20. http://www.fmprc.gov.cn/chn/pds/wjb/zzjg/yzs/dqzz/dmyzrh/zywj/t575767.htm (accessed January 14, 2011).

Ruwitch, John, and Ambika Ahuja. 2010. "China Ruffled at Security Forum over Maritime Rows." *Reuters* (Hanoi). July 23. http://in.reuters.com/article/2010/07/23/idINIndia-50356820100723 (accessed September 9, 2011).

Solingen, Etel. 2008. "The Genesis, Design and Effects of Regional Institutions: Lessons from East Asia and the Middle East." *International Studies Quarterly* 52 (2): 261–294.

U.S. Department of Defense. 1990. *A Strategic Framework for the Asian Pacific Rim: Looking Toward the 21st Century.* Washington, DC: U.S. Department of Defense.

Wan, Ming. 2003. "Economic Interdependence and Economic Cooperation: Mitigating Conflict and Transforming Security Order in Asia." In *Asian Security Order:*

Instrumental and Normative Features, edited by Muthiah Alagappa. Stanford, CA: Stanford University Press, 280–310.

Wendt, Alexander. 1999. *Social Theory of International Politics*. Cambridge: Cambridge University Press.

Xinhua Agency. 2005. "Police Officers of China, ASEAN, Japan, ROK Pledge Boosting Cooperation." August 19. http://english.peopledaily.com.cn/200508/19/eng20050819_203350.html (accessed September 8, 2011).

———. 2008. "APT Workshop on Disaster Relief Urges More Co-op." June 12. http://news.xinhuanet.com/english/2008-06/12/content_8356928.htm (accessed January 14, 2011).

———. 2010. "Military Officials from ASEAN Plus Three Mull Non-Traditional Security Challenges." October 12. http://english.peopledaily.com.cn/90001/90776/90883/7163492.html (accessed September 8, 2011).

5   Disputes over Territories and Maritime Rights and Interests

Their Political Economic Implications

Zhang Tuosheng

S INCE THE END OF THE COLD WAR, EAST ASIA HAS BEEN relatively stable and peaceful. However, various issues remain unsettled, including numerous disputes over territorial and maritime rights and interests. In the region, China and Japan are the two countries most troubled by these types of disputes. China is concerned with both land and maritime disputes, whereas Japan is concerned exclusively with maritime ones. The Chinese and Japanese disputes with neighboring countries reflect their traditional roles as land and sea powers; analyzing their claims may help us develop a better understanding of the nature of such disputes in the region.

This chapter covers six cases of disputes among China, Japan, and some of their neighbors, analyzing the causes of the conflicts; depicting the evolution of claims; and exploring the interaction of political, economic, and security factors underlying them. The latter interactions have determined the past and present course of disputes over territories and maritime rights and interests and will determine their future. The evolution of disputes in turn will also have a major impact on East Asian regional politics, economics, and security.

This study finds that since the end of the Cold War, improved political and security relations among states in East Asia have had a positive effect on the handling of regional territorial and maritime disputes. Economic factors, however, have had more mixed effects on the disputes. In general, economic developments have resulted in a trend toward relaxation, but the trend has been punctuated by periodic reintensification of these disputes. Nevertheless, as long as the main trend of improving political and economic relations in East Asia does not change, the ongoing efforts of countries in the region to address their disputes over territory and maritime rights and interests seem likely to keep these disputes manageable while gradually advancing them toward peaceful resolution.

Sino-Russian and Sino-Soviet Boundary Disputes

After the founding of People's Republic of China, there were three sets of boundary lines in effect between China and the Soviet Union: the Treaty Line, the Soviet Cartography Line, and the Line of Actual Control (the LAC). The Treaty Line was established by a series of treaties between China and Russia in the middle and late nineteenth century (among the Qing dynasty's international agreements, often referred to as unequal treaties), through which more than 1.5 million square kilometers of Chinese territories were annexed by czarist Russia. The Soviet Cartography Line was marked in the maps published by the Soviet Union. The LAC demarcated de facto control of China and the Soviet Union. From the Treaty Line to the Soviet Cartography Line and the LAC, each offered the Soviet Union more Chinese territory. The simultaneous existence of the three lines complicated disputes between China and the Soviet Union over several areas and islands that encompass a total area of thirty-five thousand square kilometers (Li 2005: 157).

In the early 1950s, China and the Soviet Union were close allies, and disagreements about boundary issues were not actively disputed. In 1958, the Chinese government set out to resolve boundary disputes with its neighbors. Initially, boundary surveys were performed smoothly in an environment of friendliness and mutual trust. However, beginning in the late 1950s, ideological differences arose between the Chinese Communist Party and the Communist Party of the Soviet Union, which soon developed into more general antagonism over conflicting national interests. This was followed by a series of boundary incidents in the early 1960s that increased the urgency of solving the boundary disputes through diplomatic negotiations.

Bilateral negotiations began in 1964 and lasted for four decades. At the time of the first negotiations, the Sino-Soviet split had not yet occurred, and the two countries reached an initial understanding on the alignment of the eastern boundary. However, no agreement was signed as a result of the resurfacing of ideological factors. A second round of negotiations occurred between 1969 and 1978, after the break in bilateral relations and several armed border conflicts. When the negotiations ended nine years later, there still had been no resolution of the issue. The third round of negotiations was held from 1987 to 1991. In the context of the normalization of Sino-Soviet relations, capped by Mikhail Gorbachev's visit to Beijing in May 1989, these negotiations were far less contentious than earlier rounds had been. In May 1991, China and the Soviet Union signed the Agreement on the Eastern Section of the Boundary, thereby surmounting the largest and most difficult obstacle in their boundary dispute.

Since the collapse of the Soviet Union, relations between China and Russia have consistently improved, and negotiations have continued to yield progress, most notably in the signing of the Agreement on the Western Section of the Boundary in 1994 and the Supplementary Agreement on the Eastern Section of the Boundary in 2004. In June 2005, the two governments exchanged the documents that ratified the Supplementary Agreement, which finalized the settlement over a 4,300-kilometer border.

On the basis of this account of the evolution of Sino-Soviet and Sino-Russian territorial disputes and settlements, it is possible to derive the following conclusions.

First, political relations between the two countries played a critical role in the evolution of the boundary dispute. Until the late 1950s, the two countries were allies, and the boundary disputes largely remained dormant. In the 1960s and 1970s, along with the deterioration of political relations, boundary disputes became increasingly serious and led to severe military crises and even armed conflicts between the two countries. Since the end of 1980s, the gradual improvement and normalization of Sino-Soviet relations created improved conditions for the resolution of boundary disputes. After the disintegration of the Soviet Union, China-Russia relations rapidly developed, and the boundary disputes were finally resolved.

Second, compared to the role of political relations, the role of economic relations was minor in the evolution and resolution of the disputes. Economic relations were significantly undermined by the deterioration of Sino-Soviet political relations, and when the boundary negotiations were reopened in the late 1980s, economic cooperation between the two countries was very limited, and prospects for economic cooperation were not a key consideration. Nevertheless, along with improvements in political relations and the mitigation of boundary disputes, there was noticeable growth in economic relations, particularly along the eastern border. This development subsequently helped foster a settlement of the disputes.

Third, the series of historical treaties between China and Russia complicated the resolution of border disputes. On the one hand, the treaties were the very reason behind the boundary disputes. On the other hand, as acts of governments of two sovereign states, they constituted an important basis for the two sides to finally achieve settlement over their border disputes. In fact, since the first round of negotiations in 1964, China's basic position was that it was still willing to negotiate a boundary line on the basis of those treaties, in spite of their unequal nature. However, as Sino-Soviet relations deteriorated, the question of the treaties' legitimacy grew in importance and border disputes escalated. With the marked improvement of political relations, the two sides were able to overcome this historical obstacle (Jiang 2005).

Fourth, the area of the territories actually disputed was relatively small in size and of neither political nor military importance. Therefore, with the normalization of Sino-Soviet relations and, in particular, with the marked development of political relations with Russia, Kazakhstan, Kyrgyzstan, and Tajikistan, the remaining issues were quickly resolved. The only exception was Heixiazi Island, which had been under Russia's de facto control. Of far more military and economic significance, it was the most contested and complicated dispute and the last to be resolved.[1]

Sino-Vietnamese Disputes over Land Borders and the Delimitation of the Beibu Gulf (Gulf of Tonkin)

China and Vietnam share a land border more than 1,300 kilometers long. In the 1880s, the Qing government of China and the French colonial government in Vietnam signed a boundary demarcation treaty on the basis of customary lines. This border was recognized by successive governments of both countries, yet there were different understandings regarding the details of the demarcation that led to disputes regarding certain stretches of territory.

From the founding of the PRC until the early 1970s, the border between China and Vietnam remained largely peaceful and served as the front line for China's assistance to Vietnam in its war against the French and the Americans. However, after 1968, as strategic breaches appeared between China and Vietnam, boundary frictions began and increased around the time of

Vietnamese unification. In the 1970s, the dispute over the Beibu Gulf (Gulf of Tonkin) emerged as evolution in the laws of the sea resulted in overlapping and conflicting claims between the two countries.

During the mid-1970s, the countries twice organized negotiations to discuss their land-border dispute and the delimitation of the Beibu Gulf. The negotiations were unsuccessful because of the deterioration of bilateral political relations. In 1979, along with the breakdown of China-Vietnam relations, the two countries fought a brief war, followed by smaller military skirmishes that persisted until the late 1980s.

After China and Vietnam normalized relations in 1991, the two countries sought to resolve their disputed land border and maritime boundaries. In October 1993, the two sides signed the Agreement on Basic Principles, which specified that the disputes should be addressed pragmatically and that the land boundary and Beibu Gulf issues should be addressed first, followed by negotiations on other maritime disputes.

In the mid-1990s, however, the political relationship between China and Vietnam cooled as Vietnam began improving its ties with the United States and increased its contacts with Taiwan. Nonetheless, the two sides gradually gained a better understanding of the importance of strengthening bilateral cooperation. In 1999, leaders of the two countries jointly identified guiding principles for the relationship, including long-term stability, future-oriented good-neighborliness, friendship, and comprehensive cooperation (Xinhua News Agency 1999). This established a framework for improving China-Vietnam relations and led to an increase in mutual trust. Ever since, China and Vietnam have stepped up their efforts to resolve their territorial disputes.

In December 1999, the two countries signed the Land Border Treaty. A year later, they signed the Agreement on the Demarcation of the Beibu Gulf Territorial Waters, Exclusive Economic Zones, and Continental Shelf and the Agreement on Fishing Cooperation in the Beibu Gulf. Thus, on the eve of the twenty-first century, they reached a final settlement demarcating land borders as well as the Beibu Gulf. Compared with the talks on the land borders, the negotiation on the delimitation of the Beibu Gulf was much more difficult, experiencing "much fluctuation" and "a frequency of negotiation very rare in Chinese diplomatic history" (Tang 2009: 262).

The following conclusions can be drawn regarding the evolution and resolution of China-Vietnam territorial and Beibu Gulf disputes.

First, there is a significant interaction between bilateral political-security relations and bilateral disputes. In the 1950s and 1960s, the China-Vietnam relationship was characterized as one of comrades and brothers who shared a common goal of resisting the United States. During that time both countries neglected the territorial issues. This changed in the mid-1970s, when, along with the deterioration of bilateral relations, territorial and maritime disputes emerged and intensified. In the post–Cold War world, however, strategic tensions faded and relations warmed, thus enabling China and Vietnam to return to a more pragmatic relationship. This opened new opportunities to resolve their border disputes as part of the broader improvement in their bilateral political and security relationship.

Second, compared with their political and security relations, economic ties between China and Vietnam had far less impact on the evolution of their territorial disputes. Although bilateral economic relations witnessed improvements, stemming in part from the amelioration of political-security relations, the scale of China-Vietnam trade and economic cooperation remained limited throughout the 1990s. Economic ties certainly were not the primary impetus for both countries to resolve their territorial and Beibu Gulf disputes, although it would be incorrect to ignore the role of economic interests completely. Indeed, in the case of the Beibu Gulf, there were considerable economic interests at stake, which made the maritime dispute far more difficult to resolve than those on land. The new century has witnessed considerable acceleration in bilateral economic and trade ties. If this trend continues, and is matched by warming political ties, it will facilitate resolution of the remaining South China Sea disputes between China and Vietnam.

Third, the asymmetries between the size (and indirectly, the power) of the countries matter. The size and power differential between China and Vietnam, in addition to the fact that the two countries had just undergone a period of military conflict, made Vietnam exceptionally vigilant and suspicious of China, particularly on security-related issues. Restoring and improving bilateral political and security relations proved difficult and slow paced. Progress in dispute resolution has largely paralleled the general quality of bilateral relations.

Fourth, the Beibu Gulf dispute was more difficult to resolve not only because greater economic interests were at stake but also because the dispute is based on a different set of legal principles. Land borders were already delimited in historical treaties and recognized by successive governments of the two countries, whereas disputes in the Beibu Gulf emerged along with the relatively recent evolution of the international laws of the sea.

South China Sea Disputes Between China and Five Southeast Asian Countries

China is currently one of several countries (including Vietnam, the Philippines, Malaysia, and Brunei) that have competing territorial claims over islands, reefs, exclusive economic zones (EEZs), continental shelves, and maritime resources in the South China Sea. In addition, China and Indonesia have a dispute over EEZs. Before the 1970s, these nations generally did not express any objections to China's sovereignty over the Nansha and Xisha islands. The nine-dashed line drawn by China in 1947, marking its traditional maritime claims in the South China Sea, also appeared on the maps of many other countries (see Li 2011). However, with the enactment of international laws of the sea and the discovery of a potentially rich reserve of oil and gas in the South China Sea at the end of 1960s, these countries began to make competing sovereignty claims.[2] At the time, China was in the midst of the Cultural Revolution and thus was barely able to offer anything more than diplomatic responses until the late 1970s, when there were two small-scale military conflicts between China and Vietnam.[3]

Since the end of the Cold War, economic development has become a priority on the agendas of most countries. With the unprecedented growth in demand for oil and gas and the subsequent increased interest in maritime resources, the disputes in the South China Sea have quickly heated up. Vietnam, the Philippines, and Malaysia all have intensified their claims over the islands, reefs, and maritime resources in the South China Sea. In response, in 1992, China promulgated its Law on the Territorial Sea and Contiguous Zone, to more effectively protect its territory, maritime rights, and interests. Just two years later, the Meiji Jiao (called Mischief Reef in the Philippines) incident broke out between China and the Philippines, drawing international attention to the disputes in the South China Sea.

In this context, China and the other countries began to seek resolutions to these disputes. In the early 1990s, China officially proposed that the South China Sea disputes be handled by shelving disputes and engaging in joint development. During the 1994 China–Association of Southeast Asian Nations'

(ASEAN) Foreign Ministers' Dialogue, China advanced this position and expressed a willingness to peacefully resolve the South China Sea disputes on the basis of international law and the principles of the UN Convention on the Law of the Sea. The ASEAN states welcomed China's proposal. In the context of strengthened China-ASEAN relations, China and the ASEAN countries signed the Declaration on the Conduct of Parties in the South China Sea in November 2002.[4] Subsequently, China and the Philippines reached an agreement in November 2004 on joint oil and gas exploration in the disputed waters. Then, in March 2005, three oil companies from China, the Philippines, and Vietnam signed the Agreement on Joint Marine Seismic Undertaking in Certain Areas in the South China Sea, a significant step toward "shelving disputes and engaging in joint development."

In 2008, as the deadline drew near for submitting claims to the UN Commission on the Limits of the Continental Shelf, the parties continued to hold sharply different positions on this question and disputes in the South China Sea again grew more heated. In this situation, implementation of the joint development agreement ran into major difficulties and trilateral cooperation stalled. Since 2010, frictions among the concerned states (especially between China and Vietnam and between China and the Philippines) over fisheries and energy exploration in disputed areas have repeatedly occurred. With the high-profile intervention of the United States in July 2010, the South China Sea disputes again drew considerable attention from the international community.[5]

In 2011, although frictions over the South China Sea have continued, the parties also redoubled their efforts to resolve their disputes through cooperation. In June and October, China and the United States held two consultations over Asia-Pacific affairs, reaching important understandings on many issues, including the South China Sea situation. Furthermore, in August, foreign ministers from China and the ASEAN countries met and agreed on guidelines for the implementation of the Declaration on the Conduct of Parties in the South China Sea. Meanwhile, high-level dialogues between China and Vietnam and between China and the Philippines resumed. All three countries reiterated that they will observe the declaration, pursue dispute resolution by peaceful means, and continue safeguarding regional peace and stability. As a result, tensions over the situation in the South China Sea eased somewhat.

This overview of the disputes in the South China Sea over the past four decades suggests the following conclusions: First, the South China Sea disputes represent complex claims of sovereignty and interests over various areas that defy simple resolution. Conflicting claims exist not only between China and the five Southeast Asian countries but also among some of the five. Yet the Southeast Asian countries tend to unite with one another in their dealings with China. Furthermore, some of the countries have launched collaborative development programs with international oil companies and some have even attempted to draw the United States into the disputes, thus further complicating the situation. This area is rich in resources and is also an important sea-lane of communication for all shipping to and from the Middle East.[6] With the expanding demands on maritime resources and global energy, as well as contrasting interpretations of historical claims and legal principles, the South China Sea disputes have intensified over past decades.

Second, South China Sea disputes, though fluctuating in intensity and seriously deteriorating at times, have been fairly well contained since the end of the Cold War. In the past two decades, the disputes have not triggered severe military crises or armed conflicts. A fundamental reason for this is the continued improvement of political and economic relations between China and the Southeast Asian countries. Furthermore, by maintaining dialogue and consultation among the parties to the conflicts and by establishing maritime security and confidence-building measures in the South China Sea, China and ASEAN have helped stabilize these disputes.

Third, as a large country that is directly involved in the South China Sea disputes, China's policies and practices carry significant weight. To maintain a favorable regional environment in which to pursue both economic reforms and modernization, China has exercised self-restraint, proposing the joint resolution of disputes through dialogues between equals and reliance on peaceful means, "shelving disputes, and engaging in joint development" on the basis of international law. In recent years, China has further proposed that the South China Sea be transformed into a "sea of peace, cooperation, and friendship."[7] Collectively, these policies have helped mitigate the disputes.

Fourth, the China-ASEAN relationship has evolved from one of dialogue to one of strategic partnership, a trend highlighted by the establishment of the China-ASEAN Free Trade Agreement. This transformation of relations is likely to have a significant impact on how maritime and territorial disputes are settled. All concerned parties have incentives to take into consideration long-term mutual political and strategic interests, try to subordinate clashes of economic interests between individual countries to the common interests of regional economic cooperation, and actively explore win-win solutions to the disputes. This provides a basis for optimism about the prospects for managing the South China Sea disputes.

Fifth, despite all this, there is still a long way to go before a final settlement of the dispute can be reached in the South China Sea. The immediate and midterm goals for the relevant nations are to implement the Declaration on the Conduct of Parties in the South China Sea, to formulate a code of conduct so that the disputes will be kept controllable, and to actively advance joint development. Only by so doing can the necessary conditions for a final resolution of the disputes be created.

East China Sea Disputes Between China and Japan

The disputes between China and Japan in the East China Sea embody two separate issues: the Diaoyu Islands (called the Senkaku Islands by Japan) and the demarcation of the East China Sea.

China's claim to the Diaoyu Islands dates from the sixteenth century.[8] Before Japan occupied them, the Diaoyu Islands had been recognized as belonging to China on the maps of Japan, Great Britain, France, the United States, Spain, and other countries. Approximately 6.3 square kilometers in size, the islands were occupied by Japan in early 1895, during the first Sino-Japanese War. According to the Cairo and Potsdam proclamations, after World War II they were to be returned, along with Taiwan, to China. However, the United States administered the Diaoyu Islands for more than two decades, transferring control of them (and Okinawa) to Japan in 1971. Both the Chinese government and the authorities on Taiwan strongly protested this move.

When China and Japan restored diplomatic relations and signed the Treaty of Peace and Friendship in the 1970s, the Diaoyu Islands dispute presented an obstacle during negotiations. However, on the basis of a Chinese proposal, the two sides agreed to set aside the dispute for later settlement and, in the interest of Sino-Japanese friendship, to proceed with improving their relations. In 1979, the Chinese leader Deng Xiaoping proposed that China and Japan "shelve the disputes and jointly develop" the islands (Ministry of Foreign Affairs 2000); Japan did not directly respond to this suggestion.

During the 1980s, a period during which China and Japan enjoyed fairly good relations, the dispute caused only limited friction between the two countries. After the mid-1990s, however, relations between the two countries fluctuated and then worsened, and frictions over the Diaoyu Islands increased. In contrast, when bilateral relations improved considerably in the fall of 2006, the dispute eased somewhat. However, toward the end of 2008, frictions increased again, and a ship collision that occurred in the sea close to the islands in September 2010 caused serious damage to bilateral relations.[9] Because neither side wished to aggravate the situation, tensions gradually eased after Japan released the Chinese captain. By the first half of 2011, bilateral relations basically returned to normal.

The dispute over demarcation of the East China Sea involves issues regarding EEZs, the continental shelf, and offshore oil and gas exploration and development. According to the 1982 UN Convention on the Law of the Sea, the EEZs of China and Japan overlap in the East China Sea. The two sides have since issued sharply contrasting claims based on their interpretations of the convention.[10]

Aiming to address these issues, in the 1990s China proposed that the area be jointly developed with Japan, but to no avail. Earlier this century, with the deterioration of China-Japan relations, China began exploring and drilling to the east of the so-called median line in the East China Sea, which intensified the dispute. As a result, both sides have launched frequent military operations in the contested waters, which increases the risk of unintentional armed clashes.

At China's urging, the two sides began negotiations in October 2004. In the first few rounds of consultations, the two sides articulated sharply different claims.[11] In October 2006, the political relationship took a turn for the better, with both countries making efforts to develop strategic and mutually beneficial relations. Their leaders agreed to develop the East China Sea into a "sea of peace, cooperation, and friendship" (Ministry of Foreign Affairs 2006). Since then, progress has been made in bilateral consultations. In June 2008, with enormous effort, the two countries reached a principled understanding on the question of the East China Sea,[12] taking a critical step toward the goal of joint development.[13]

From this overview of China-Japan disputes in the East China Sea, the following conclusions and predictions can be made. First, despite the fluctuations in China-Japan relations, shared political and economic interests have consistently tempered tensions and encouraged both countries to pursue solutions that prevent these disputes from escalating. In the 1970s and 1980s, to restore diplomatic relations and address the Soviet threat, the two countries decided to set aside their dispute over the Diaoyu Islands. In the aftermath of the Cold War, Sino-Japanese relations suffered from severe political and security instabilities, and in turn, bilateral competitions and clashes escalated. However, bilateral economic ties continued improving at a steady pace, which helped limit the East China Sea disputes.[14] In fall 2006, the two countries began to coordinate their political and economic relations in a far more extensive manner. Since then, although the East China Sea disputes still surface from time to time, consultation between the two countries has produced an important consensus on principles. In the future, if the political-economic relations between the two countries continue to improve, the two sides will be able to make concerted efforts on the basis of this and gradually make progress toward resolving the disputes.

Second, as the Diaoyu Islands dispute has political, economic, security, and legal implications, it is the most difficult to resolve of the disputes between China and Japan regarding the East China Sea. Politically, the dispute not only is a matter of sovereignty but also is closely related to historical antagonisms between the two countries. Economically, the surrounding sea areas are endowed with rich resources of oil, natural gas, and fishing. In terms of security, its geographic location is of critical importance.[15] Legally, it may have significance for the delimitation of the East China Sea as a whole. The islands are currently under the de facto control of Japan, and Tokyo flatly denies the existence of a bilateral dispute and defines the islands as Japanese territory covered by the U.S.-Japan mutual defense treaty. Given this stance, it is unlikely that the dispute will be resolved any time soon, and future frictions seem unavoidable. Nonetheless, the situation should remain manageable, as China's policy is to moderate rather than intensify the dispute,[16] and Japan similarly seeks to prevent the intense situation surrounding the Diaoyu Islands from damaging the overall Japan-China relationship. Both sides seek to draw on lessons of the 2010 ship collision to set up a crisis management mechanism.

Third, compared with the Diaoyu dispute, the dispute over delimitation of the EEZ and the continental shelf in the East China Sea should be easier to address. Although it concerns significant economic and natural resources and reflects diverging interpretations of international law, this dispute has less of an impact on sovereignty and security and is not related to any unresolved historical disputes. It becomes an issue arousing nationalist passions only when political relations between China and Japan deteriorate. When the political atmosphere recovers, the maritime dispute subsides. Thus, as long as strategic relations continue to improve and both governments gain greater latitude in their negotiations, a breakthrough in the joint development of the

East China Sea is likely. Progress will help establish conditions for the delimitation of the East China Sea and perhaps set the stage for similar progress on joint development of the Diaoyu Islands.

Fourth, the three major points of tension between China and Japan—namely history, Taiwan, and the East China Sea—are closely related to one another. The questions of both Taiwan and the Diaoyu Islands are closely related to the history of Japanese aggression, whereas the sea-lane of communication in the East China Sea is also closely related to the issue of Taiwan. Thus, as long as the issues of history and Taiwan remain a bilateral irritant, it will be difficult to resolve the disputes in the East China Sea. Yet tensions between China and Japan over history and Taiwan have markedly decreased in recent years. If the salience of the disagreements over the two issues continues to decline, the prospects for progress in resolving the East China Sea disputes will brighten.

Japanese–South Korean Disputes in the East China Sea

Disputes between Japan and South Korea in the East China Sea are twofold: they involve Dokdo (called Takeshima by Japan) and the continental shelf and maritime delimitation in the East China Sea.

Dokdo (which comprises an area of 0.18 square kilometers) is located to the east of the Korean Peninsula and is composed of two islets and a dozen reefs. Although the islets have been part of Korea since the fifteenth century, Japan claimed sovereignty over them in 1905 after its occupation of the Korean Peninsula. After World War II, Dokdo was administered by U.S. troops and then returned to Seoul in 1948. There are fertile fishery resources around the islets and potential petroleum and gas reserves in the seabed. Currently, South Korea has de facto control over Dokdo.

Since 1954, Japan has repeatedly presented protests to the South Korean government asserting Japan's sovereignty over Dokdo and demanding the end of South Korea's presence there. In response, South Korea has reiterated that Dokdo is indisputably sovereign Korean territory. South Korea has also refused the Japanese proposal to conduct negotiations over the matter or to refer the dispute to the International Court of Justice in The Hague. Since the beginning of the twenty-first century, the Dokdo dispute has intensified and, along with disputes over history, has gained increasing prominence. Japan has repeatedly sought to demonstrate sovereignty over the island, which has triggered an uncompromising response from South Korea. Despite these clashes, however, the two parties have managed to maintain control over the situation, and the dispute has not decisively undermined bilateral political or economic ties.

Beginning in the late 1960s, following the discovery of petroleum and gas resources in the East China Sea, Japan and South Korea became involved in continental shelf and maritime delimitation disputes. At the time, both countries set up exploitation zones in the disputed waters, resulting in more than twenty thousand square kilometers of overlapping claims. To settle this issue and start development, the two governments decided to begin diplomatic negotiations to delimit the continental shelf.

After multiple rounds of intense negotiations between November 1970 and September 1972, the two sides finally agreed to set aside their competing legal claims and establish a joint development zone in which they would share the oil and gas output.[17] In 1974, the two countries signed two agreements that delimited the continental shelf in the north and defined a joint development zone of about twenty-four thousand square nautical miles on the continental shelf in the south.

Japan and South Korea rushed to reach an agreement on the continental shelf even before the new framework of the International Law of the Sea was firmly established, because both sides sought to exploit the gains from the rich offshore oil reserves in the disputed areas. However, neither side has actually realized these gains from the joint development zone (Zhu 2006). Even so, Japanese–South Korean relations improved significantly, and their disputes have been kept relatively contained since they established a joint development zone.

We can therefore conclude the following regarding the East China Sea dispute between Japan and South Korea: First, bilateral political and economic cooperation has been essential to containing the dispute. After World War II, both countries were within the U.S. sphere of influence and became its military allies. In spite of enormous obstacles, the two countries managed to normalize diplomatic relations in 1965 through a series of negotiations. Following this, bilateral political and security relations have improved significantly alongside economic relations. Although their political relationship has weathered more friction since the end of the Cold War, their economic and trade ties have continued to grow, and both countries have remained important East Asian allies of the United States. Security and economic co-operation will continue playing a role in restraining their territorial disputes.

Second, with regard to the Dokdo dispute, legal principles and political interests are both relevant. The islets are insignificant in size, and whether they are economically significant stems from their position in the boundary delimitation. The dispute is certainly politically relevant, as it is closely re-lated to the legacy of Japanese occupation and colonial control of the Korean Peninsula. In the long term, because South Korea has de facto control over Dokdo and because there is a growing international consensus against the use of contested islets as a baseline for maritime delimitation, it is likely that the dispute over Dokdo will dissipate.

Third, Japan and South Korea must overcome considerable challenges be-fore they will be able to realize joint development and delimitation in the East China Sea. The energy resources in the disputed areas are increasingly im-portant to both Japan and South Korea, each of which heavily depends on en-ergy imports. The old agreement on joint development that was so hurriedly concluded has not yielded tangible results. If progress is to be made on its implementation, the two sides will have to overcome additional difficulties. Furthermore, the existing agreement covers areas in the East China Sea over which China has asserted sovereign rights to continental shelves. Therefore, Japan and South Korea will also need to address China's interests if they are to reach a lasting resolution of this dispute.

Fourth, along with changes in international law, there are new develop-ments in both Japanese and South Korean claims over the East China Sea, which may aid resolution of the dispute. First, the importance of islands is restricted in maritime delimitations and disputed islands do not enjoy EEZ or continental shelf status. Second, a single boundary line needs to be estab-lished in the East China Sea on the basis of the length of the coastline. In ad-dition, some South Korean scholars have stopped advocating for the principle of the natural prolongation of the continental shelf and instead have turned to the median-line principle applied by Japan (Zhu 2006). It is noteworthy that some of these proposals contradict the Chinese position. It clearly remains a tough task for all three countries to reach an agreement.

The Islands Disputes Between Russia and Japan

The Northern Islands comprise four territories—Etorofu Island, Kunashiri Island, Shikotan Island, and Habomai Island—located between Hokkaido,

Japan, and the Kuril Islands, Russia. Approximately five thousand square kilometers in total size, the islands are called the Northern Territory by Japan and the Southern Kuril Islands by Russia.

Historically, Japan began exercising jurisdiction over the Northern Islands as early as the thirteenth century. In the mid- and late nineteenth century, Japan and Russia signed boundary treaties that recognized Sakhalin Island as belonging to Russia and the Kuril Islands as belonging to Japan.[18] During the Russo-Japanese war of 1904–1905, Japan seized a part of Sakhalin Island. In 1945, to convince the Soviet Union to participate in military actions against Japan in the Far East, the United States and United Kingdom recognized Soviet claims to Japanese land at the Yalta Conference. Around the time of the Japanese surrender, the Soviets occupied Sakhalin Island and the Kuril Islands, including the four Northern Islands. As stipulated in the 1951 San Francisco Peace Treaty, Japan renounced all rights to the Kuril Islands as well as all rights and claims to Sakhalin Island and its nearby islets that derived from the September 5, 1905, Treaty of Portsmouth.

When Japan and the Soviet Union signed a joint declaration in 1956, the Soviet Union agreed to return Habomai and Shikotan to Japan once a peace treaty was signed. However, the Soviet Union retracted its offer because Japan insisted on the return of the four islands together and because Japan had signed a new security pact with the United States.

After the end of the Cold War, as political relations warmed and Tokyo and Moscow became interested in expanding economic cooperation (Japan sought oil, gas, and other natural resources from Russia, whereas Russia sought Japanese capital and technology), the leaders of both governments sought to resolve their territorial disputes. The two sides have offered proposals, but no agreement has been reached.

This brief overview of the Russia-Japan territorial disputes suggests the following: First, the Northern Islands dispute is shaped by several different factors that make it complicated and difficult to resolve. The bilateral delimitation treaties were arrived at under quite different historical circumstances: some through peacetime diplomacy, and others as a result of Japan's military victory over Russia. In addition, the dispute reflects the legacy of World War II and international treaties signed after its conclusion. The Russians and the Japanese have very different views about the legitimacy of the Soviet occupation of the Northern Islands and, in particular, the Yalta Agreement and San Francisco Peace Treaty. Moreover, in the international community there is no consensus regarding the merits of the competing views about the dispute.

Second, given the political, economic, and military significance of these islands, neither side is likely to facilitate resolution of the dispute by compromising. Politically, the disputes are highly sensitive and subject to nationalist sentiments in both countries, where leaders tend to employ tough rhetoric to please public opinion. Economically, as maritime territories, the Northern Islands are all habitable,[19] and they are large enough for their owner to gain significant maritime resources through contiguous EEZs. Militarily, they are strategically located, guarding Russia's access to the western Pacific, which previously served as the outpost for the Soviet Pacific Fleet throughout the Cold War. At the same time, Japan regards these islands as part of its already relatively limited sovereign territory and thus seeks every possible means to reclaim them.

Third, the two countries approach the resolution of the dispute with contrasting attitudes. Japan has taken the initiative in proposing solutions, whereas Russia has reacted with unhurried indifference. Their proposed solutions are far too different to enable compromise. The four Northern Islands are regarded by the Japanese as their rightful territory, and their reunification is on the top of every Japanese cabinet's agenda. In contrast, Russia wishes only to acquire Japanese financial aid through mitigating the disputes rather than making any real territorial concessions. Russia has clearly expressed its unwillingness to cede all four islands, with the relinquishing of Shikodan and Habomai being its most generous offer. Japan, however, has insisted on the reclamation of all four islands. These fundamental differences are highly unlikely to be resolved in the foreseeable future (He 2003).

Fourth, having fought several wars against each other and having been adversaries throughout the Cold War, relations between Russia and Japan remain cool. The two countries' territorial disputes remain an obstacle preventing them from successfully negotiating a peace treaty. Although there have been improvements in bilateral diplomatic relations since the end of the Cold War, Russia-Japan relations remain less fruitful than their Russia-Europe and Russia-U.S. equivalents. Moreover, when Russia's relations with Europe or the United States deteriorate, its relations with Japan follow suit. Bilateral trade and investment between Russia and Japan have also been slow to develop. This weakness in Russia-Japan economic cooperation is both a reason for and a consequence of weak political relations.

Fifth, difficulty in resolving the dispute is exacerbated by the intricate geopolitical environment in this region. Geopolitics in Northeast Asia is entangled by the complicated relationship among Russia, Japan, and the United States, which was antagonistic throughout the Cold War period and remains tense even now. For the United States, it is a core security and strategic goal to both monitor any revival of Russian power and keep Japanese development within a permissible range. The United States also maintains a close watch on improvements in Russia-Japan relations to monitor any potential effects on the U.S.-Japan alliance.

Conclusion

On the basis of the preceding discussion of these major cases involving China, Japan, and their respective neighbors, we can arrive at the following four broad conclusions about East Asian territorial and maritime disputes in the post–Cold War era.

First, after the end of Cold War, the disputes over territories and maritime rights and interests in East Asia can be put in three different categories that reflect the primary types of interaction between the dispute and the political and economic relations between the relevant countries.

The first category is disputes that have been completely resolved by the relevant countries, such as the China-Russia boundary disputes and the China-Vietnam disputes over their land border and the Beibu Gulf. Their resolution followed a general pattern of improved bilateral political and security relations, which facilitated the dispute resolution and in turn supported further bilateral economic and political cooperation.

The second category includes disputes that are kept under control and have some prospects for gradual or partial resolution despite periodic clashes. Examples include the East China Sea disputes between China and Japan, the South China Sea disputes between China and the five Southeast Asian countries, and the East China Sea disputes between Japan and South Korea. The dynamics embodied in these situations are as follows: healthy bilateral political and economic cooperation or strong economic ties become a significant driving force that shapes the scope of the disputes and prevents them from escalating. At the same time, as the disputes are brought under control, bilateral political and economic relations further expand.

The third category is disputes that remain stalemated, such as the Russia-Japan territorial disputes. Although both sides would like to improve political relations and develop economic ties, the stakes involved in the dispute are so significant that they present insurmountable obstacles. In such situations, the prospect for resolving disputes is rather slim.

This categorization indicates that the overall state of political and economic relations between contending parties is vitally important in determining the prospects for the resolution of disputes over territories and maritime rights and interests. For disputes involving minor conflicts of economic or security interest, improvements in overall political relations may be sufficient to facilitate a resolution. For those that involve considerable economic and/or security interests, although a steady improvement of bilateral political and economic relations alone is unlikely to ensure their settlement, it may help keep them under control and improve the prospects for moving toward a gradual resolution.

Even when political relations are cold and economic relations are warm, the countries still have a fairly strong desire to keep their disputes under control, as neither side wants to see a disruption of critical bilateral economic cooperation and a consequent deterioration of overall relations. In this sense, warm economic relations are also important in constraining the disputes.

However, when there are critical political, security, and economic interests involved in the disputes, the extent of improvement will be limited. Weak political and economic relations also reduce the ability and incentives for the parties to resolve their disputes, and in such circumstances, they become extremely difficult to resolve.

A second broad conclusion is that one can distinguish four types of disputes by the varying levels of political, security, and economic interests involved. The first type involves significant political, security, and economic interests. Examples include the Northern Islands disputes between Russia and Japan, and the South China Sea disputes between China and the five Southeast Asian nations. The second type involves primarily political and security interests, with economic interests playing a comparatively minor role. Examples include the Diaoyu Islands dispute between China and Japan, and the Dokdo-Takeshima dispute between Japan and South Korea. The third type involves principally economic interests, in which political and security interests are either absent or of secondary importance. The Beibu Gulf delimitation dispute between China and Vietnam, the East China Sea delimitation dispute between China and Japan, and the East China Sea dispute between Japan and South Korea fit this type. The fourth type involves no important political, security, or economic interests. The Sino-Soviet and Sino-Russia boundary dispute and the China-Vietnam land-border dispute both fit this type.[20]

There are, of course, many other factors besides political, security, and economic interests that affect territorial and maritime disputes in East Asia. These factors include the origins of the disputes, the political and cultural traditions of the countries involved, the role of third parties, the evolution of international law, and changes in regional and international circumstances. Yet the influence of these variables is typically realized through the core factors of political, security, and economic interests.

It is obvious that the four categories of disputes are vastly different in their nature, content, and severity. In the future, countries will need to work together for dispute resolution, moving from easier-to-resolve and urgent disputes to more difficult and less urgent ones.

A third broad conclusion is that East Asian territorial (land) disputes are nearing settlement, whereas maritime disputes will continue to exist for quite some time, thus constituting a major challenge for countries in the region. Most disputed territories on land are small in size, remote in location, and already delimited in historical territorial or demarcation treaties. There are also well-established international laws that govern the delimitation of such territory. Thus, it is relatively easy to address territorial disputes on land. China was previously most troubled by these sorts of territorial disputes with its neighbors, but along with the delimitation of its borders with Russia, Kazakhstan, Kyrgyzstan, Tajikistan, and Vietnam, all its land boundary disputes in East Asia have been resolved. Presently, the Thai-Cambodia boundary dispute is the only unsettled territorial dispute on land in East Asia.

However, in recent decades, maritime disputes have become a growing source of insecurity in East Asia. The reasons for this include the following: (1) besides their own value, maritime territories may determine the delimitation of continental shelves and EEZs; (2) sea lines of communication are increasingly critical for East Asian nations;[21] (3) resource shortages and advancements in science and technology, especially in oceanographic studies, have contributed to more intense competition over maritime resources (a large portion of which are still inaccessible with current technology); (4) some of the bilateral maritime disputes (such as those over the South China Sea and the East China Sea) are further complicated by the involvement of third parties; and (5) contemporary international laws of the sea are still evolving.

To maintain long-term peace and stability in East Asia, it is imperative for East Asian countries to explore effective ways to resolve maritime disputes at an early date.

Fourth and finally, in general, since the end of the Cold War, economic issues have gained importance while the significance of political and security issues have decreased. This change is reflected not only in the increased relative importance of economic interests but also in the improvement of state-to-state relations, which has an effect on the handling of these disputes. The decreasing significance of political and security considerations has contributed to easing and may facilitate the eventual resolution of territorial and maritime disputes in East Asia. However, the rise in importance of economic factors has two seemingly contradictory implications for these disputes. On the one hand, countries attach greater importance to economic development, discouraging disruptive escalation of their territorial and maritime disputes. On the other hand, intensified competition over economic resources in the disputed areas increases the difficulty of resolving such disputes and becomes a main reason for their rising salience.

It is worth mentioning that in the current international environment, contending parties may have greater opportunity for compromise, cooperation, and mutual gain in resolving conflicts of economic interest than they do in resolving conflicts of political and security interests. In the latter, the conflicting parties have little leeway for compromise or concession and zero-sum attitudes still prevail.

All in all, it is likely that with additional effort to resolve the territorial and maritime disputes in East Asia through dialogue, the disputes will remain under control and some will move toward resolution. Near-term efforts should focus on realizing joint development programs, establishing confidence-building measures for maritime security, and enhancing crisis management to prevent potential military conflicts that result from competition over maritime resources. In the medium term, countries need to expand joint development and strengthen maritime security cooperation so that disputes may gradually fade in importance. In the long term, with sustained improvements in political and economic relations, major breakthroughs in new energy, and improved international laws and regional security mechanisms, the prospect for resolving disputes over territories and maritime rights and interests in East Asia should improve. Resolving these outstanding disagreements would not only enhance bilateral relations between the states that are parties to the disputes but also contribute to a broader, more sustainable peace in the region.

Notes

1. This island is located at the junction point of the Wusuli and Heilongjiang Rivers. In addition, it is a gateway of the Trans-Siberian Railway, and it is adjacent to Khabarovsk, Russia's political and economic center in the Far East. After deterioration of bilateral relations, the Soviet Union reinforced military infrastructure on the island, built an international airport in Khabarovsk on the banks of the Heilongjiang River, and set up a manually controlled pontoon bridge to restrict watercourse usage. In addition, Heixiazi Island is rich in natural resources.

2. The United Nations started to establish the international law regime for the sea in 1958, and officially adopted the Convention on the Law of the Sea in 1982.

3. Namely, the fighting over Xisha in 1974 and Nansha in 1988.

4. According to the declaration, each party undertakes to exercise restraint and refrain from taking any action that would complicate or expand the disputes while seeking ways to establish mutual trust in the spirit of cooperation and understanding.

5. At the ASEAN Regional Forum conference in July 2010, U.S. Secretary of State Clinton stressed in her statement the importance and urgency of maintaining freedom of navigation in the South China Sea and expressed U.S. opposition to coercion, use of force, and threat of use of force on the question of the South China Sea, which some perceived as taking the side of Vietnam, the Philippines, and other claimants. Chinese Foreign Minister Yang Jiechi immediately refuted Clinton's statement.

6. According to some studies, the geological reserves of oil in the South China Sea are between 23 billion and 30 billion tons (data from 2009). Proven natural gas reserves are 323.5 million cubic meters (data from 2008). There are also very rich fishery resources

7. In 2010, media around the world reported the Chinese statement that the South China Sea was a "core interest" and claimed that a major change had taken place in Chinese maritime security policy. Such allegations are completely groundless. China adopts different policies toward territorial and maritime rights and interests on the one hand and Taiwan on the other hand. For the former, the Chinese policy is to seek a peaceful resolution through dialogue without resort to force, and for the latter China will make all efforts for a peaceful reunification while retaining the right to use force.

8. The Diaoyu Islands officially became part of Chinese territory as early as 1562 during the Ming dynasty (see Jia 2010).

9. In late 2008, China dispatched an ocean surveillance ship to nearby waters, to which Japan strongly responded. In early 2009, Prime Minister Aso reiterated in a

congressional meeting that the Treaty of Mutual Cooperation and Security Between the United States and Japan is applicable to the Diaoyu Islands, to which China expressed strong discontent.

10. On the question of boundary demarcation in the East China Sea, China insisted on the principle of equity and natural prolongation of the continental shelves, whereas Japan advocated the principle of median line or equidistant line.

11. Besides holding different principles of demarcation, with regard to the Chinese proposal to "shelve disputes and engage in joint development," Japan first rejected the concept and later expressed willingness to discuss it, while still insisting that the median-line principle serve as the basis for demarcation.

12. The two sides agreed that during the transition period before a final delimitation is realized, the two countries will cooperate with each other to develop the disputed areas, collaboratively or jointly, without jeopardizing the legal positions of either country. They also preliminarily defined the joint development zones.

13. After the consensus on principles was announced, strong opposition appeared in public opinion in both countries, which led to stagnation of consultation on implementation. In July 2010, negotiation on implementation of the consensus was restarted. In September of the same year, the Chinese side announced suspension of negotiations due to the ship collision incident.

14. This pattern of Sino-Japan relations is referred to as cold political and warm economic relations.

15. Some people in Japan have always regarded it as an indispensable part of the so-called first island chain that prevents Chinese naval power from going into the Pacific.

16. Because Japan denies the existence of the dispute over Diaoyu Islands and has constantly strengthened its actual control over the islands, China has taken measures to demonstrate its presence in the disputed area, such as sending ocean surveillance ships and fishing administration ships to nearby seas.

17. At that time, Korea advocated the principle of natural prolongation of the continental shelf, whereas Japan insisted on the median-line principle.

18. Japan and Russia signed the Treaty of Shimoda and Treaty of Saint Petersburg, respectively, in February 1855 and May 1875.

19. After Soviet occupation, almost all Japanese residents on the islands withdrew, which has weakened the Japanese position in the dispute. Currently, the total number of Russian residents is fewer than twenty thousand. There were more Russians before 1994, when one-third of the residents left after an earthquake.

20. During the Cold War, because of a deterioration in political relations, both became major disputes.

21. For example, the South China Sea has become a very important sea-lane of communication linking East Asian countries with the rest of the world (e.g., West Asia, Africa, Europe) and an ocean corridor linking the Pacific Ocean and the Indian Ocean.

Works Cited

He Yuexiang. 2003. "E Ri Ling Tu Jiu Fen Nan Yi Jie Jue Yuan Yin Fen Xi" [Territorial Dispute Between Russia and Japan: Why Is It a Hard Nut to Crack]. *Dang Dai Ya Tai* [Journal of Contemporary Asia-Pacific Studies] 3: 38–43.

Jiang Changbin. 2005. *Zong E Bian Jing Tan Pan Nei Mu* [Inside Story of China-Russian Boundary Negotiation]. *Bridge of Century* 12: 50–53.

Jia Yu. 2010. "Ri Ben Guan Yu Diao Yu Dao Zhu Quan Yi Ju Bu Cheng Li" [The Japanese Evidence of Its Sovereignty over Diaoyu Islands Does Not Hold Water). *People's Daily.* October 3.

Li, Danhui. 2005. "Comrades Plus Brothers: Sino-Soviet Border Relations in the 1950s." *Social Sciences in China* 26 (2): 156–168.

Li Guoqiang, 2011. "Zhong Guo Nan Hai Jiang Yu Xing Cheng De Li Shi Kao Cha" [An Investigation into the History of Forming of Chinese Boundaries in the South China Sea], *Zhong Guo She Hui Ke Xue Bao* [Newspaper on Social Sciences in China]. June 23, p. 13.

Ministry of Foreign Affairs of the People's Republic of China. 2000. "Set Aside Dispute and Pursue Joint Development." November 17. http://www.fmprc.gov.cn/eng/ziliao/3602/3604/t18023.htm (accessed January 21, 2012).

———. 2006. "China and Japan Issue Joint Press Communiqué." October 8. http://www.fmprc.gov.cn/eng/wjdt/2649/t276184.htm (accessed January 21, 2012).

Tang Jiaxuan. 2009. *Zhong Yue Lu Di Bian Jie He Bei Bu Wan Hai Yang Hua Jie Tan Pan* [China-Vietnam Negotiation on Their Land Border and Maritime Delimitation in the Beibu Gulf]. *Jin Feng Xu Yu* [Heavy Storm and Gentle Breeze]. Beijing: World Knowledge Press.

Xinhua News Agency. 1999. "Zhongyue Lianhe Shengming" [Sino-Vietnamese Joint Declaration]. February 27. http://www.gmw.cn/01gmrb/1999-02/28/GB/17981%5EGM3-2803.HTM (accessed April 18, 2012).

Zhu Fenglan. 2006. "Ri Han Da Lu Jia Xie Din Ji Qi Dui Dong Hai Hua Jie De Qi Shi" [Continental Shelf Agreement Between Japan and South Korea and Relevant Thoughts on East China Sea Delimitation]. *Dang Dai Ya Tai* [Journal of Contemporary Asia-Pacific Studies] 11: 32–40.

6   The Cult of Energy Insecurity and Great Power Rivalry Across the Pacific

Danielle F. S. Cohen and Jonathan Kirshner

MOST STATES THAT ARE DEPENDENT ON IMPORTED ENERGY fret about the domestic and international political consequences implied by that dependence—supply disruptions can wreak havoc with the economy, rattling support for the regime in power, and they can expose countries to national security threats by limiting their ability to fight wars or by leaving them vulnerable to extortion. States, perhaps not unrealistically, view energy as the lifeblood of their economies and, somewhat less rationally, worry about the precariousness of that flow the way one would worry about a jugular vein in a knife fight.

Great powers do more than fret. They seek, proactively and often aggressively, to do whatever it takes to ensure energy security. States have clashed over energy resources throughout modern history, and since the Second World War, the Persian Gulf region has attracted the attention of great powers as a consequence of the massive oil reserves to be found there (Yergin 1991; Barnhart 1987; Painter 1986). In contemporary politics, several factors have led some analysts to expect an increasingly dangerous clash over energy security among the United States, China, and Japan (Klare 2004: esp. 175–179; Kleveman 2003: 9, 98, 101, 192, 263). These concerns derive from claims, especially in popular accounts, that global petroleum production will soon reach peak levels, after which it will gradually diminish over time, while at the same time, global demand for oil is on the rise, with new actors in emerging economies (like India and China) elbowing their way for space at the table (Goodstein

2005; Roberts 2004; Deffeyes 2001). Also alarming was the doubling of oil prices from 2003 to 2006, and their doubling again from 2006 to 2008, a seemingly inexorable rise that finally crested and receded as a result of the global economic crisis. Finally, there is the distinct salience of energy security for three principal states hungry for the world's oil: Japan, which depends on imports, by sea, for virtually all the 4.4 million barrels of oil it consumes each day; China, a late entrant to crowded world markets with soaring demand for imported oil; and the United States, the elephant at the watering hole. Even in 2009, after two years of dismal economic growth, the United States still consumed more oil than the total consumption of the next four biggest players, and it remained the world's dominant oil importer, bringing in more foreign oil than China and Japan combined (Energy Information Administration 2009c, 2009d).

Nevertheless, we argue that energy insecurity is a myth; that is, concerns by states that they will not be able to ensure adequate energy supplies, thus presenting leaders with economic and political crises, are misguided. States need not be worried about this problem, with the exception of a few unlikely scenarios (about which more below), especially if short-term disruptions (easily managed by relatively modest contingency planning) are excluded from consideration. However, and this is a big *however*, although the political stability of the international system is not threatened by energy insecurity, it is threatened by what can be called "the cult of energy insecurity," that is, the erroneous belief that national security requires ambitious and vigilant foreign policy measures to assure adequate access to energy.

The cult of energy insecurity is the result of two great and commonly held exaggerations. The first exaggeration is to overstate the extent to which the supply of oil to any given state can actually be threatened. The second exaggeration is to greatly overestimate the extent to which states can redress problems of energy security through foreign policy measures. Most threats to energy security are imagined, but even for those few concerns that are real, there is little (with regard to foreign policy) that states can do about it.[1] Most international political measures designed to enhance energy security only marginally enhance it at best, and they invariably generate costs and negative international political externalities that outweigh the benefits of any marginal increase in security produced.

The cult of energy insecurity is akin to the "cult of the offensive" before the First World War. Before that war, defensive military postures and tactics had the advantage over the offense, but the widespread, erroneous belief that the advantage was with the offense contributed to both the proximate and underlying causes of the war (Van Evera 1984; Snyder 1984). Similarly, although there is little objective reason to be concerned about the availability of energy, the cult of energy insecurity could bring about dysfunctional policies and unnecessary political conflicts among states over energy.

Also like the cult of the offensive, the cult of energy insecurity is a latent danger. That is to say, on a day-to-day basis, overt patterns of behavior might not look cultlike, although they will reflect its underlying dispositions, capabilities, and implicit hair-trigger responses. Thus, the true pathologies of the cult are less visible until a moment when some spark or crisis sets states off on a self-defeating, aggressive scramble to ensure energy security, with the greater danger coming from the scramble rather than from a real threat to needed supplies. Leading states have the capacity to take measures that would take the edge off this implicit tension. In fact, the financial crisis of 2007–2008 and the global recession that followed created a window of opportunity (by creating slack in previously tight world energy markets) during which states could calmly revisit their energy strategies. But inherent anxiety about energy security (coupled in some cases with regrettable shortsightedness) makes them reluctant to take such measures.[2]

Nevertheless, to the extent that energy insecurity exists, there are much better, cheaper, less internationally politically dysfunctional measures that can be taken than the foreign policy efforts that are typically advanced under this banner. Wise energy security management invariably begins (and almost always ends) at home. In addition, it bears repeating that with regard to some level of energy insecurity, the hard truth is that there is nothing that states can productively do about it. As with many things in life, there are ultimately no guarantees, and some level of insecurity is simply part of international anarchy. The sooner states recognize this, the better off they, and world politics, will be.

Even if states manage to become deprogrammed and let go of the cult of energy insecurity, the politics of energy will nevertheless still likely generate three areas of political friction among great power rivals: First, China's growing economic relationships with oil-producing states that are in political conflict with the United States will be a source of irritation for Sino-American relations. Second, the irretrievably central importance of Persian Gulf oil, transported now and into the future primarily by tanker, will contribute to an emerging naval security dilemma. Finally, rivalries are likely to simmer over the construction of pipelines and haggling over the disposition of the oil and gas that is shipped through them. There are simply more (if still often overstated) opportunities for political maneuvering about energy that must be moved from one fixed terminus to another under the sovereign control of states, as opposed to the undifferentiated oil that moves freely about at sea, directed by apolitical spot markets.

This chapter continues in five parts. First, we locate the foundational errors at the root of the cult of energy insecurity: the failure to fully understand the concept of opportunity cost (which renders the physical control over energy supplies virtually meaningless) and, secondarily, the failure to appreciate the relative efficiency of world energy markets. Three sections that follow assess the energy concerns and strategies of the United States, China, and Japan. A final discussion considers those three areas where, despite our generally optimistic disposition, we believe that energy competition could likely lead to increased international political conflict (though still not likely war).

Why the Cult of Energy Insecurity Is a Cult: Efficient Markets and Opportunity Costs

Recent concerns about supply-side and demand-side pressures on world oil markets have added some stress to the cult; though plausible, they are largely overstated, at least with regard to their relevance as significant national security issues in the coming decades.[3] In its *World Energy Outlook* for 2004, the International Energy Agency (IEA) estimated that, even though global energy demand was expected to continue to grow over the coming quarter century, from 75 million barrels a day (mbd) in 2000 to 120 mbd in 2030, global production should be able to meet that demand (IEA 2003: 8, 12; 2002: 92). It is possible to contest (and perhaps even ridicule) the expectations of the IEA. After all, in 2002, the IEA estimated that oil prices would remain at about $21 per barrel through 2010 before rising to $29 through 2030; two years later it updated its projection with the expectation of oil at an average price of $35 per barrel between 2005 and 2030. Obviously, prices would quickly soar beyond anything their experts imagined, almost before the ink was dry on their publications. (In 2007, the IEA predicted the price would be $59 in 2010 and $62 in 2030; in 2008, it settled on predictions of $100 and $122, respectively.) But the IEA's errors actually underscore one of the two reasons the adherents to the cult of energy insecurity have it so wrong: the "threat" of oil comes from its price, not from its availability (IEA 2004: 33; 2002: 37; 2007: 64; 2008: 68; Verleger 2005: 209–210, 212).[4]

This is because of the remarkable efficiency of world oil markets. One does not need to be a flag-waving free marketeer to acknowledge how well markets work in this particular area. Oil is an essentially homogeneous, fungible product that will seek out its highest dollar level. And energy markets are not only extraordinarily efficient (and rich in information and remarkably institutionally complete); they are also distinctly equilibrating. They are efficient in that, unlike many markets, prices are extremely flexible, both up and down. (In constant 2008 dollars, the price of oil declined, in fits and starts, from nearly $100 per barrel in 1980 to less than $16 in 1998; from 2003 it was on the rise, soaring in 2008 to more than $140 before tumbling (not all the way) down to earth in the wake of the global economic crisis.) They are equilibrating in that the behavior of market participants is price sensitive in the appropriate direction. In addition, large increases in the price of oil are further self-correcting in that they tend to have a recessionary impact on consumer economies, further tamping down demand (Guo and Kliesen 2005; Lescaroux and Mignon 2008).

There are three quick lessons here. First, the fact that the IEA guessed so wrong, over and over again, about the price of oil should actually give us more confidence in its optimistic assessments of the availability of supply—those guesses were based on $35-per-barrel oil—all other things held constant, oil at $100 (or more) will likely call forth more supply (from oil sands and other sources that become profitable at higher prices) and tamp down demand from its original expectations. Indeed, the IEA has already revised its demand estimates considerably downward in the light of higher price expectations (IEA 2008).[5] Second, demand and supply shocks will be further adjudicated by the price mechanism; if market conditions push oil to $150, then that is where the price will go.[6] Third, although global demand seems likely to rise, it is wise to remember that oil prices are not easy to predict and can (and have) gone down; caution should be taken in projecting linear trends into the future.

The efficiency of the price mechanism with regard to oil does come at an (economic) cost; oil prices are relatively volatile, and this can be problematic for states. But that volatility does not alter the basic national security picture presented here.[7] The overall supply of oil for the coming decades, at least, will almost certainly be ensured by the functioning of the price mechanism, and more likely than not, oil prices will remain relatively high in historical perspective and rise further as global economic recovery emerges. So concerns for supply are overstated: the oil will be there, at a price. But the cult of energy insecurity rests on two interrelated blunders: underestimating the power and efficiency of energy markets, as just discussed, is one; the other, and even more consequential for questions of national security, is ignoring the inescapable power of opportunity costs.

It is often said that the theory of comparative advantage is the most important (and elegant) economic theory that noneconomists should understand and appreciate. For students of international relations and especially for specialists in strategy and security studies, however, the most important contribution of economics is the concept of opportunity cost, which means, essentially, that the "true" cost of something is measured not by its price tag but by the opportunities forgone by making one choice instead of another.[8]

To recognize the inescapable implications of opportunity costs is to recognize that for consumers of oil (setting aside the issue of emergency supplies to deal with short-term disruptions and military contingencies), the physical control or legal claim to oil is largely irrelevant.[9] Choices about how oil will be allocated—that is, where it goes and to what uses it is put—will be decided, if not dictated, by what economists call the shadow price of oil; that is, its opportunity cost, what is forgone elsewhere by using it here. This will be established by the world price of oil set on international markets. This holds true even for oil that is domestically produced or under the proprietary or physical control of a consuming state. Governments can dictate, by fiat, the retail price that oil will sell for within their borders (the United States did it for years), but they are servants to the real cost of using it—the opportunity cost—which is set on world markets.[10] For consuming states, the control of oil is a myth. But that has not stopped them from trying.

U.S. Energy "Strategy" and Its Pathologies

From the perspective of the United States (and, to a large extent, of the world more generally), there is only one real threat to energy security, defined as some assurance of access to needed oil supplies: an interruption of the flow of oil from the Persian Gulf region.[11] There appear to be two, but only two, plausible scenarios by which this could occur: through the control of the Persian Gulf supplies or the disruption of its transshipment. If a single hostile power were to gain control—physical control or even political domination—over the entire resources of the Persian Gulf, this would be a real national security threat to the United States and is therefore something that the United States directs its power and influence to help avoid. Given the (essentially) undifferentiated nature of oil, and the fact that it is mostly transported by ships at sea (as opposed to natural gas, which is delivered by pipeline), in general it is exceedingly difficult for one nation or even a group of nations to wield oil power, that is, to target a specific adversary for an oil embargo. Targeted oil sanctions have a history of failure, and for good reasons (Stern 2006; Crane et al. 2009: 41). Oil pretty much sloshes around the world, and if one country refuses to sell oil to another, that oil will be sold elsewhere, displacing other sales and thus freeing up other supplies, which will find their way to the nominal target of the oil sanction. The pattern of distribution might be affected, but not the essentials of supply and demand or the availability of oil more generally. And even if one country tried to affect these essentials by cutting back its own production, it would bear the brunt of the cost of such a sanction, still fail to target the object of its wrath directly (all consuming states would share any increased costs), and create incentives for other producers to profit from increasing their own production.[12]

The only two countries that could conceivably rattle world markets generally by refusing to sell oil, Saudi Arabia and Russia, are each utterly dependent on oil revenues to keep their governments afloat. But dominating the entire Persian Gulf region would be different: because so much of the world's reserves are concentrated there, controlling them would be a game changer. Targeted sanctions would still be of limited practicability, but the concentration of resources and thus power that such control would provide to one single political entity would be considerable, thus creating a dangerous and capacious force to be reckoned with. Moreover, control of that much oil would, very uncharacteristically, create a real oil weapon that could be a force in world politics. Turning off the spigot, or even just strategically wreaking havoc with it, would still be costly to the (now hegemonic) oil supplier, but the potential political payoffs would be much greater, and it is easy to imagine scenarios under which the political objectives would be considered worth the economic costs (which, in this context, would also probably be easier for the supplier to bear).

This is the logic behind the Carter doctrine, which formalized the commitment of the United States to use force to ensure that Persian Gulf oil would not come under the control of any single hostile power. This rhetoric was put to the test during the first Gulf War and in its aftermath (Carter 1980; Eilts 1980; Lieber 1992). If Iraq had been allowed to conquer Kuwait unopposed, it might have been able to achieve political domination over Saudi Arabia and the smaller Gulf States even without formal military conquest of them. Such domination would have been a real threat to the U.S. national interest.[13]

As a distinct but nevertheless related matter, a sustained blockage of the Strait of Hormuz would also represent a real threat to energy security. The strait is a vulnerable choke point, and 17 million barrels of oil flow through it each day If there was a serious impediment to the flow of oil through this passage, it could cause a major disruption on world energy markets, and it would take some time before alternative routes could be established. Although in practice it would appear to be quite difficult to shut down the strait, in the short term, significant interference with the flow would be truly uproarious for the global economy, and potentially threatening to the conduct of military operations. Coupled with some other political crisis or coordinated military attack, this scenario could become quite dangerous (Talmadge 2008; Gholz and Press 2008, Gholz and Press 2010: 477–481).

Given the significance of the strait, and the possibility of a short-term disruption in world oil supplies, two American practices follow logically: some U.S. naval presence in the region, both as a deterrent and, if necessary, as a force to protect tanker traffic and suppress threats to it, and the existence of the U.S. strategic petroleum reserve. That reserve is currently at approximately 700 million barrels (or enough to replace about fifty days of imports at current rates of consumption); plans to expand the reserve have been put on hold by the huge spike in oil prices over the past few years. In any event, a robust reserve makes sense. With the reserve, oil on tankers at sea, reductions in demand that would accompany sudden and giant spikes in prices, and likely production increases elsewhere (to take advantage of those higher prices), the United States should be able to endure a significant short-term disruption in oil supplies without crippling essential services at home or military operations abroad (Beaubouef 2007; Gholz and Press 2010: 461–462).

The United States, then, faces little by way of direct threat to its natural security deriving from energy concerns. Two potential problems—domination of the Gulf resources by a single power or a disruption of the flow of oil through the Strait of Hormuz—are, respectively, very unlikely and manageable at a fairly modest cost. Absent either of those threats, price, not power, will determine where the world's oil will go and how it will be used. But this sanguine conclusion belies the extraordinarily dysfunctional nature of U.S. energy policy, which, of its own accord, actually harms U.S. national security. Some of the problematic policies derive from the cult, but others are even more puzzling, at least from the perspective of most international relations theory, which expects states to more or less rationally assess their interests.

The United States has, almost stubbornly it seems, refused to take simple (and even profitable) measures to reduce its profligate consumption of oil.[14] This, rather than any external threat to supplies, ironically does present national security problems. In practice, the United States has borne enormous costs from the fact that it is so dependent on oil. With the world's reserves concentrated in the Persian Gulf region, the global dependence on Middle Eastern oil has complicated U.S. foreign policy and generated what can technically (if somewhat euphemistically) be called negative security externalities, which include (but are not limited to) the military enforcement of the Carter doctrine.[15]

In addition, although it is difficult to predict the price of oil, the best and eminently plausible guess is that the secular trend will be for world prices to rise in the coming years (Hamilton 2009). Simply put, high oil prices empower states and regimes that are political opponents of the United States, and American consumption is the single most important driver of the world price. Three of the big winners from high oil prices, for example, are Russia, Iran, and Venezuela. U.S. (non)energy policy is particularly puzzling for a student of international security because it is a choice that is actively and obviously empowering U.S. enemies and subsidizing U.S. geopolitical rivals. The biggest political challenge to the United States is not the axis of evil; it is the axis of oil, a troublemaking monster created by an America in the role of Dr. Frankenstein. It matters not whether the United States buys its oil directly from these sources. Indeed, it is correct to observe, for example, that Russia and Iran are not major suppliers of oil to the United States; rather, its four biggest suppliers are Canada, Mexico, Saudi Arabia, and Venezuela. But this ignores the fungibility of oil. Consumption in the United States contributes (indeed, it is by far the single biggest contributor on the demand side of the equation) to the world price of oil. If its policies (or lack of policy) cause the world price to rise, then that affords benefits to net oil exporters everywhere. An increase in the price of oil, from, say $30 per barrel to $100 per barrel, at current rates of export, provides Russia with a windfall of about $175 billion annually, Iran with $64 billion, and Venezuela with $54 billion. Saudi Arabia, a country whose geopolitical interests are not obviously in accord with those of the United States (the mutual bond and level of respect is closer to that of junkie and drug dealer), picks up about $217 billion. Were oil to sell at $150 per barrel, at current rates of export the total annual receipts from oil sales for those four countries would be approximately $372 billion, $136 billion, $115 billion, and $465 billion, respectively.[16]

This is all in accord with a recent RAND assessment, which concludes that the risks to the United States from economic coercion by oil exporters or from competition with other states are "minimal" and are less significant than the related military costs or the "increased income for rogue states"; profligate U.S. consumption is also alarming for the general wealth transfer it implies (U.S. imports of petroleum products tipped the financial scales at $333 billion in 2007) (Crane et al. 2009: 23, 43, 50, 57, 77). The United States has a real energy and security problem. But it can see the source of the threat only by looking in the mirror.

The New Kid in Town: China
Hits the World Energy Scene

Chinese policy makers are card-holding members of the cult of energy insecurity. Although, as for the United States, the underlying facts supporting the existence of energy insecurity are suspect, Chinese strategists believe that China faces a two-part challenge: First, like leaders from other states, they believe that China's desire for an adequate and reliable supply of energy resources at an affordable price necessitates a particular foreign policy (Yergin 1988; Deese 1979–1980). These energy resources underpin the continued growth of the Chinese economy, which they believe to be necessary for the continued legitimacy of the Chinese Communist Party (CCP). Unlike their peers in the United States and Japan, however, Chinese strategists are also acutely concerned about the security of oil transports as they travel across the Indian Ocean and through the Strait of Malacca. These analysts worry that the United States might impose a blockade in the event of a crisis, most likely over Taiwan.

Although imported oil accounted for approximately 10 percent of China's total primary energy demand in 2008, it is at the center of Chinese discussions of their energy security (Zhang 2011: 8–9; Collins and Murray 2008: 90).[17]

We focus here on oil as the most significant aspect of China's energy security strategy for three reasons.[18] First, although the IEA projects that the percentage of China's total primary energy demand supplied by oil will increase only slightly through 2030, the percentage of that oil demand fulfilled by imports will rise dramatically. Demand for oil will grow at an average annual rate of 3.7 percent between 2005 and 2030, but domestic crude oil production will peak at approximately 4 mbd at the beginning of this decade, before declining (IEA 2007: 123, 125; Wu and Storey 2008: 194). China will fill the gap between its rising demand and its fairly constant domestic supply with foreign imports. Today, China imports approximately half of its oil; by 2030, it will import approximately three-quarters (Downs 2004: 21; Central Intelligence Agency 2009a; IEA 2007: 123, 125, 288).[19] In absolute terms, Chinese oil imports are expected to increase from 3.1 mbd in 2005 to 13.1 mbd in 2030 (IEA 2007: 288).

Second, although imported petroleum products are not essential for industrial or residential power, they are essential for transportation, which is rapidly growing both in absolute terms and as a share of the country's total energy consumption. The legitimacy of the CCP rests on its ability to deliver the economic goods—it does not want to ever be in the position of telling urban drivers and business truckers that the gas has run out (Bader 2008: 98–99; Energy Information Administration 2009b: 21, 29, 49, 97, 120, 122, 126, 128; Cooper 2008; Bergsten et al. 2008: chap. 7). The IEA estimates that the transportation sector will account for more than two-thirds of the increase in Chinese oil consumption between 2005 and 2030 (IEA 2007: 288). By 2030, Chinese oil demand for the transportation sector alone will amount to at least twice as much oil as the country is able to produce domestically (IEA 2007: 123, 125, 288, 297). As China develops its car culture, the government will need to ensure that its population remains satisfied by assuring ready access to affordable gasoline.[20]

Finally, oil is the aspect of China's energy security strategy that is likely to have the greatest implications for international politics. According to Wu Lei and Lu Guangsheng, China's increased demand for oil has accounted for approximately one-third of the total world increase in demand for oil over the past decade (Wu and Lu 2008: 53). At a minimum, therefore, China's oil demands are a major driver of world oil prices. At the same time, however, members of the Chinese cult of energy insecurity express concerns that their foreign purchases may not make it safely to the mainland. To the extent that this concern about transportation security motivates a naval strategy or increased attention to the sea lines of communication (SLOCs), Japan and the United States will need to stay alert.

China's Efforts to Diversify Suppliers

As part of an overarching desire to ensure affordable, reliable energy resources, China has pursued a diversification strategy. Supply security may be achieved through several policies, including the diversification of energy trading partners, energy conservation that aims to decrease overall demand, and increased research and development of alternate energy sources like wind, nuclear, or hydropower. With regards to oil, China has focused in particular on its perceived need to diversify suppliers. After first becoming a net oil importer in 1993, China quickly became a major international client; in 2009, it was the world's third-largest oil importer after the United States and the European Union (Central Intelligence Agency n.d.a). Concerned, as are other states, about overdependence on Middle Eastern oil, China has sought to diversify its oil suppliers. As of the first half of 2006, the Middle East accounted for 45 percent of Chinese oil imports, with 32 percent coming from Africa, 13 percent from Central Asia, and 7 percent from Central and South America (Rosen and Houser 2007: 31; Energy Information Administration 2009a).[21] Nevertheless, there are hard limits to the energy security this diversification implies: China's demand for oil will grow much faster than these non–Middle Eastern states can supply it; over the coming decades, Persian Gulf oil will only increase its share of world supply; and there remain the inescapable implications of opportunity costs—the world market price of oil—which for China, as for the United States, dictates energy politics regardless of where they import their oil from or who physically controls it (Bader 2008: 100; Wu and Storey 2008: 195, 198; Energy Information Administration 2009b: 29, 31; IEA 2008: 86, 91, 197, 249, 274).

Lurking in the tall weeds as a possible exemplar of the latency of the cult are China's national oil companies (NOCs), and their penchant for "equity oil" deals. Media accounts suggest the Chinese leadership has encouraged the three major NOCs to engage in a policy of locking up oil at its source. In these equity deals, a Chinese company forms an agreement with a foreign government regarding the production of oil from already discovered fields. The foreign government owns the oil in its territory; the Chinese company purchases the right to extract the oil, and the output is split with the foreign government

(Downs 2004: 35). As Erica Downs argues, the Chinese government favors "equity oil" because it believes, not necessarily correctly, that equity oil deals can provide oil at a lower than market price, eliminate market price risk, and negate the chance that an intermediary could cut off supply in a crisis (Downs 2004: 35; Traub 2006).[22]

Yet the threat from these equity deals is easily overstated; in fact, if not for the cult, it would not be a threat at all. Despite the perceived advantages of equity oil, the vast majority of Chinese equity oil is sold on the international market to the highest bidder (Energy Information Administration 2009a; Houser 2008: 162). Furthermore, any oil that China is reputed to take off world markets simply displaces oil that would have been purchased elsewhere. Actually, China's going-out strategy, through which it has pursued energy treaties in thirty countries, has put more energy on world markets (although the effect of Chinese investments on increased global supplies seems to be fairly marginal for now; Wu and Lu 2008: 54; Ghazvinian 2007: 151, 154, 274–279; Zha 2009: 28; Downs 2007: 43, 47, 51; Zhao 2009: 95, 97, 101).

But problems loom. The latency of the cult means that the true nature of China's NOCs will not be known until they are tested in a real crisis, exactly the moment when the dysfunctions of the cult would become most consequential. Will China's big, state-owned companies, with executives chosen by and beholden to the CCP, behave like "good" U.S. companies, choosing business over country? Will the NOCs' leaders choose their own advancement in the CCP over the interests of their businesses? Or will they exacerbate the cult at the worst possible moment (say, by holding, rerouting, or seizing supplies in an emergency; Bader 2008: 101, 103, 106; Friedberg 2006: 34)?

Even if China's efforts to obtain equity oil do not have negative effects on the position of other states in global markets, China's efforts to diversify suppliers still draw global attention because of the nature of its resource diplomacy. China has offered huge loans and developmental assistance packages to oil-rich countries and has demonstrated a willingness to work with regimes that are spurned by the international community. As a late entrant to global oil markets, China must face the reality that international oil companies have already laid claim to the best, established oil sources. Chen Fengying, an analyst at the China Institutes of Contemporary International Relations, phrased the policy succinctly: "China confronts foreign competition. . . . Chinese companies must go places for oil where American [and] European companies are not present" (Chen, in Goodman 2004: A01).[23]

China's energy deals with various African countries have drawn particular notice, although the size and quality of Chinese possessions relative to those held by the West are often overemphasized (Downs 2007: 42–43). In 2004, for example, China announced a $2 billion oil-backed loan to Angola, a country that by 2006 was China's single largest source of African oil imports (Traub 2006). Nevertheless, in light of the credit crunch produced by the current economic crisis, China's continued willingness to make loans to state-owned oil companies in exchange for oil deserves attention. Since the beginning of 2009, China has announced oil-for-loan deals with Russia, Brazil, Kazakhstan, and Venezuela (Carew 2009). The $25 billion, twenty-year deal with Russia's Rosneft and Transneft will yield China 15 million tons of crude oil each year (Barboza 2009).

China's quest for oil has led it to pursue business relations with countries whose status as international persona non grata have prevented international oil companies from pursuing relationships with them. In the past five years, China's Sinopec has signed two deals with the Iranian government for the development of the Yadavaran oil field (Ying and Sethuraman 2007; "China to Develop Iran Oilfield" 2004). The China National Offshore Oil Company (CNOOC) has named Myanmar (Burma), a regime that was long condemned by the international community for its silencing of political opposition, as one of its two main areas of investment for the medium term (Perlez 2006a; Perlez 2006b; "China-Myanmar Oil Pipe Work to Begin This Year" 2007).[24] In response to international pressure, China has recently begun to take a harder line on Sudan, but it remains Sudan's largest oil customer (Downs 2007: 60–62; Kahn 2006; Pan 2007).[25]

Transportation Security: Implications for China's Naval Strategy

With so much of China's oil coming by sea, China has been especially sensitive to the security of the supply chain. Chinese strategists have devoted much attention to addressing these issues (Guan and He 2007; Li 2004; Zhang 2003; Ross 2009: 68–75). Concerns about transportation security arise from the geography of the Strait of Malacca, a six-hundred-mile-long waterway among Singapore, Malaysia, and Indonesia that is only one and a half miles wide at its narrowest point. Some 80 percent of Chinese oil imports travel through the strait. The strait is beset by a host of problems arising from its geographical constraints, including the possibility of a ship running aground, an oil spill, or a collision between ships, and it is also threatened by pirates (Ebel 2005: 56, Khalid 2006).

In addition to these concerns, shared by neighboring importers like Japan and the Philippines, the CCP also fears that a third party might manipulate Chinese access to oil imports, which would challenge the country's economic stability and undermine the regime. A commonly discussed scenario features a U.S. blockade of the Strait of Malacca in the event of a crisis over Taiwan (Wu and Shen 2006: 40; Li 2004: 18).[26] On the basis of these concerns, some analysts suggest that the Chinese may be seeking to enhance their naval capabilities to protect the SLOCs and the tankers that travel along them, although steps in this regard are preliminary at best. Chinese policy proposals that connect the development of a blue-water navy to energy insecurity are designed to provide China with the naval capabilities to patrol the strait and to protect Chinese imports. As Li Xiaojun argues, "For China, whoever controls the Strait of Malacca controls the pathway for China's oil and can threaten China's national security. Without a doubt, the sea power to guarantee the security of the SLOCs is the key to the oil security problem" (Li 2004: 18). It is notable that the works of the U.S. naval strategist Alfred T. Mahan are increasingly invoked in debates about China's emerging role in international trade. Writes Zhang Wenmu, "The modern navy appeared along with international trade, and naval predominance was the basic route by which England and the United States achieved the expansion of international trade. Now, China is expanding international energy markets at a rapid pace, but its ability to protect the international energy interests it has already obtained are seriously lagging behind" (Zhang 2003: 16). Although other goals, such as reunification with Taiwan, are more immediate drivers of Chinese naval modernization, energy security may, at the least, provide a useful argument for naval proponents who wish to persuade the Chinese government to invest more heavily in its development.[27]

Despite Chinese concerns that the United States might blockade the Strait of Malacca in the event of a Sino-U.S. crisis, the effectiveness of such a strategy remains in doubt. On the basis of their comprehensive analysis of possible strategies for blockading Chinese energy imports, two Naval War College researchers conclude, "An energy blockade of China would not only fail to achieve its objective but also send destructive shock waves through the global economic and political landscape" (Collins and Murray 2008: 80). The United States has conventional military superiority over the still-developing Chinese Navy, but a variety of factors would make a "distant" blockade of the Strait of Malacca ultimately ineffective. The Chinese Navy could promote its interests through asymmetric warfare by laying mines, attacking regional targets with short- or medium-range missiles, or using its submarines to threaten replenishment ships (Collins and Murray 2008: 83).

Even if the Chinese Navy were too weak to take these defensive measures, the blockading navy would still face a number of challenges. According to Collins and Murray, only 10 percent of Chinese oil imports are carried on Chinese tankers; the blockading navy would therefore need to interdict non-Chinese tankers carrying non-Chinese personnel, which would cause serious diplomatic complications. In addition, because a single tanker can carry oil meant for multiple destinations, the blockading navy would need to separate oil destined for China from oil destined for other countries in the region like Japan or South Korea. Even then, because oil is often bought and sold on the market, oil that was destined for a non-Chinese country as it passed the strait might be bought by China once it cleared the checkpoint (Collins and Murray 2008: 84). To oversee this process, the blockading navy would need to board each of the fifty-two tankers that pass through the Strait of Malacca per day, which would require a large commitment of resources (Collins and Murray 2008: 87). Firing on a ship would be problematic, unless the level of conflict was severe, because this would cause a major oil spill and create an environmental disaster (Collins 2006: 25). Were a blockade of the strait to succeed, the blockading navy would also need to be prepared to blockade alternate routes through the Lombok and Sunda straits and around Australia (Collins and Murray 2008: 86). In this context, Collins and Murray argue, "China is not fundamentally vulnerable to a maritime energy blockade in circumstances other than global war" (Collins and Murray 2008: 93).[28]

In short, the concerns expressed by some Chinese that the United States might blockade the Strait of Malacca in a crisis over Taiwan seem unfounded. Given the immense cost and difficulty of such an action, it is hard to imagine a Taiwan scenario in which the United States would single-handedly impose an energy blockade. The only plausible scenario would be one in which China suddenly invades Taiwan and the United States becomes involved in the war. This type of Chinese maneuver seems unlikely at present. And were China to make such a move, the United States might be able to persuade Kazakhstan and Russia to clamp down on Chinese overland oil imports as well, because they might be concerned by the new aggression of their neighbor. Nevertheless, this assessment is unlikely to assuage the concerns of Chinese military planners. If the roles were reversed, the United States would take the prospect seriously.[29] On the positive side, from the perspective of global stability, Chinese concerns about a potential blockade give the Chinese an incentive to prevent a serious breakdown in their relations with the United States (Friedberg 2006: 23, 27; Zha 2006: 7–8, 9, 15; Blair, Chen, and Hagt 2006: 39–40; Zhang 2006: 22–23).

Pipelines

In light of Chinese concerns about the security of the transport of oil imports by sea, Chinese strategists hope to diversify the means by which their imports are transported. Broadly speaking, oil can be transported via three methods: rail, pipeline, and tanker. Tankers provide the most cost effective form of transportation, but Chinese strategists worry that they may be vulnerable to interdiction by the U.S. Navy. Consequently, the Chinese planned to decrease the percentage of oil imports shipped by tanker from 93.5 percent in 2005 to 83 percent in 2010 (Ebel 2005: 29). At the same time, transportation via rail is vastly more expensive than any other form of transportation, and the Chinese expressed a desire to decrease the percentage of their imports that were transported by rail, already quite low, to 2 percent by 2010 (Erickson and Collins 2010: 92; Ebel 2005: 29). This leaves pipelines as the best alternative for the diversification of the means of transportation; Chinese strategists hoped to raise the percentage of oil imports transported by pipelines to 15 percent by 2010 (Ebel 2005: 29).

Recently, China has negotiated several important pipeline deals. As part of the February 2009 loans-for-oil deal between Russia and China, Russia agreed to build a pipeline spur from Skovorodino, Russia, to Daqing, China ("Russia Starts Construction of Oil Pipeline to China" 2009). The pipeline officially opened on January 1, 2011, after a two-month test period. It is expected to carry approximately three hundred thousand barrels per day for the next twenty years ("Russia-China Oil Pipeline Opens" 2011). The path of the East Siberia–Pacific Ocean (ESPO) pipeline was a source of contention for years, with the Chinese advocating successfully for the Daqing spur to be built first and the Japanese pushing for an extension, which is now under construction, across Siberia to the port city of Nakhodka, from which oil will travel the short distance to Japan by tanker (Myer 2005: C3).[30] Meanwhile, in 2007, China and Kazakhstan agreed to extend the Atasu-Alashankou pipeline westward to the Caspian Sea, thus opening up Chinese access to a resource-rich area (Golovnina 2007). The Atasu-Alashankou pipeline was the first oil pipeline to China, and carried 102,600 barrels per day, about half its capacity, into Xinjiang as of December 2007 (Erickson and Collins 2010: 94). These two pipeline deals represent responsible economic decision making—transportation of oil over land via pipeline is cheaper than via railroad—and allow China to diversify its means of transporting oil.

Other pipeline projects make far less strategic sense and represent behavior consistent with the cult. In June 2010, construction began on an oil pipeline from Kyaukphyu, Myanmar, to Kunming, Yunnan Province, China, thus allowing Chinese oil imports to avoid the Strait of Malacca (Kong 2010: 57).[31] According to Erickson and Collins, although this project might be economically feasible, it will not improve Chinese energy security (Erickson and Collins 2010: 99).[32] The pipeline will be vulnerable to internal instability in Myanmar, and the Chinese were criticized for engaging in a major economic deal with the ruling junta (Erickson and Collins 2010: 100). Still under discussion is a proposal to build a China-Pakistan energy corridor from Gwadar, Pakistan, to Xinjiang, China. Although this pipeline would bypass all choke points but the Strait of Hormuz, it would be expensive to build in such difficult terrain. Furthermore, the pipeline would pass through Baluchistan, one of the most troubled and instable parts of Pakistan (Wu and Storey 2008: 202). Another proposal, to build an "Asian Panama Canal" across Thailand seems to have disintegrated (Wu and Storey 2008: 202; Erickson and Collins 2010: 101).

Although these latter three pipelines would avoid some of the potential problems posed by the Strait of Malacca, they present their own complications. First, pipelines are fixed in location. This means they are vulnerable to nonstate (terrorist) or state-based threats in a way that tankers may not be (Erickson and Collins 2010: 105). These concerns are particularly relevant in Myanmar and Pakistan. Given Chinese concerns about the political instability of many Middle Eastern and African oil producers, investing in major pipeline projects in politically unstable regions is a curious strategy. Second, in each of these cases, oil would still be shipped by tanker from its point of origin in Africa or the Middle East to a port at the start of the pipeline. Erickson and Collins argue that this would conveniently focus a potential adversary's attention on key strategic points. Targeting a specific port would be easier than targeting numerous tankers at sea (Erickson and Collins 2010: 100).

China's anxiety over energy is understandable, if ultimately unwarranted. A country long accustomed to energy self-sufficiency, China's demand for energy, and for imported oil, has been growing rapidly and will only continue to do so over the years. It would be a mistake to dismiss the psychological influence that foreign dependence on energy plays in domestic debates and policy (Zhao 2009: 106; Zhang 2006: 17, 19–20; Blair, Chen, and Hagt 2006: 34, 36; Wu and Storey 2008: 191–192, 196). Worse, unlike the United States, China has plausible fears about the potential for a consequential interruption of world oil flows, however unlikely those fears are to be realized in practice. With the bulk of China's imports coming by ship, and the modest capabilities of China's navy compared to that of the United States, these are contingencies that must be contemplated. Yet the bottom line is that there is little that can be done about Chinese energy dependence or its worst-case scenarios.

Islands of Vulnerability: Japan's Search for Foreign Oil

Whereas China's need for oil imports is a fairly recent result of its economic development, Japan is a resource-poor island nation that has long relied on foreign imports to satisfy its energy needs. Today, Japan is one of the world's largest coal and natural gas importers and the fourth-largest oil importer (Central Intelligence Agency 2011). Japan's search for energy resources has long been a significant driver of its foreign policy. During the 1930s and 1940s, Japan's pursuit of the euphemistic Greater East Asia Co-Prosperity Sphere was motivated by its need for important resources, including oil, particularly after the U.S. oil embargo began in August 1941. As industrialization picked up again in the 1970s, Japan began to seek foreign energy partners in a manner similar to China's current strategy, although it also emphasized energy conservation and alternative energy sources such as nuclear power. Japan's notion of energy security is similar to China's in terms of supply security; like China, Japan seeks to diversify the suppliers of its oil so that it is not overly dependent on Middle Eastern oil. Nevertheless, because of its security alliance with the United States, Japan does not have concerns about the transportation security of its oil beyond those experienced by other states. Although it has increased its participation in ensuring security in the Strait of Malacca, Japanese strategists have not felt the need to focus on naval measures to secure their oil imports (Khalid 2006).

Efforts to Diversify Suppliers

Japan has fought a long and moderately successful battle to wean itself off oil. Oil currently represents approximately half of Japan's total energy demand, down from 80 percent during the 1970s (Energy Information Administration 2011; Rosen and Houser 2007: 17). Japan's success at diversifying its oil suppliers has been more uneven. Before the oil shocks of the 1970s, Japan imported approximately 90 percent of its oil from the Middle East. With concerted effort, Japan reduced Middle Eastern oil as a percentage of total oil imports to slightly more than 70 percent by the early 1980s by increasing oil imports from Asia. Today, despite Japan's continued efforts to diversify suppliers, the Middle East supplies approximately 80 percent of Japan's oil imports (Energy Information Administration 2011).

Faced with this renewed dependence on Middle Eastern oil, the Japanese government is actively seeking to diversify its oil suppliers. Recent developments suggest that Japan is revitalizing its efforts to explore and develop potential oil sites. During the first half of the 2000s, Prime Minister Junichiro Koizumi replaced the Japan National Oil Corporation (JNOC), established in 1967, with the Japan Oil, Gas and Metals National Corporation (JOGMEC) and spun off the most successful units of JNOC into private companies in which the state maintained an equity stake (Energy Information Administration 2011).[33] Among JOGMEC's key responsibilities is providing Japanese companies with "capital required for: oil and natural gas exploration overseas and in the coastal waters of Japan (including oil sand and oil shale), development and/or liquefaction of natural gas overseas, and acquisition of overseas oil and natural gas assets" (JOGMEC 2007). Japan's New National Energy Strategy, released in May 2006, further highlights the renewed attention to foreign exploration and development and the desire to build strong relations with oil-producing states. Notably, the strategy report suggests that the Japanese should seek to increase the percentage of imported crude oil that derives from exploration and production by Japanese companies from 15 percent to 40 percent by 2030 (Ministry of Economy, Trade, and Industry 2006: 13–14, 26–27).[34] The vast majority of the projects funded by JOGMEC are concentrated in Russia, Eurasia, and Southeast Asia, but the 2006 energy strategy also highlights Africa (particularly Libya and Nigeria), South America, and Canada as key targets for further oil exploration and development (JOGMEC 2007; Ministry of Economy, Trade, and Industry 2006: 26).

Pipelines

Similar to China, Japan is interested in importing more oil from Russia and the Caspian Sea region and was consequently very involved in discussions over the route of the ESPO pipeline during the 2000s. China and Japan engaged in competitive diplomacy with Russia during the mid-2000s, with both seeking to persuade the Russians to build the pipeline in their direction. Shortly before the first section of the pipeline, from Taishet to Skovorodino, was completed in 2009, Russia finally decided to begin work on a spur from Skovorodino to Daqing, China, in exchange for Chinese loans to two Russian oil companies ("Russia Starts Construction of Oil Pipeline to China" 2009). More recently, construction began on the second stage of the pipeline, to be completed in 2013, which will connect Skovorodino to a port in Kozmino Bay, southeast of Nakhodka (Watkins 2010: 43).[35] In the meantime, oil will be transported via railroad from Skovorodino to the Pacific Ocean, from where it will be relatively simple and cost effective to then ship it to Japan (Energy Information Administration 2008a).

Although the Japanese continue to show measured interest in developing energy relations with Russia, the extent of their interest in the ESPO project seems to have cooled somewhat since the mid-2000s. Anticipating the construction of the second phase of the pipeline, JOGMEC and Russia's Irkutsk Oil reached a $95.8 million deal in April 2008 to jointly explore a block at Severo-Mogdinksy, approximately ninety miles from the path of the ESPO pipeline ("Jogmec Saddles Up" 2008). In 2009, JOGMEC and Irkutsk Oil began survey work at two additional locations, Zapadno-Yaraktinsky and Bolshet-irsky, both even closer to the ESPO pipeline (Motomura 2010). Nevertheless, Russia has been hard pressed to attract large-scale Japanese investment in the ESPO project, given uncertainty about the amount of proven oil reserves in East Siberia and decreasing political support in Tokyo for investment in Russian energy projects (Itoh 2010: 23). To the extent that Japan continues to pursue its pipeline interests with Russia, it will do so through a combination of sweetened business deals and diplomacy, not through coercive measures.

Beyond the Cult of Energy Insecurity: Three Paths to International Political Conflict

In summary, we do not expect competition among the great powers in East Asia (China, Japan, and the United States) to lead to militarized disputes among them. However, despite our conclusion that states need not engage in security competition over energy, rooted in the cult, we do see three possible sources of potentially consequential international political conflict among these states. One indirect consequence of China's energy strategy (and of its increased importance as a player on world markets more generally) is, as noted above, its cultivation of close ties with resource-rich nations in conflict with the United States, including Sudan and Iran. This will likely create new and nontrivial Sino-American conflicts of interest. In addition, no matter how successful China is in its efforts at efficiency in use and diversification of supply, in the future most of China's oil will nevertheless come from the Middle East and Russia. The growing importance of China as a market for energy exporters will enhance its political influence in many parts of the world, which again will at times create new conflicts of interest that, though unlikely to cause war, will contribute to frustrations and new sources of political frictions between the two states.

China, with its late entry into the global oil business, its no-questions-asked approach to diplomatic relations, and its traditional sensitivity to sovereignty issues, embraces close relations with regimes that are in political conflict with the United States. China's leeriness of sanctions in general, combined with its strong desire to keep good ties and in some cases curry favor with oil-exporting countries will continue to work at cross purposes to U.S. foreign policy objectives. This has already been evident with the Darfur crisis in Sudan (China purchases half of Sudan's oil exports, which account for 10 percent of its oil imports), and it will likely be even more problematic with regard to Iran (China is its second-largest export market, a relationship almost certain to grow in importance over time). Potential irritants down the line include closer ties with Venezuela (China's increasing influence in Latin America more generally could ruffle U.S. feathers); also, if the United States has a falling out with Saudi Arabia, or if it looks like it might, China would be more than happy to enhance its relations with the Kingdom (Zha 2006: 13; Shen 2006: 56, 58, 61; Ghazvinian 2007: 286–288; Wu and Storey 2008: 200, 204; Bader 2008: 97, 105, 107; Friedberg 2006: 28, 30, 34).[36] Even well short of a breach of relations with the United States, it would not be surprising if the Saudis were the next country to try to play the China card.[37]

Second, there is potential for a security dilemma over naval competition (Fravel 2008). Here each state's ambitions appear to encroach on others' perceived interests. Following the end of the Second World War, the U.S. Navy

enjoyed dominance in the Pacific Ocean. The Seventh Fleet, based in Yoko-
suka, Japan, ensures U.S. interests regarding Korea and Taiwan, and its mem-
orable positioning during the 1995–1996 Taiwan Strait crisis was an important
indicator of U.S. strength. As an island nation facing great maritime vulnerability, Japan's Self-Defense Forces have cooperated with the United States,
although the extent to which Japan should bear the burden for its own defense
is a continual source of friction. Against the background of U.S.-Japan cooperation in the Pacific, the increasing power and ambitions of China's navy
and its discordant goals present security challenges for the United States and
Japan (Christensen 1999). Although China's desire to unify with Taiwan is the
most important motivator of its plans for military modernization, concerns
about the security of the SLOCs are often raised as an important secondary
goal. As China expands its naval reach beyond its immediate coastline, it will
enter areas of the sea that the United States currently dominates (Fravel 2009:
14). Although China's military is currently far weaker than the United States',
it seeks to enhance its submarine force, a development that would greatly
strengthen its military posture (Reuters 2009). In 2011, China launched its
first aircraft carrier (a refurbished Russian model; "US Satellite Snaps China's
First Aircraft Carrier at Sea" 2011). Concern about future Chinese military
capabilities may motivate the United States in turn to enhance its military
capabilities in the region and may be the development that finally ends Japan's adherence to article 9 of its postwar constitution, which has long limited
its remilitarization. Taylor Fravel argues that Chinese intentions are not ex-
pansionist, but the potential for misperception and mistrust by U.S. military
planners could result in a security dilemma in the Pacific (Fravel 2008: 135).

Finally, although we have focused mainly on the security challenges posed
by the pursuit of oil, the pursuit of natural gas, an increasingly important
resource for China and Japan, poses another challenge to relations in East
Asia. The transportation of gas through pipelines further opens the door for
political competition over pipeline construction and increases the opportunities (as with Russia's heavy-handed pipeline politics) for states to fear vulnerabilities (Stern 2006). Access to natural gas fields in the East China Sea
has also been a source of heated debate between China and Japan. China and
Japan have disputed the exact borders of their respective exclusive economic
zones (EEZs), and Japanese officials have argued that Chinese development of
the Chunxiao field might drain gas from the Japanese side (Energy Information Administration 2008b). Following sharp tensions in 2005–2006, the two

states agreed in 2008 to jointly develop the Chunxiao field (Bristow 2008). Regional tensions spiked again in the fall of 2010, when the Japanese arrested the captain of a Chinese fishing boat that had collided with two Japanese Coast Guard boats near the disputed Diaoyu (Senkaku) Islands (Fackler and Johnson 2010). This resurgence of animosity highlights the unresolved nature of important territorial questions in the East China Sea.

In summary, the cult of energy insecurity derives from two big, widely shared exaggerations about how vulnerable states are to supply disruptions and the extent to which states can redress their energy concerns through foreign policy measures. International political stability would be enhanced if states were to recognize the inescapable role of opportunity costs and the efficient nature of the price mechanism in determining the disposition of the world's oil. Nevertheless, it must be recognized that even without the problems generated by the cult, these three potential flash points could produce true security challenges for the countries involved. It remains to be seen whether the diplomatic skills of great powers will be up to the task of navigating these (political) minefields, as well as diffusing tensions generated by the security dilemma.

Notes

1. Domestic measures, like energy taxes and tax rebates for efficiencies, in contrast, hold considerable promise at no cost to society as a whole and do not generate negative security externalities. In fact, because the United States is such a large consumer of foreign oil, a gasoline tax would be a moneymaker for the United States; it would have the same effect as an optimal tariff and would transfer wealth from exporters of oil.

2. The endurance (and breadth) of the cult of energy insecurity presents something of a puzzle, as it suggests that states are making systematic and persistent errors, which contribute to policies that make them less secure. This is inconsistent with a rational-actor model of the state, and with a realist conception of an autonomous, capacious state. It is possible to construct logics that try to rehabilitate the logic of cult-driven choices: elite decision makers might be extremely risk averse to certain types of crises that they fear being held accountable for; they may have very short time horizons; they might be choosing the best policies available in the context of the limits to their autonomy presented by domestic political pressures. But it may also be that our definitions of rationality are unrealistically strict, or that states are simply less competent and capable than might be expected.

3. This section draws on Kirshner (2008).

4. The International Energy Agency remains certain that "resources are more than adequate to meet demand until 2030 and beyond. Less certain is how much it will cost" (IEA 2004: 29). One thing that never changes in these reports is that production and reserves are seen as adequate to meet expanding global demand until 2030 and beyond.

5. The International Energy Agency (2008) estimates that global energy demand will grow from 85 mbd in 2007 to 106 mbd in 2030.

6. These two factors also take some of the edge off the peak oil arguments. For an example of peak oil skepticism based on market responses, see Aguilera (2009).

7. Oil price volatility, especially with regard to sudden spikes in the price of oil, can cause real political problems for states. Since the mid-1980s, oil prices have been more volatile than those of other commodities, and oil price spikes are associated with economic downturns. Thus, especially in states (e.g., China) where the legitimacy of the government rests on good economic performance, it is possible to see why volatility might appear to be a national security issue. However, our basic conclusions about energy security still hold. If the problem is truly volatility (prices bouncing around), then there are simple measures states can take to contain it: buffer stocks, overlapping long-term contracts, and domestic regulations and controls. These measures would all be economically inefficient and money losers, but the cost in economic efficiency might be well worth it to a leadership especially wary of the political consequences of oil price volatility. To the extent that *volatility* is used imprecisely to mean "large sustained increases in the world price of oil," we are back in the world of opportunity costs, and there is simply nothing that states can do about this type of insecurity. Even the physical control of oil will not change the economic laws that will govern its shadow price. On the volatility of oil prices and its effects on real economic activity, see Guo and Kliesen (2005); Regnier (2007); Kilian (2008).

8. For a nice introduction to this concept, see Frank (2000: 8–13). Frank (p. 9) identifies the failure to consider opportunity costs as the number-one "pitfall in decision making" people make (number two is the failure to ignore sunk costs); see also Schumpeter (1954: 917).

9. Indeed, as we note elsewhere in this chapter, virtually all Chinese equity oil is sold in the international market to the highest bidder.

10. On U.S. price controls and the international pressures that contributed to decontrol, see, for example, Ikenberry (1988).

11. To paraphrase Willie Sutton, the Persian Gulf matters because that is where the oil is, and where it will be found, increasingly, in the future (Central Intelligence Agency n.d.b).

12. For a more general discussion of these types of issues, see Kirshner (1997).

13. This is not to endorse any particular policy or course of action by the United States—the full range of costs and benefits of a variety of policy options need to be considered—but it does acknowledge the logic of the national security interest of the United States that no single power dominates the region.

14. And the retreat of oil prices in 2008–2009 would present yet another opportunity to seize the initiative with a big gas tax.

15. Regardless of one's opinion regarding the first and second Persian Gulf wars and their motivations, it is extremely unlikely that they would have occurred if the oil were not there. To be clear, this is not to say that the wars were "wars for oil." Rather, it is to observe that Saddam Hussein's behavior mattered more (and was more dangerous) because it occurred in the Gulf—had Iraq been situated in West Africa or Latin America, there is a good chance he would still be in power. A short primer on externalities can be found in Frank (2000: 585–614). For efforts to assess the costs of U.S. oil dependence, including military spending devoted to the effort, see Duffield (2007) and Crane and colleagues (2009).

16. U.S. imports and calculations of windfalls are based on import and export data of the U.S. Department of Energy, Energy Information Administration.

17. That same year, coal accounted for slightly less than 63 percent of total primary energy demand, and natural gas a mere 2.4 percent. Biomass accounted for some 13 percent.

18. For a contrasting view, see Ross (2009).

19. In contrast, the IEA (2007: 317) projects that China will import only 3 percent of its coal in 2030. Moreover, China has recently begun to seek gas deals to broaden its energy supplies. Although natural gas accounted for only about 3 percent of total energy consumption in China in 2004, its popularity is expected to increase. In addition to tapping China's large domestic supply of natural gas (proven natural gas reserves were conservatively estimated at 53.3 trillion cubic feet as of January 2006), China is looking to make gas pipeline deals with Kazakhstan and Russia.

20. Chinese analysts themselves focus on oil as the crucial aspect of their country's energy security challenges (see, e.g., Yang [2008]; Wu and Lu [2008]). See Zha (2008) for a criticism of this narrow focus. Although China's domestic oil production is currently sufficient to meet its commercial transportation needs, it cannot also satisfy the demands of the growing number of individual drivers.

21. In 2008, the proportion of oil imported from the Middle East rose to 50 percent, whereas the percentage imported from Africa declined slightly to 30 percent. Whether China can maintain its diversification success given the large stores of oil in the Persian Gulf remains to be seen, especially given Japanese inability to maintain its diversification strategy. As China has diversified its suppliers of oil, it has had to build and upgrade refining capacity to handle crude oil of varying qualities. Today, Chinese refineries must process light and sweet domestic crude oils, heavy and sour Middle Eastern crude oils, and high-acid crude oils from places like Sudan and Bohai Bay (Energy Information Administration 2009a).

22. Although some analysts argue that China is less inclined to overspend on its energy deals than it once was, anecdotal evidence suggests that overspending still occurs. Sinopec's spring 2006 $2.2 billion bid for rights to develop two deepwater blocks in Angola dwarfed the bids made by Western countries for similar areas.

23. For a more partisan representation of this view, see Xia, in Jaffe and Lewis (2002: 126–127).

24. The other country is Nigeria.

25. Nevertheless, there are some indications that the situation in Darfur has affected Chinese thinking (Guan and He 2007: 46; Wu and Lu 2008: 57–58).

26. Concerns about a U.S. blockade of oil imports are based at least in part on historical memories of the U.S.-led trade embargo against China following the Korean War. As elaborated below, however, such concerns are overstated.

27. For an overview of the motivations behind China's naval program, see Fravel (2008).

28. Nevertheless, during wartime the United States would be more willing to accept the large costs related to attempts to impose a blockade. We believe that tensions over energy are likely to be limited to the three scenarios described below, and even then would likely stop short of war.

29. For the naval nationalism argument, see Ross (2009).

30. This pipeline project is discussed in further detail below.

31. Construction of a gas pipeline began simultaneously.

32. Although shipping by tanker is generally cheaper than transportation via pipeline, in this case the alternative is for oil to travel via tanker to China's southeast coast, before being transported via pipeline through China to the southwest. This pipeline would offer a shortcut that would deliver oil directly to the southwestern region.

33. The two biggest companies spun off from JNOC are Inpex and Japex.

34. Whether this ambitious goal can be met remains to be seen. When government officials created JNOC, they had a slightly lower target for the percentage of oil to be obtained from fields explored and developed by Japanese countries, which they failed to reach.

35. Given the frequency with which the Russians renegotiate deals related to ESPO, the prospects for the completion of the ESPO pipeline should be regarded as uncertain.

36. As Zha (2006: 12) notes, "To ensure access to a Middle Eastern supply of oil, China finds itself in the uncomfortable position of having to cater to the political demands of some of its suppliers there."

37. That is, Saudi Arabia could actively cultivate closer economic and political ties with China, in an effort not to have all of its international political eggs in one basket, and/or simply signal this capacity to the United States.

Works Cited

Aguilera, Robert F., Roderick G. Eggert, Gustavo Lagos C. C., and John E. Tilton. 2009. "Depletion and the Future Availability of Petroleum Resources." *Energy Journal* 30 (1): 141–174.

Bader, Jeffrey A. 2008. "Rising China and Rising Oil Demand: Real and Imagined Problems for the International System." In *The Global Politics of Energy*, edited by Kurt Campbell and Jonathon Price. Washington, DC: Aspen Institute, 96–111.

Barboza, David. 2009. "With Cash to Spend, China Starts Investing Globally." *New York Times*. February 20.

Barnhart, Michael A. 1987. *Japan Prepares for Total War: The Search for Economic Security, 1919–1941*. Ithaca, NY: Cornell University Press.

Beaubouef, Bruce A. 2007. *The Strategic Petroleum Reserve: U.S. Energy Security and Oil Politics, 1975–2005*. College Station: Texas A&M University Press.

Bergsten, C. Fred, Charles Freeman, Nicholas R. Lardy, and Derek J. Mitchell. 2008. *China's Rise: Challenges and Opportunities*. Washington, DC: Institute for International Economics.

Blair, Bruce, Chen Yali, and Eric Hagt. 2006. "The Oil Weapon: Myth of China's Vulnerability." *China Security* (Summer): 32–63.

Bristow, Michael. 2008. "Pragmatism Triumphs in China-Japan Deal." *BBC News*. June 19. http://news.bbc.co.uk/2/hi/asia-pacific/7463492.stm.

Carew, Rick. 2009. "China Lends Abroad to Ease Oil Deals." *Wall Street Journal*. April 20.

Carter, Jimmy. 1980. State of the Union Address. January 23.

Central Intelligence Agency. N.d.a. "Country Comparisons: Oil—Imports." *CIA World Factbook*. https://www.cia.gov/library/publications/the-world-factbook/rankorder/2175rank.html.

———. N.d.b. "Country Comparisons: Oil—Proved Reserves." *CIA World Factbook*. https://www.cia.gov/library/publications/the-world-factbook/rankorder/2178rank.html.

———. 2009a. "China." *CIA World Factbook*. April 23. https://www.cia.gov/library/publications/the-world-factbook/geos/ch.html.

———. 2011. "Japan." *CIA World Factbook*. November 15. https://www.cia.gov/library/publications/the-world-factbook/geos/ja.html.

"China-Myanmar Oil Pipe Work to Begin This Year." 2007. *Reuters*. April 22. http://uk.reuters.com/article/oilRpt/idUKPEK7637220070422.

"China to Develop Iran Oilfield." 2004. *BBC News*. November 1.

Christensen, Thomas J. 1999. "China, the U.S.-Japan Alliance, and the Security Dilemma in East Asia." *International Security* 23 (4): 49–80.

Collins, Gabriel B. 2006. "China Seeks Oil Security with New Tanker Fleet." *Oil and Gas Journal* 104 (38): 20–22, 24–26.

Collins, Gabriel B., and William Murray. 2008. "No Oil for the Lamps of China?" *Naval War College Review* 61 (2): 79–95.

Cooper, Richard N. 2008. "China's Coming Demand for Energy." In *China, Asia, and the New World Economy*, edited by Barry Eichengreen, Charles Wyplosz, and Yung Chul Park. Oxford: Oxford University Press, 1–17.

Crane, Keith, Andreas Goldthau, Michael Toman, Thomas Light, Stuart E. Johnson, Alireza Nader, Angel Rabasa, and Harun Dogo. 2009. *Imported Oil and U.S. National Security*. Santa Monica, CA: RAND Corporation.

Deese, David A. 1979–1980. "Energy: Economics, Politics, and Security." *International Security* 4 (3): 140–153.

Deffeyes, Kenneth S. 2001. *Hubbert's Peak: The Impending World Oil Shortage*. Princeton, NJ: Princeton University Press.

Downs, Erica S. 2004. "The Chinese Energy Security Debate." *The China Quarterly* 177 (March): 21–41.

———. 2007. "The Fact and Fiction of Sino-African Energy Relations." *China Security* 3 (3): 42–68.

Duffield, John S. 2007. *Over a Barrel: The Costs of U.S. Foreign Oil Dependence*. Stanford, CA: Stanford University Press.

Ebel, Robert E. 2005. *China's Energy Future: The Middle Kingdom Seeks Its Place in the Sun*. Washington, DC: Center for Strategic and International Studies.

Eilts, Herman F. 1980. "Security Considerations in the Persian Gulf." *International Security* 5 (2): 79–113.

Energy Information Administration. 2008a. "Country Analysis Briefs: Russia: Oil Exports." May. http://www.eia.doe.gov/emeu/cabs/Russia/Oil_exports.html.

———. 2008b. "East China Sea: Oil and Natural Gas." March. http://www.eia.doe .gov/cabs/East_China_Sea/OilNaturalGas.html.

———. 2009a. "Country Analysis Briefs: China: Oil." http://www.eia.doe.gov/emeu/ cabs/China/Oil.html.

———. 2009b. *International Energy Outlook 2009*. May. http://www.eia.gov/forecasts/ archive/ieo09/pdf/0484%282009%29.pdf.

———. 2009c. "Overview." http://www.eia.gov/countries/index.cfm?topL=imp.

———. 2009d. "Overview: Oil Consumption." http://www.eia.gov/countries/index .cfm?view=consumption.

———. 2011. "County Analysis Briefs: Japan." March. http://www.eia.gov/countries/ cab.cfm?fips=JA.

Erickson, Andrew S., and Gabriel B. Collins. 2010. "China's Oil Security Pipe Dream: The Reality, and Strategic Consequences, of Seaborne Imports." *Naval War College Review* 63 (2): 89–111.

Fackler, Martin, and Ian Johnson. 2010. "China and Japan Escalate Standoff over Fishing Captain." *New York Times*. September 19. http://www.nytimes.com/ 2010/09/20/world/asia/20chinajapan.html?ref=territorialdisputes.

Frank, Robert H. 2000. *Microeconomics and Behavior*. 4th ed. Boston: McGraw-Hill.

Fravel, M. Taylor. 2008. "China's Search for Military Power." *Washington Quarterly* 31 (3): 125–141.

———. 2009. "China, Rising Power and Expansion: Can Conquest Pay?" Paper presented at Peace Studies Program, Cornell University, Ithaca, NY, April.

Friedberg, Aaron. 2006. "'Going Out': China's Pursuit of Natural Resources and Implications for the PRC's Grand Strategy." *NBR Analysis* 17 (3): 5–34.

Ghazvinian, John. 2007. *Untapped: The Scramble for Africa's Oil*. Orlando, FL: Harcourt.

Gholz, Eugene, and Daryl Press. 2008. "All the Oil We Need." *New York Times*. August 20.

———. 2010. "Protecting 'The Prize': Oil and the U.S. National Interest." *Security Studies* 19 (3): 453–485.

Golovnira, Maria. 2007. "Kazakhstan, China Agree on Pipeline from Caspian." *Reuters UK.* August 18. http://uk.reuters.com/article/2007/08/18/kazakhstan-china-idUKL1872705320070818.

Goodman, Peter S. 2004. "China Invests Heavily in Sudan's Oil Industry: Beijing Supplies Arms Used on Villagers." *Washington Post.* December 23: A01. http://www.washingtonpost.com/wp-dyn/articles/A21143-2004Dec22.html.

Goodstein, David. 2005. *Out of Gas: The End of the Age of Oil.* New York: Norton.

Guan Qingyou and Fan He. 2007. "Zhongguo de Nengyuan Anquan yu Guoji Nengyuan Hezuo" [China's Energy Security and International Energy Cooperation]. *Shijie Jingji yu Zhengzhi* [World Economics and International Politics] 11: 45–53.

Guo, Hui, and Kevin L. Kliesen. 2005. "Oil Price Volatility and U.S. Macroeconomic Activity." *Federal Reserve Bank of St. Louis Review* 87 (6): 669–683.

Hamilton, James D. 2009. "Understanding Crude Oil Prices." *Energy Journal* 30 (2): 179–206.

Houser, Trevor. 2008. "The Roots of Chinese Oil Investment Abroad." *Asia Policy* 5 (January).

Ikenberry, G. John. 1988. "Market Solutions for State Problems: The International and Domestic Politics of Oil Decontrol." *International Organization* 42: 151–177.

International Energy Agency. 2002. *World Energy Outlook 2002.* Paris: Organisation for Economic Co-operation and Development and International Energy Agency.

———. 2003. *Findings of Recent IEA Work, 2003.* Paris: Organisation for Economic Co-operation and Development and International Energy Agency

———. 2004. *World Energy Outlook 2004.* Paris: Organisation for Economic Co-operation and Development and International Energy Agency

———. 2007. *World Energy Outlook 2007.* Paris: Organisation for Economic Co-operation and Development and International Energy Agency

———. 2008. *World Energy Outlook 2008.* Paris: Organisation for Economic Co-operation and Development and International Energy Agency

Itoh, Shoichi. 2010. "The Geopolitics of Northeast Asia's Pipeline Politics." In *Pipeline Politics in Asia: The Intersection of Demand, Energy Markets, and Supply Routes,* edited by Edward C. Chow, Leigh E. Hendrix, Mikkal E. Herberg, Shoichi Itoh, Bo Kong, Marie Lall, and Paul Stevens. National Bureau of Asian Research Special Report 23. Seattle: National Bureau of Asian Research, 17–28.

Jaffe, Amy Myers, and Steven W. Lewis. 2002. "Beijing's Oil Diplomacy." *Survival* 44 (1): 115–134.

JOGMEC. 2007. "JOGMEC's Activities." http://www.jogmec.go.jp/english/activities/financial_oil/equitycapital.html.

"Jogmec Saddles Up at Severo-Mogdinsky." 2008. *Upstream.* April 28. http://www.upstreamonline.com/live/article153296.ece.

Kahn, Joseph. 2006. "China Courts Africa, Angling for Strategic Gains." *New York Times* November 3: A1.

Khalid, Nazery. 2006. "Burden Sharing, Security and Equity in the Straits of Malacca." *Japan Focus.* November 17. http://www.japanfocus.org/products/topdf/2277.

Kilian, Lutz. 2008. "The Economic Effects of Energy Price Shocks." *Journal of Economic Literature* 46 (4): 871–909.

Kirshner, Jonathan. 1997. "The Microfoundations of Economic Sanctions." *Security Studies* 6 (3): 32–64.

———. 2008. "The Cult of Energy Insecurity and the Crisis of Energy Security." Paper presented at the Tobin Project Conference, "America and the World: National Security in a New Era." Airlie House, VA, November 14–16.

Klare, Michael T. 2004. *Blood and Oil: The Dangers and Consequences of America's Growing Petroleum Dependency.* New York: Metropolitan Books.

Kleveman, Lutz. 2003. *The New Great Game: Blood and Oil in Central Asia.* New York: Grove Press.

Kong, Bo. 2010. "The Geopolitics of the Myanmar-China Oil and Gas Pipelines." In *Pipeline Politics in Asia: The Intersection of Demand, Energy Markets, and Supply Routes,* edited by Edward C. Chow, Leigh E. Hendrix, Mikkal E. Herberg, Shoichi Itoh, Bo Kong, Marie Lall, and Paul Stevens. National Bureau of Asian Research Special Report 23. Seattle: National Bureau of Asian Research, 55–66.

Lescaroux, Francois, and Valerie Mignon. 2008. "On the Influence of Oil Prices on Economic Activity and Other Macroeconomic Variables." CEPII Working Paper No. 2008-05. April. http://www.cepii.fr/anglaisgraph/workpap/pdf/2008/wp2008-05.pdf.

Li Xiaojun. 2004. "Lun Haiquan Dui Zhongguo Shiyou Anquan de Yingxiang" [On the Influence of Sea Power upon China's Oil Security]. *Guoji Luntan* [International Forum] 6 (4): 16–20.

Lieber, Robert J. 1992. "Oil and Power After the Gulf War." *International Security* 17 (1): 155–176.

Ministry of Economy, Trade, and Industry. 2006. "New Energy Security Strategy." May.

Motomura, Masumi. 2010. *Japan's Participation in East Siberia Oil and Gas Development.* PowerPoint presentation at the 3rd Japan-Russia Energy Dialogue. May 13. Khabarovsk, Russia. http://www.erina.or.jp/jp/Research/dlp/2010/pdf/J-R/KN/motomura.pdf.

Myer, Steven Lee. 2005. "World Business Briefing Europe: Russia: Pipeline to End Near Japan." *New York Times.* January 1: C3.

Painter, David S. 1986. *Oil and the American Century: The Political Economy of U.S. Foreign Oil Policy, 1941–1954.* Baltimore: Johns Hopkins University Press.

Pan, Esther. 2007. "China, Africa, and Oil." January 26. New York: Council on Foreign Relations. http://www.cfr.org/publication/9557/.

Perlez, Jane. 2006a. "China Competes with West in Aid to Its Neighbors." *New York Times.* September 18. http://www.nytimes.com/2006/09/18/world/asia/18china.html.

———. 2006b. "Myanmar Is Left in Dark, an Energy-Rich Orphan." *New York Times.* November 17: A1.

Regnier, Eva. 2007. "Oil and Energy Price Volatility." *Energy Economics* 29 (3): 405–427.

Reuters. 2009. "China Navy Spells Out Long-Range Ambitions." *Washington Post.* April 15.

Roberts, Paul. 2004. *The End of Oil: On the Edge of a Perilous New World.* Boston: Houghton Mifflin.

Rosen, Daniel H., and Trevor Houser. 2007. *China Energy: A Guide for the Perplexed.* Washington, DC: Center for Strategic and International Studies and Peterson Institute for International Economics.

Ross, Robert S. 2009. "China's Naval Nationalism: Sources, Prospects, and the U.S. Response." *International Security* 34 (2): 46–81.

"Russia-China Oil Pipeline Opens." 2011. *BBC.* January 1. http://www.bbc.co.uk/news/world-asia-pacific-12103865.

"Russia Starts Construction of Oil Pipeline to China." 2009. *Reuters.* April 28.

Schumpeter, Joseph. 1954. *History of Economic Analysis.* New York: Oxford University Press.

Shen, Dingli. 2006. "Iran's Nuclear Ambitions Test China's Wisdom." *Washington Quarterly* 29 (2): 55–66.

Snyder, Jack. 1984. *The Ideology of the Offensive: Military Decision Making and the Disasters of 1914.* Ithaca, NY: Cornell University Press.

Stern, Jonathan. 2006. "Natural Gas Security Problems in Europe: The Russian-Ukrainian Crisis of 2006." *Asia Pacific Review* 13 (1): 32–59.

Stern, Roger. 2006. "Oil Market Power and United States National Security." *PNAS* 103 (5): 1650–1655.

Talmadge, Caitlin. 2008. "Closing Time: Assessing the Iranian Threat to the Strait of Hormuz." *International Security* 33 (1): 82–117.

Traub, James. 2006. "China's African Adventure." *New York Times Magazine.* November 19. http://www.nytimes.com/2006/11/19/magazine/19china.html?pagewanted=all.

"US Satellite Snaps China's First Aircraft Carrier at Sea." 2011. *Guardian.* December 15. http://www.guardian.co.uk/world/2011/dec/15/us-satellite-china-aircraft-carrier.

Van Evera, Stephen. 1984. "The Cult of the Offensive and the Origins of the First World War." *International Security* 9 (1): 58–107.

Verleger, Philip K., Jr. 2005. "Energy: A Gathering Storm?" In *The United States and the World Economy: Foreign Economic Policy for the Next Decade*, edited by C. Fred Bergsten. Washington, DC: Institute for International Economics, 209–246.

Watkins, E. 2010. "Russia Plans to Start Extending ESPO Crude Oil Pipeline in 2011." *Oil and Gas Journal* 108 (12): 43.

Wu, Kang, and Ian Storey. 2008. "Energy Security in China's Capitalist Tradition." In *China's Emergent Political Economy*, edited by Christopher A. McNally. New York: Routledge, 190–208.

Wu Lei and Lu Guangsheng. 2008. "Guanyu Zhongguo-Feizhou Nengyuan Guanxi Fazhan Wenti de Ruogan Sikao" [Some Thoughts on the Development of Sino-African Energy Relations]. *Shijie Jingji yu Zhengzhi* [World Economics and Politics] 9 52–58.

Wu, Lei, and Shen Qinyu. 2006. "Will China Go to War over Oil?" *Far Eastern Economic Review* 169 (3): 38–40.

Yang Zewei. 2008. "Zhongguo Nengyuan Anquan Wenti: Tiaozhan yu Yingdui" [China's Energy Security: Challenges and Responses]. *Shijie Jingji yu Zhengzhi* [World Economics and International Politics] 8: 52–60.

Yergin, Daniel. 1988. "Energy Security in the 1990s." *Foreign Affairs* 67 (1): 110–132.

———. 1991. *The Prize: The Epic Quest for Oil, Money and Power.* New York: Simon and Schuster.

Ying, Wang, and Dinakar Sethuraman. 2007. "China, Iran Sign $2 Billion Oil Production Agreement." *Bloomberg.com.* December 10. http://www.bloomberg.com/apps/news?pid=newsarchive&sid=akJh5.VKopoU.

Zha, Daojiong. 2006. "Energy Interdependence." *China Security* (Summer): 2–16.

———. 2008. "Tuozhan Zhongguo Nengyuan Anquan Yanjiu de Keti Jichu" [Expanding the Bases for Research on Chinese Energy Security]. *Shijie Jingji yu Zhengzhi* [World Economics and International Politics] 7: 79–80.

———. 2009. "The China Factor in Global Energy Dynamics." *Contemporary International Relations* 19 (March): 24–31.

Zhang, Jian. 2011. *China's Energy Security: Prospects, Challenges, and Opportunities.* July. Brookings Institution. http://www.brookings.edu/~/media/Files/rc/papers/2011/07_china_energy_zhang/07_china_energy_zhang_paper.pdf.

Zhang Wenmu. 2003. "Zhongguo Nengyuan Anquan yu Zhengzhi Xuanze" [China's Energy Security and Policy Choices]. *Shijie Jingji yu Zhengzhi* [World Economics and International Politics] 5 (May): 11–16.

———. 2006. "Sea Power and China's Strategic Choices." *China Security* (Summer): 17–31.

Zhao, Hongtu. 2009. "China's Overseas Energy Investment: Myth and Reality." *Contemporary International Relations* 19 (March): 89–120.

7 Economic Growth, Regime Insecurity, and Military Strategy

Explaining the Rise of Noncombat Operations in China

M. Taylor Fravel

I N THE PAST DECADE, NONCOMBAT OPERATIONS HAVE EMERGED as a new component of China's evolving military strategy. To be sure, preparing to fight a high-technology and "informationized" war remains the focus of the People's Liberation Army's (PLA) modernization and reforms. Nevertheless, China's armed forces have started to stress the importance of conducting a wide range of noncombat operations (*feizhanzheng junshi xingdɔng*) or the use of the military for purposes other than waging war.[1] These operations include disaster relief and peacekeeping, among others. As demonstrated in Figure 7.1, the discussion of noncombat operations in the *Jiefangjun Bao*, the official newspaper of the PLA, began in the late 1990s and has increased dramatically since 2008.

The growing role of noncombat operations in China's military strategy presents a theoretical and empirical puzzle. Within the study of international security, scholars widely believe that states will use their growing wealth to generate conventional military capabilities for traditional combat missions, especially wars with other states (Gilpin 1981; Kennedy 1987; Mearsheimer 2001; Waltz 1979; Zakaria 1998). In addition, the majority of past rising powers have conformed to this theoretical expectation, investing solely or primarily in combat capabilities. The United States, for example, began to develop doctrine for "military operations other than war" only following the collapse of the Soviet Union. In China, however, the majority of noncombat operations described in authoritative PLA texts emphasize domestic missions, such

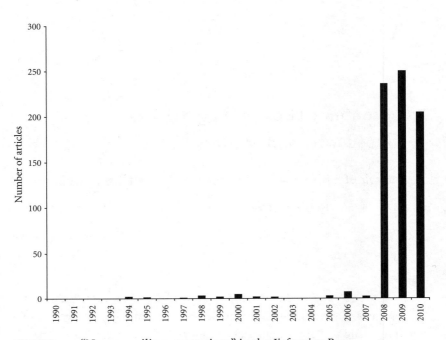

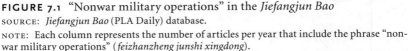

FIGURE 7.1 "Nonwar military operations" in the *Jiefangjun Bao*
SOURCE: *Jiefangjun Bao* (PLA Daily) database.
NOTE: Each column represents the number of articles per year that include the phrase "nonwar military operations" (*feizhanzheng junshi xingdong*).

as managing natural disasters and social unrest, although international missions such as peacekeeping also receive attention. Moreover, China has begun to emphasize noncombat operations even though the modernization of its force for traditional combat operations is far from complete. In 2010, the Pentagon classified only 25 percent of China's naval surface combatants and fighter aircraft as "modern" (Office of the Secretary of Defense 2010: 45).

I argue that the rise of noncombat operations in China's military strategy is principally a response to internal threats to regime security that are a byproduct of rapid economic growth. Concerns about domestic stability have created a new dimension of China's defense policy. I begin with the assumption that leaders craft national policies to deal with the most pressing threats that they face, including not just external threats to the security of the state but also internal threats to a leader or a regime's political survival. Survival at home is as important as survival abroad. Growth, especially rapid growth, is usually a source of legitimacy for leaders in developing countries such as

China. Such growth, however, also generates new sources of instability, such as income inequality and corruption that can fuel societal unrest, which, in turn, may jeopardize continued growth and ultimately legitimacy. Under these conditions, as Samuel Huntington (1968) noted several decades ago, the need for continued growth creates a powerful interest in maintaining domestic political order and preventing the spread of social unrest. The armed forces provide leaders with one important tool for achieving these goals. Thus, for developing countries, economic growth can create a strong incentive for a state's military to develop capabilities to conduct noncombat operations.

My starting point is the military strategy that China adopted in 1993. This strategy emphasized the ability to fight and win "local wars under modern especially high-technology conditions" and was revised in 2004 to highlight the role of information technology in modern warfare (Jiang Zemin 2006: 278). The basic goals of the strategy were defending the Chinese Communist Party (CCP) against internal threats, safeguarding China's sovereignty and territorial integrity, promoting national unification, protecting maritime interests, and supporting regional stability (Fravel 2008a). What President Hu Jintao described in 2004 as China's "development interests" accounts for the PLA's new emphasis on noncombat operations. Since then, the goals of China's military strategy have reemphasized the importance of internal security and maintaining domestic political order. The scope of regional stability has broadened to include a new global dimension, especially in regions where China trades heavily. Ensuring the ability to access resources for future development has been underscored. To achieve these goals, China's military strategy has stressed the role of noncombat operations to maintain stability both at home and abroad to promote continued economic growth.

Several implications follow from my argument. First, I identify a new causal pathway through which domestic politics can influence the goals and content of a state's military strategy, especially in the developing world. To be sure, the role of regime insecurity in a state's military strategy is only a partial one and cannot account for all aspects of a state's military strategy. Nevertheless, it can help explain the noncombat dimension of a state's military strategy, especially the domestic component, that existing approaches emphasizing external factors cannot.

Second, I suggest an alternative perspective on the relationship between rising powers and the likelihood of armed conflict. Most approaches to the study of power shifts in international politics, including variants of power transition theory, assess the propensity for conflict at the systemic level of analysis (e.g., Choucri and North 1975; Copeland 2000; Gilpin 1981; Kugler and Lemke 1996; Organski 1958; Organski and Kugler 1980). In general terms, conflict is more likely to occur because uneven economic growth alters the relative position of states, which can create incentives for either rising or dominant powers to use force. I suggest that the conversion of material capabilities into military power is far from automatic. Instead, domestic factors such as regime security also shape the type of military capabilities that rising powers choose to develop.

Third, the growing role of noncombat operations in China's military strategy demonstrates the continued domestic role for China's armed forces, which includes the PLA, whose principal mission is external defense, and the paramilitary People's Armed Police (PAP), charged with maintaining internal stability. By contrast, scholars frequently view the PLA's focus on noncombat operations principally as a tool of statecraft designed to strengthen China's international influence (e.g., Chase and Gunness 2010; Holsag 2009; Nodskov 2009; Office of the Secretary of Defense 2010: 19; Watson 2009). The emphasis on noncombat operations by both the PLA and the PAP suggests that China will develop combat capabilities more slowly than might otherwise be the case, especially if the sources of regime insecurity remain in the coming decade. Although detailed budgetary data is unavailable, the organizational changes that have been implemented to conduct noncombat operations indicate that the PLA is devoting fewer resources to long-range force projection than analysts expected a decade ago. To be sure, China still remains involved in conflicts and disputes that could escalate to war, especially over Taiwan and various maritime disputes in East Asia. Nevertheless, the continued domestic orientation of China's armed forces may help dampen spirals of hostility with other great powers associated with the security dilemma.

The chapter proceeds as follows. The first section outlines how economic growth can create incentives to develop noncombat capabilities by increasing political instability that then threatens future growth and legitimacy. The second section surveys Chinese language sources on military affairs to identify and discuss the three goals of China's military strategy that are shaped by concerns about economic growth and regime security. The third section examines in detail the noncombat capabilities that the PLA has sought to develop and shows how these aim to address the internal and external sources of instability created by economic growth.

Economic Growth, Regime Insecurity, and Military Strategy

Why would economic growth create incentives for a developing country such as China to develop noncombat military capabilities, especially for domestic missions? One answer can be found in the relationship between economic growth and regime security. In developing countries, especially authoritarian ones, economic growth is an important source of legitimacy for the state. The process of growth, however, can increase political instability, which jeopardizes future growth and ultimately the security of the ruling regime. When political instability increases, leaders may choose to use their country's armed forces internally, which can broaden the goals and content of military strategy from external defense to include regime security.

The logic of political instability and regime insecurity as a source of military strategy extends earlier work on the relationship between domestic politics and foreign policy. To explain alliance formation in the developing world, Steven David (1991) argues that leaders "omni-balance" by forming alliances to counter the most pressing threat that they face. For many leaders in the developing world, especially in authoritarian states, the most pressing threats to their political survival emanate from internal political challenges, including coups, rival factions, riots, and rebellions. As a result, a leader may seek to form an alliance with an adversary abroad to balance more immediate internal threats at home. Leaders design their foreign policies to deal with domestic problems as well as foreign ones. If internal threats can explain alliance formation, then they may also explain other national policies, including military strategy.

For leaders in developing countries, economic growth creates several powerful reasons for using their armed forces to maintain internal political stability. First, despite bolstering legitimacy, the process of rapid economic growth also creates new challenges for the state and sources of political unrest, which, if not addressed and managed, can limit future growth and ultimately threaten legitimacy. As Samuel Huntington (1968) noted several decades ago, leaders in developing countries pursuing high-growth strategies place a premium on stability and order because of the social upheaval of modernization. Sources of instability associated with rapid growth include internal migration, urbanization, income inequality, and corruption, among others, all of which can spark or stoke social unrest. Second, the ongoing societal transformation and sources of instability that growth creates increase the vulnerability of the economy to external shocks, which can also further increase instability and jeopardize future growth. These shocks can include negative developments in the global economy beyond the control of individual leaders, such as the 2008 financial crisis and the loss of jobs in export sectors around the world, and other events such as natural disasters and pandemics that call into question the capacity and legitimacy of the state.

Political instability can shape the goals and content of a state's military strategy in several ways. At the most general level, it suggests that one goal in the military strategies of developing countries will be maintaining domestic political order, in addition to the traditional emphasis on defense against foreign enemies. States may design their military strategy not only to maximize security against external threats and combat with other armed forces but also to manage and reduce internal threats. Key tasks required to achieve these domestic goals might include containing outbreaks of social and political unrest or providing relief and maintaining order when natural disasters occur. Whatever the specific circumstances, the general goal of maintaining domestic stability requires the capability to perform a variety of noncombat operations, including disaster relief, search-and-rescue, riot control, counterinsurgency, counterterrorism, and other operations. Such operations tend to be manpower intensive and require specialized training because the tasks involved are not those typically used in combat (although some are, such as logistics, communications, and command and control).

Threats to economic growth and regime security, of course, can also occur beyond a state's borders, especially for developing countries that pursue growth through integration with the global economy. Through the process of development, such states acquire new interests overseas in those factors that facilitate or hinder future growth, which can also shape the goals and content of a state's military strategy. Two such interests stand out. The first is access to the key inputs for future growth, especially natural resources. Countries that depend on world markets for these inputs may consider using their armed forces to help ensure their ability to access them. The second is the stability of the world trading system, including the security of sea lines of communication and access to foreign markets. To be sure, the relationship between new overseas interests and economic growth is consistent with structural approaches. At the same time, these interests can arise not just because of competition among states for relative power but also because they can negatively affect growth, increase political instability, and threaten regime security. New overseas interests that developing countries acquire often have a domestic basis in addition to an international one.

These external interests that influence growth and political stability can also shape the goals and content of a state's military strategy in several ways. The main goal is maintaining stability in the international system to ensure the ability to gain access to resources in other countries, protection for overseas investments, and the uninterrupted flow of trade. At a minimum, these goals require the ability to project and sustain at least a small number of forces overseas to perform noncombat operations, such as peacekeeping, disaster relief, and noncombatant evacuation, as well as combat operations such as sea-lane security. The ability to "show the flag" in regions in which a state has investments or trades heavily can also be useful to ensure that its interests are taken into account in those regions during periods of instability.

My argument about the effect of economic growth and regime security on military strategy offers two contributions. First, it can explain a phenomenon that existing theories about rising powers cannot, namely, why a rising power would seek to develop capabilities for noncombat operations, especially domestic ones, when its military modernization for traditional war fighting is far from complete. Second, it also suggests that some externally oriented goals are more closely related to domestic political concerns than just international competition among states. Of course, growth ultimately enables a state to increase its power in the international system, but the domestic incentives for growth and how they can shape military strategy at home and abroad should not be overlooked. The relationship between growth and regime security is especially relevant for developing countries because of the fragility of their institutions and vulnerability to political instability. Whereas the state in advanced industrialized societies can take internal security for granted, the state in the developing world cannot. For these states, internal regime security is as important as external state security.

As a rapidly developing country, China offers a rich environment in which to explore the relationship between economic growth and military strategy. First, since the start of opening and reform, the percentage of the population living in urban areas increased from 19 percent in 1979 to 43 percent in 2008 (World Bank 2010). Likewise, internal migration has mushroomed. Although the "roving population" of migrant workers is hard to count, it appears to include more than 17 percent of the population, or approximately

221 million people (Xinhua 2011). Second, given the ongoing societal change, the government faces constant pressure to provide jobs in both urban and rural areas. In 2007, only 71 percent of college graduates were able to find work (China Labor Bulletin 2007). Although the official jobless rate measures only a portion of the labor force, a 2010 white paper suggested that true unemployment, including surplus labor in rural areas, hovered around 20 percent (State Council Information Office 2010).[2] Third, the level of inequality has increased steadily. When Deng Xiaoping started his reforms, the Gini coefficient (which measures the distribution of income in a state) was 0.30, which suggested a relatively equal distribution. By 2010, however, it had jumped to 0.47 (Chen 2010). Although lower than other developing countries such as Brazil (0.59) and Mexico (0.55), this jump nevertheless reflects a fairly substantial change in society (Naughton 2007: 217). Finally, the economic foundations of growth are shaky. In recent years, and especially since the global financial crisis in 2008, local governments borrowed heavily from China's banks, and their debt is one-third of China's gross domestic product (GDP), a fact that significantly increases the overall debt-to-GDP ration from 20 percent to more than 50 percent (Shih 2010). The emphasis on growth through investment and not consumption continues to run the risk of high levels of inflation, which would only heighten the pressure on employment (Fewsmith 2009).

In recent years, Chinese officials have expressed growing concern about maintaining stability. In February 2011, the Central Party School convened a special and unprecedented study and discussion session (*yantao ban*) for provincial and ministerial level cadres that the entire Politburo attended. During his speech at the opening session, President Hu Jintao noted the importance of "social management" (*shehui guanli*) amid China's rapid social and economic development. Hu stressed that improved social management was needed to "maintain social order, promote social harmony, [and] ensure that people can live and work in peace" (Xu Jingyue 2011). At around the same time, China's security services reacted swiftly and sharply to appeals from overseas activists to launch a "jasmine revolution" (*molihua geming*) following the popular revolutions in Tunisia and Egypt in early 2011. Reporting in the Chinese media is also consistent with growing leadership concerns about instability. As Figure 7.2 shows, the number of articles in *Jiefangjun Bao* that mention "safeguarding stability" (*weiwen*) has increased dramatically since 2000.

Below, I trace how economic growth and concerns about regime security have affected the goals and content of China's military strategy. Toward this

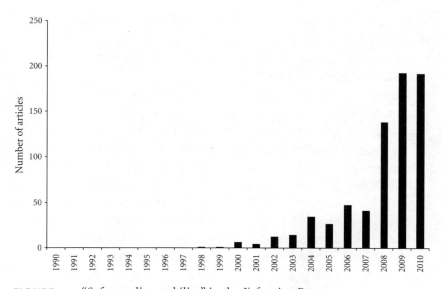

FIGURE 7.2 "Safeguarding stability" in the *Jiefangjun Bao*
SOURCE: *Jiefangjun Bao* (PLA Daily) database.
NOTE: Each column represents the number of articles per year that include the phrase "safeguarding stability" (*weiwen*).

end, I tap new and original data from Chinese-language sources. The use of Chinese military writings poses several challenges for scholars, including assessment of the authoritativeness of any particular work and determination of the degree to which it represents mainstream military viewpoints. I address these challenges in two ways. First, I use a collection of previously unpublished speeches given by Hu Jintao to various military audiences in the PLA in his capacity as the chair of the Central Military Commission (CMC; Zong zhengzhi bu 2006). These speeches offer insight into how China's senior leaders view the utility of military power, as well as the goals and content of China's military strategy. That these speeches were not openly published matters for two reasons. First, the views contained in the speeches were not tailored for the ears of foreign audiences. Second, the speeches were disseminated as part of a campaign to educate the PLA about its "historic mission in the new phase of the new century" (*xinshiji xinjieduan wojun lishi shiming*).[3] The concept of a new historic mission described how the need to ensure China's continued development required that the PLA shoulder new tasks known as the "three provides and one role" (*sange tigong, yige fahui*). These tasks are (1) to maintain the CCP's status as the ruling party, (2) to provide a security guarantee to safeguard China's continued development, (3) to help safeguard China's expanding national interests, and (4) to play a role in fostering world peace (Zong zhengzhi bu 2006: 76–83).

Second, I examine professional military writings by Chinese military strategists in the PLA. In particular, I use writings primarily from two authoritative and influential institutions that play a central role in developing the PLA's military strategy. The first is the Academy of Military Science (AMS), which is a research institute for military theory directly under the CMC. Scholars from the AMS, for example, led the drafting of the combat regulations that were published in 1999. The second institution is the National Defense University, which is the PLA's main teaching and training organization for senior officers across the military services (Gill and Mulvenon 2002). Both organizations maintain active publishing houses for works on military affairs along with flagship journals, including *Zhongguo junshi kexue* (*China Military Science*) and the *Guofang daxue xuebao* (*Journal of the National Defense University*), respectively (e.g., Fan Zhenjiang and Ma Baoan 2007; Peng Guangqian and Yao Youzhi 2001; Wang Wenrong 1999).

Broadening Strategic Goals: From Survival to Development

In the past decade, the goals of China's military strategy have increasingly emphasized development in addition to survival. The effect of economic growth on China's military strategy can be observed in three goals that expand and broaden the 1993 strategy. These goals include reemphasizing internal security and maintaining domestic political order, widening the scope of regional stability to include a new global dimension, and highlighting access to resources that China views as necessary for continued growth. To be sure, the importance of other goals, such as achieving Taiwan's unification or defending claims in territorial disputes, have not diminished. The PLA is developing the capabilities to pursue multiple objectives simultaneously. Nevertheless, the effect of growth has been to stress factors related to development in addition to China's traditional security concerns. As Hu Jintao explained in 2004, China's armed forces "must pay attention not only to protecting national survival interests but also to protecting national development interests" (Zong zhengzhi bu 2006: 80).[4]

The concept of a "new historic mission" for China's armed forces demonstrates how growth has broadened the scope of China's military strategy to include noncombat operations. Hu Jintao introduced the concept of a new historic mission in December 2004 in his first major speech as chair of the CMC (a position he assumed from Jiang Zemin in September 2004). As detailed by Hu, the concept outlined the role of the armed forces in ensuring China's continued economic growth. Moreover, and underscoring the link to regime security, the CCP tasked the PLA and PAP with this new historic mission. When Hu introduced the concept, he described how it was necessary to support the CCP's own "three great tasks" of continuing China's economic modernization, completing national unification, and safeguarding world peace and promoting common development. According to Hu, "Amid this great historic process, what kind of historic mission our army should undertake is a great task that must be deeply considered" (Zong zhengzhi bu 2006: 76). The overarching purpose of identifying a new historic mission for China's armed forces has been to further the CCP's own objectives, which, in turn, remain centered on economic development, for its own survival as well as for its political objectives.

The emphasis in descriptions of the historic mission concept on protecting economic development reflects greater attention in the PLA to China's growing economic interests. In many military publications, discussions of the economic dimension of security have become increasingly prominent (Fan Yuejiang 2003; Liu Xingliang 2004). According to the noted AMS scholar Major General Li Jijun, for example, "traditional security with national defense as dominant is the pillar of national security." At the same time, however, "nontraditional security with economics at the core is the foundation of national security" (Li Jijun 2004: 38). Likewise, reflecting the growing emphasis on economics, scholars from the PLA's Nanjing Political Academy conclude that, "at present, China's most important national interests are the promotion of economic development and the achievement of national unification" (Huang Zaisheng and Zhang Kenan 2008: 7). Such statements are perhaps a natural reflection of China's steady economic growth over the past three decades.

Internal Security and Political Order

As my argument about political instability and regime security suggests, authoritative PLA sources emphasize the many internal threats to China's continued development, especially domestic unrest and instability. Indeed, in Hu Jintao's introduction of the PLA's new historic mission, concerns about regime security receive as much attention as external interests. As a result, the first task that Hu Jintao assigned to the PLA as part of its new historic mission is, unsurprisingly, "to provide an important powerful guarantee to consolidate the party's ruling status" (Zong zhengzhi bu 2006: 77). Although defense of the CCP and regime survival have been a long-standing goal for China's armed forces that predates even Deng Xiaoping's reforms, it was re-emphasized by Hu because of the new challenges that the party faces as the transition from a planned economy to the market continues. It also demonstrates that China's leaders believe that political instability can not only disrupt economic growth in a variety of ways but also pose a clear challenge to legitimacy of the CCP.

During a speech at an enlarged meeting of the CMC in December 2005, Hu Jintao described how China's rapid economic development and integration into the world economy created new threats to the CCP's power. His statement is worth quoting at length:

> In the current stage, our country's social contradictions and problems are increasing, and contradictions and problems in society are increasing. International and domestic hostile forces constantly scheme to use these contradictions and problems to stir up trouble. As our country's connections with the outside world increasingly expand and deepen, the interactive quality of internal security and international security strengthens. If not handled well, some internal problems could evolve into international problems; some international problems may also be transmitted internally and bring out problems of social instability. We must have a clear understanding of this new characteristic of the national security situation.

Hu then described the various actors that threatened China, especially those that targeted the CCP, such as "separatist forces," democratic movements, and *falun gong* activists (Zong zhengzhi bu 2006: 197).

In one of the first PLA studies of its new historic mission, internal threats to the regime are prominent. According to scholars from the National Defense University, "the pounding of complex social problems" exerts the greatest influence on China's development. The scholars note that income inequality poses an especially serious threat because it decreases public trust in government, undercuts support for domestic reform, increases social unrest, and weakens the government's authority (Zheng Weiping and Liu Mingfu

2005). In light of these complex challenges, an editorial in the *Jiefangjun Bao*, the PLA's official newspaper, observes that "social contradictions are influencing one another, and the number of factors harmful to social stability have increased. Whatever aspect is not prevented or is mismanaged will influence and strain [development goals]" (Jiefangjun bao bianjibu 2006: 5). Political order remains central for economic growth and regime security.

For China's leaders, internal threats to domestic stability and political order are easy to find. Indeed, many of these threats would be classified as nontraditional because the source is not another state but nonstate actors (including societal groups) and the natural environment. The first set of internal threats includes the sharp increase in mass incidents, whereby citizens protest against local governments over a range of social issues associated with reform and rapid development, including corruption, land seizures, and environmental degradation. The number and scope of demonstrations, protests, and riots classified as mass incidents in China has increased dramatically from 8,700 in 1993 to potentially as high as 170,000 in 2009 (Mi Aini 2010; Tanner 2004).[5] The second set includes terrorism and ethnic unrest, such as the large-scale protests in Lhasa and throughout Tibetan areas in March 2008 and the ethnic violence in Urumqi, the capital of Xinjiang, in 2009. Ethnic unrest is especially worrisome for China's leaders because many ethnic groups reside in frontier regions adjacent to China's international boundaries (Chen Yong 2006). The third set of threats include natural disasters, such as the 2008 earthquake in Sichuan that killed more than 87,000 people (and wounded more than 374,000),[6] the snow and ice storms in January 2008 that threatened to cripple national transportation networks, and the earthquakes and droughts in 2010. Other threats include pandemics such as the severe acute respiratory syndrome crisis in 2003 and China's own vulnerability to cyberattack.

All of these, especially if more than one occurs at the same time, are perhaps the threats most likely to derail China's continued growth and, as a consequence, threaten regime survival. Moreover, China's leaders clearly recognize the potential threat. During the National People's Congress (NPC) in 2009, Hu Jintao called on China's armed forces "to provide mighty support for national interests and social stability" (Wang Hongjiang 2009). Similarly, in March 2010, Premier Wen Jiabao's report at the NPC noted the "major task of safeguarding stability in key areas" for the PLA and PAP (Wen Jiabao 2010).

External Stability

The importance of external stability is a commonly discussed factor in scholarly analysis of China's grand strategy. This was a goal in the 1950s during the Bandung era and received renewed attention after Deng Xiaoping launched China's reform drive in 1979. The goal of external stability remains today but assumes an even broader scope and greater importance than before because of China's integration into the global economy. In the past, China sought stability abroad to conserve resources for domestic policy initiatives. The primary concern was that conflict abroad would drain resources and attention away from reform. This concern remains today. Yet with China's gradual shift to a market economy amid deepening integration with the global economy, China is more vulnerable to instability abroad than ever before, especially in regions beyond its immediate periphery.

At the sixteenth party congress in 2002, Jiang Zemin put forth the notion of a period of strategic opportunity for China's development in which to build a "moderately well-off" (*xiaokang*), or middle-class, society. The opportunity for such development existed because the odds of a great-power war over the coming two decades were deemed to be low and Deng's reforms had created a foundation for further growth. Since becoming general secretary, Hu Jintao has embraced this goal and has instructed the PLA to "provide a strong security guarantee for protecting the great period of strategic opportunity for national development" as part of its new historic mission (Zong zhengzhi bu 2006: 78). As a *Jiefangjun Bao* editorial noted, "the key to maintaining and seizing this period [of strategic opportunity] lies in creating a stable and dependable security environment" (Jiefangjun bao bianjibu 2006: 1). Threats to stability that authoritative military publications identify include the escalation of China's outstanding territorial and maritime disputes with its neighbors as well as the conflict over Taiwan (Liu Xiaoli 2009). According to the *Jiefangjun Bao*, the PLA can safeguard the period of strategic opportunity against these threats by "using the deterrent role created by military power to prevent or postpone the outbreak of war" (Jiefangjun bao bianjibu 2006: 5). The implication is not that China would necessarily settle these disputes through force, but that with a strong military it would deter others from challenging China on these issues, thus diverting attention away from continued economic development.

Beyond these traditional security interests, however, another component of the PLA's new historic mission includes contributing to the protection of the global commons and hedging against the spread of armed conflict. On the one hand, a stable external environment for China requires not only peace on its immediate periphery, where China has active disputes with other states, but also stability in other regions where China has new interests such as investments and where instability could adversely affect China's development. Toward this end, Hu Jintao instructed China's armed forces in December 2004 to "play an important role in maintaining world peace and promoting common development" (Zong zhengzhi bu 2006: 80). As a *Jiefangjun Bao* editorial echoed, the PLA "must undertake more duties and play a bigger role in all kinds of activities for safeguarding world peace," such as through peacekeeping or international disaster relief operations (Jiefangjun bao bianjibu 2006: 5). At the same time, many military publications observe that economic globalization will also increase friction, especially among developing countries, which can threaten stability worldwide. According to the *Jiefangjun Bao*, "The more opportunities [developing countries] have to enter the international arena, the more opportunities they will have for clashes and conflicts with hegemony [and] power politics" (Jiefangjun bao bianjibu 2006: 5).

The emphasis on the global dimension of China's external security environment reflects the vulnerability of China's economy to threats beyond its borders in addition to domestic political instability. Greater integration brings less national autonomy and control over domestic affairs. The commandant of the Nanjing Ground Forces Academy, Major General Chen Yong, notes, for example, that economic globalization produces a "butterfly effect" (*hudie xiaoying*) in international security affairs. Because globalization deepens interdependence among states, an incident in any one area can influence other states and other regions, "creating a global shock" (Chen Yong 2006: 20). The recent global financial crisis, for example, underscored China's vulnerability to the whims of the global economy, with implications for employment and central government tax collection (Sun Huangtian 2009). Discussions of nontraditional security threats highlight other problems from domestic terrorism to environmental security that globalization creates or intensifies (Bao Bin and Wang Guifang 2006: 12).

A final component of external stability is the security of trade routes and sea lines of communications. Sea-lane security is a traditional combat mission, but in Chinese writings it has received new attention in the context of concerns about domestic stability. The vast majority of China's trade is transported via the sea, as China relies on overseas markets for its exports (Ling

Shengyin and Hua Ren 2005). As the rise of piracy in the Gulf of Aden demonstrates, trade routes require protection and are part of the global commons. The security of maritime transportation routes affects all seaborne trade, but it is especially salient for energy resources. Hu Jintao reportedly highlighted the problem of sea-lane security with his November 2003 remark about the so-called Malacca dilemma, which referred to the large proportion of China's imported energy supplies traveling through the Strait of Malacca, a narrow waterway plagued by piracy (Shi Hongtao 2004). A study from the PLA's National Defense University indicates that more than 50 percent of ships flowing through the Strait of Malacca are bound for China (Liu Xiaoli 2009: 44).

Access to Resources and Markets Overseas

Authoritative PLA writings on military affairs have identified access to resources and markets overseas for continued growth as a new interest that affects growth and needs protection. International competition, not domestic stability, is the dominant driver of this set of concerns, but discussion of these concerns in the context of China's domestic instability only increases their importance. As several military economists note, China's economic development increasingly depends on access to overseas markets and resources, such as petroleum (Ling Shengyin and Hua Ren 2005). The AMS scholar Wang Guifang, for example, argues that "the unimpeded supply of resources" is a "main interest" (*zhuyao liyi*) for the nation (Wang Guifang 2006: 79). Energy, perhaps unsurprisingly, was one of the key resources that Wang highlights. Likewise, General Li Jijun reaches a similar conclusion, stressing the importance of access to overseas resources for continued development (Li Jijun 2004).

More generally, descriptions of the PLA's new historic mission notes new interests in resources that China has acquired. In the December 2004 speech, Hu Jintao described this task as "providing powerful strategic support for safeguarding national interests" (Zong zhengzhi bu 2006: 79). The first set of interests concern maritime resources. In introducing the historic mission concept, Hu Jintao described the ocean as "a treasure chest of strategic resources for the continued development of mankind" (Zong zhengzhi bu 2006: 80). Other military publications over the past decade have echoed this theme by underscoring the importance of securing China's "maritime rights and interests" (*haiyang quanyi*; Wang Shumei, Shi Jiazhu, and Xu Mingshan

2007; Zhang Wei 2007; Zheng Weiping and Liu Mingfu 2005: 139–151). The importance of maritime security has increased because the ocean contains abundant resources, whose importance scholars note will grow only with the continuation of globalization (Wang Shumei, Shi Jiazhu, and Xu Mingshan 2007; Zhang Wei 2007). In addition, China's disputes over offshore islands and maritime demarcation, especially in the South China Sea, cannot be separated from a concern for resources.

The second and third areas in which Hu Jintao noted that China's interests in resources have expanded are in space (*taikong anquan*) and the "electromagnetic sphere" (*dianci kongjian*). When compared with the maritime domain, China's interests in these areas are driven more by the dominant military position of the United States than by specific economic interests. Both space-based sensors and information networks are key components of U.S. military power, whose "command of the commons" constrains the PLA (Posen 2003). Nevertheless, space is also considered "a vast vista for the development of mankind," with resources for development (Zheng Weiping and Liu Mingfu 2005: 152–171; Zong zhengzhi bu 2006: 80). Likewise, the increasing role of information technology in China's economic development increases the vulnerability of its own economy to cyber attack (Zheng Weiping and Liu Mingfu 2005: 172–189). Military publications express concern that if China fails to develop capabilities in these areas, then it will be marginalized and unable to tap their potential in the future (Chen Yong 2006; Wang Shumei, Shi Jiazhu, and Xu Mingshan 2007; Zhang Wei 2007). Indeed, Hu referred to space and the electromagnetic sphere as new "development security interests" (Zong zhengzhi bu 2006: 85).

New Methods for New Goals: The Rise of Noncombat Operations

The content of a state's military strategy describes the ways or methods for achieving its strategic goals. When Hu Jintao introduced the concept of a new historic mission for the PLA, he also outlined the capabilities that it should possess. During an enlarged meeting of the CMC in December 2005, he said: "Starting from the overall international and domestic situation, we must . . . take strengthening the ability to win local wars under modern conditions as the core, and continuously raise the ability to deal with multiple security threats to ensure that our army can deal with crises, maintain peace, contain wars, and win wars under different kinds of complicated situations" (Zong zhengzhi bu 2006: 196). During a 2006 meeting with PLA delegates to the NPC, Hu similarly instructed the PLA to "work hard to develop capabilities to deal with many kinds of security threats and complete diversified military tasks" (Zong zhengzhi bu 2006: 253).

In Hu's speeches, the phrase "many kinds of security threats" refers to the goals discussed in the previous section. By contrast, "diversified military tasks" means using China's growing military capabilities in two different ways. The first highlights traditional combat operations and war-fighting capabilities. Although China's economic growth through integration with the global economy increases the potential costs of conflict, China has not slowed its military modernization drive.[7] Instead, the PLA continues to stress the need to fight and win short wars as well as the importance of "strategic deterrence," so that the costs of conflict may be contained (Peng Guangqian and Yao Youzhi 2001: 241).[8] The second way of using military power emphasizes noncombat operations to enhance regime security and promote economic development by maintaining stability at home and abroad. Despite the continued, and primary, importance of combat operations, the broadening of the goals of China's military strategy has focused attention on developing new capabilities for noncombat operations to conduct diversified military tasks.

Types of Noncombat Operations

Consistent with a focus on regime security and the primacy of maintaining domestic stability, the types of noncombat operations most frequently discussed by Chinese military strategists are internal missions to help the state maintain public order and, ultimately, defend the CCP. Table 7.1 displays the results of a survey of sixteen books published by the PLA on noncombat operations since 2004.[9] These books represent studies by research groups at different military institutions, including the Academy of Military Science and the National Defense University, and many were published for internal use only (which enhances their authoritativeness on the subject). The survey demonstrates the dominant role of domestic noncombat operations in PLA writings on the subject, which can be grouped into three broad categories. The first is disaster relief and rescue, such as the operations that the PLA conducted after the 2008 Wenquan earthquake in Sichuan. The second is maintaining social stability, including containing demonstrations,

TABLE 7.1 PLA research on noncombat military operations

Source	Domestic operations							International operations				
	Disaster relief	Social stability maintenance	Counter-terror	Border control	Garrison operations	Nuke-chem-bio	Local development	Peace-keeping	Disaster relief	Military cooperation	Show of force	SLOC protection
Zhang (2004)	Y	Y	Y					Y				
Wang et al. (2006)	Y	Y	Y	Y			Y	Y				
Fu, Zhang, and Yang (2008)	Y	Y	Y		Y			Y			Y	
Han and Yue (2008)	Y	Y	Y	Y	Y			Y		Y		
Jundui tufa shijian guanli yanjiu xiaozu (2008)	Y	Y	Y									
Ran (2008)	Y	Y	Y					Y				
Yang, Xu, and Xu (2008)	Y	Y			Y		Y	Y	Y	Y	Y	
(No author) (2009)	Y	Y	Y		Y			Y				
Liu Xiaoli (2009)	Y	Y	Y	Y	Y	Y			Y		Y	Y
Liu Yuan (2009)	Y	Y	Y	Y				Y	Y	Y		
Shou and Xu (2009)	Y	Y	Y			Y		Y	Y	Y		
Song, Shi, and Yang (2009)	Y		Y	Y				Y	Y			
Wang Naichang (2009)	Y					Y						
Xiao and Li (2009)	Y	Y	Y	Y				Y	Y	Y		Y
Zhao (2009)	Y	Y	Y	Y	Y			Y	Y	Y		
Wu (2010)	Y	Y	Y	Y	Y			Y				Y
Total mentions	16	14	14	8	7	3	2	13	7	6	3	3

NOTE: This table reports the results of a survey of sixteen books on noncombat military operations that were written by teams of scholars from different PLA institutes. All but two were published since 2008.

riots, uprisings, rebellions, and large-scale mass incidents that would upset social order, especially in China's ethnic-minority regions. A third category includes counterterrorism, which primarily addresses domestic terrorism, such as the attacks against government officials in many areas of Xinjiang in the 1990s or the heightened concerns about terror attacks during the 2008 Olympics and the sixtieth anniversary of the People's Republic in October 2009. What unites these types of operations, along with others such as border security and garrison operations, is that they all stress bolstering regime security through maintaining social order and managing internal challenges to the CCP (Tan Wenhu 2008: 12).

As Table 7.1 shows, not all the new noncombat operations identified for China's armed forces are domestic. The two most frequently discussed international noncombat operations are peacekeeping and disaster relief. Peacekeeping is the only international noncombat operation that receives as much attention in Chinese writings as the domestic ones. In addition to enhancing China's image in international society, these operations play an important role in maintaining a stable external environment that facilitates China's development and bolsters regime security indirectly. Peacekeeping has attracted the most attention, and it is the one international noncombat operation in which the PLA and PAP have accumulated the most experience.

In the past decade, the deployment of PLA and PAP soldiers in noncombat operations is consistent with the emphasis on domestic and not international missions contained in doctrinal writings. Table 7.2 lists the number of soldiers who participated in major noncombat operations since 1998. Four events involved the deployment of more than one hundred thousand troops. During the ice storms that swept through twenty-one provinces in China in January 2008, for example, Chinese soldiers helped to clear thirty-two thousand kilometers of roads and restore power throughout the provinces (Xiao Tianliang 2009: 192). Likewise, following the 2008 earthquake in the Wenquan region of Sichuan, Chinese soldiers rescued 3,338 individuals and evacuated more than 1.4 million people (State Council Information Office 2009: 56). As Dennis Blasko (2010) notes, these deployments represent the largest use of Chinese soldiers since China's 1979 invasion of Vietnam. Overall, between 2005 and 2010, 2,785,000 PLA and PAP troops participated in disaster relief efforts, including 1,845,000 in 2009 and 2010 alone (State Council Information Office 2006, 2009, 2011).[10]

TABLE 7.2 Major troop deployments for domestic noncombat operations

Year	Event	PLA and PAP troops	Reserve and militia
1998	Major flooding of the Yangtze, Songhua, and Nen Rivers	300,000	5,000,000
2002	Flooding in Shanxi, Fujian and 19 other provinces	20,000	170,000
2003	Flooding of the Huai River in Jiangxi, Hunan, and Shanxi provinces	48,000	410,000
2008	Snow and ice storms in 21 provinces	224,000	1,036,000
2008	Earthquake in Wenquan, Sichuan	146,000	75,000
2008	Security for the Olympics	131,000	NA
2010	Earthquake in Yushu, Sichuan	16,000	NA
2010	Mudslides in Zhouqu, Gansu	7,600	NA

SOURCE: Liu and Cai (2010), State Council Information Office (2008), and Xiao (2009).
NOTE: Reliable data on PLA and PAP deployments in Tibet in 2009 and Urumqi in 2009 is unavailable.

By contrast, PLA and PAP involvement in international noncombat operations and the scope of their activities is limited. Between 1990 and 2010, 17,390 Chinese troops participated in UN peacekeeping operations—a small fraction of the number that has participated in domestic noncombat operations (State Council Information Office 2011: 71). China's first deployment of peacekeepers occurred in 1990, when five observers were dispatched to the UN Truce Supervision Organization mission in the Middle East, and such deployments have increased substantially in the past decade. As of December 2010, China had 1,955 peacekeepers overseas, primarily engineering troops and civilian police officers (State Council Information Office 2011). Although China has dispatched medical or search-and-rescue teams to ten different natural disasters in other countries since 2001, the total number of personnel involved was fewer than one thousand (Xiao Tianliang 2009: 193–195).[11] Likewise, roughly 7,040 sailors and marines have participated in antipiracy patrols in the Gulf of Aden since December 2008.[12] Finally, in February 2011, China's military conducted its first noncombatant evacuation operation when it dispatched four IL-76 transport aircraft from Xinjiang to Libya. The PLA Navy (PLAN) sent a frigate that was conducting escort missions in the Gulf of

Aden to the Mediterranean to escort civilian ships that had been chartered to evacuate Chinese citizens from Libya.

Chinese writings also discuss two other types of noncombat operations. The first is military cooperation, which includes military exchanges, joint military exercises, and military aid (Chen Yong 2006; Liu Xingliang 2004; Wang Guifang 2006). Broadly speaking, these efforts can help demonstrate China's growing military power, which is useful for strategic deterrence. At the same time, these activities also strengthen the PLA's ability to conduct domestic noncombat operations because many of the joint military exercises strengthen the PLA's ability to conduct counterterrorism or disaster relief operations at home. The majority of China's joint military exercises with other countries have emphasized counterterrorism operations and maritime operations (mostly search and rescue). For example, the largest such exercise, Peace Mission 2007, involved the deployment of 1,600 Chinese troops to Russia to conduct counterterrorism exercises. From 2003 to 2010, China has participated in thirty-three joint military exercises, most of which were based either around maritime search and rescue (fourteen) or counterterrorism (fourteen).[13] As Scott Tanner (2009) suggests, both peacekeeping and joint military exercises focusing on counterterrorism and search and rescue strengthen China's ability to conduct such operations within its own borders.

The second type of operation emphasizes border security. Broadly speaking, border security operations are designed to maintain stability along China's periphery, including the vast ethnic-minority frontiers in China as well as areas adjacent to China's land and sea borders. As discussed above, enhanced interdependence suggests new challenges to China's interests. One type is border closure and control operations (*fengkong xingdong*) designed to prevent the flow of illicit materials, weapons, and other contraband into China. According to one source, China conducted its first closure and control operation on its borders with Afghanistan, Pakistan, Tajikistan, Kyrgyzstan, and Nepal after the United States attacked the Taliban following September 11, 2001 (Liu Xiaoli 2009: 142). In 2005, for example, Hu Jintao specifically called for greater funding for frontier and coastal defense forces (Zong zhengzhi bu 2006: 207). Another type is what Chinese sources refer to as garrison operations, which include law enforcement in frontier regions and maritime areas as well as other operations designed to defend its interests on its immediate periphery. Border security is manpower intensive, involving two hundred thousand soldiers from local PLA units in various provincial military districts in addition to one hundred thousand border defense troops from the PAP (Blasko 2007: 310; Fravel 2007: 724, 727). Although border security is an old mission for the PLA and PAP, it has received renewed attention because of concerns about limiting flows across borders that might increase domestic instability.

As the example of border security illustrates, noncombat operations involve soldiers from both the PLA and the PAP. Although the PAP is a paramilitary force tasked with maintaining social stability, it cannot fulfill its missions without substantial support from the PLA.[14] During the 2010 earthquake in Yushu, Qinghai, for example, 12,798 troops were deployed in the first ten days of the disaster. Sixty-three percent of that force, or 8,143 soldiers, were PLA troops, primarily from the Lanzhou Military Region, and the others were from the PAP (Dong Qiang 2010: 10). During the unrest in Tibet in 2008 and the riots in Urumqi in 2009, soldiers from PAP units were deployed visibly, riding in armored vehicles or suppressing demonstrations (Tanner 2009). At the same time, consistent with its operational doctrine, PLA units were most likely sealing off affected areas to contain the spread of unrest, even though they were not observed in media reports (Chen Yong, Xu Guocheng, and Geng Weidong 2003: 490–505).

Organizing for Noncombat Operations

Organizational change to develop capabilities for noncombat operations is consistent with the domestic emphasis in Chinese doctrine and troop deployments for noncombat operations. The first area of change concerns training, an important indicator of priorities in any military organization. In 2001, a new *Program for Military Training and Evaluation* included, for the first time, noncombat operations. In September 2002, a new generation of military training regulations issued to implement the 2001 *Program* introduced training for noncombat operations, focusing on flood, rescue, and relief operations (Yang Jin, Xu Feng, and Xu Lisheng 2008: 3). Emphasis on training for these operations continued throughout the decade. In January 2008, for example, the General Staff Department's annual training directive highlighted training for noncombat operations in addition to combat-oriented training. The directive instructed the PLA to "strengthen training for non-war military operations" for counterterrorism, dealing with "sudden incidents," safeguarding stability, and disaster relief—all domestic operations. The directive also included, for the first time, a section for training for peacekeeping operations in addition to disaster relief and domestic stability operations (Liu Fengan 2008: 3). In June 2009, the PLA opened a peacekeeping training center for pre-deployment training for units formed to engage in peacekeeping operations (Lu Desheng 2009: 1). Starting in 2009, several large-scale exercises for noncombat operations were held, including Great Wall-6 on counterterrorism and Land-Sea 2009 on maritime search and rescue.

A second area of change emphasizes command mechanisms and force structure. In March 2005, a leading small group for emergency responses to sudden incidents was formed along with an Office for Emergency Response in the Operations Department of the General Staff Department (Tian Yixing 2009: 5). In 2006, the CMC and State Council called for strengthening coordination among the military and local governments, which resulted in a master plan for managing sudden incidents that was published in November 2006. Afterward, the General Staff Department established liaison mechanisms for coordinating with twenty ministries and agencies (Yang Zhongxu 2010). In January 2009, the CMC approved a force-building plan for noncombat operations (Dong Qiang 2010). By July 2010, the PLA had created eight specialized units, including maritime search and rescue teams; rapid response teams for floods, earthquakes, nuclear or chemical disasters, pandemics, and transportation emergencies; and rapid air transport and mobile communications support (Zhu Jiashu and Yaobao 2010: 4). These specialized emergency forces include almost one hundred thousand soldiers, with roughly fifty thousand soldiers at the national level and forty-five thousand soldiers at the provincial level (Xiong Zhengyan and Guochang 2010: 3).

The third area of organizational change to support noncombat operations concerns the creation of a legal regime. Relevant regulations and laws governing the PLA's activities in these areas have been issued in recent years, including the PLA's 2005 regulations (*tiaoli*) for participation in disaster relief and rescue operations and a 2007 law on handling domestic crises (*tufa shijian*; Liu Xiaoli 2009: 346–363).

The fourth and final area of change includes a dramatic increase in government spending on public security, which includes civilian police as well as the PAP. In 2009 alone, for example, spending on public security increased by more than 47 percent, to 129 billion yuan. In 2010, such spending increased by another 14 percent (Ministry of Finance 2010).[15] China's official defense expenditure also includes costs associated with noncombat operations. According to a 2010 white paper on national defense, one of three reasons listed for the growth of China's defense budget was "increased investment in improving capabilities for non-war military operations" (State Council Information Office 2011).

Long-range power projection capabilities are less prominent in writings on China's noncombat operations than perhaps might be expected. Interestingly, the National Defense University study discussed above does not identify aircraft carriers as a key capability for the PLAN to acquire, nor do other authoritative military publications on China's economic interests or maritime interests heavily stress aircraft carriers.[16] In the 2006 edition of *The Science of Campaigns* (*Zhanyi xue*), for example, the discussion of campaigns for sea-lane security focuses almost exclusively on counterblockade operations around China's ports, not on the projection of combat power in distant waters (Zhang Yuliang 2006: 539–546). In other discussions of China's maritime strategy, many military publications give less weight to developing naval combat power versus other means for protecting China's interests in various regions of the world (Tang Fuquan, Ye Xinrong, and Wang Daowei 2006: 66). To be sure, some power projection capabilities will be developed for peacetime operations such as peacekeeping and disaster relief, but in general new economic interests linked with development have not been mobilized to emphasize the long-range projection of combat power.

In addition, even discussions of naval modernization include noncombat operations. In a study from the National Defense University, scholars identified three main drivers for naval modernization: trends in naval modernization among the great powers; China's own maritime challenges including maritime sovereignty disputes, maritime resource conflicts, and sea-lane security; and Taiwan (Liu Xiaoli 2009). The most important new requirement for PLAN to meet these challenges was "comprehensive planning and development for peacetime and wartime" (Zheng Weiping, Wang Jianwei, and Liu Mingfu 2005: 229). This requirement stressed improving the strategic uses of PLAN in peacetime for activities such as maritime security cooperation, naval exchanges, disaster relief, fisheries protection, counterpiracy, and countersmuggling in addition to maritime deterrence. Although the scholars note that the same forces must have a wartime purpose, the focus on peacetime activities reflects an effect of expanding economic interests in the maritime domain. China's deployment of eight task forces to participate in counterpiracy patrols in the Gulf of Aden highlights the role that PLAN can play in noncombat operations.

Conclusion

This chapter examines why China's armed forces have sought to strengthen their ability to conduct noncombat operations, especially domestic ones, even though China's military modernization for traditional combat operations is far from complete. The answer lies in the relationship between economic growth and political instability. Although key to the legitimacy of leaders in developing countries, growth also creates new sources of domestic unrest and increases the vulnerability of the economy to external shocks, both of which, if unchecked, can harm future growth. Thus, developing countries such as China may use their armed forces to manage or prevent domestic unrest as well as to provide services that the state lacks, such as emergency disaster relief. For this same reason, they may also use their forces to help maintain stability in their international security environment, as such stability allows leaders to concentrate resources on domestic affairs. The logic linking economic growth and regime insecurity with noncombat operations is not unique to China and should apply to other countries undergoing similar transformations.

The role of regime insecurity in China's military strategy should not be overstated. China's economic growth continues to generate additional resources for the PLA's modernization drive, which emphasizes potential contingencies around its immediate periphery, especially Taiwan and increasingly the South China Sea. China spends more on defense than any other country apart from the United States. Nevertheless, to date, the principal effect of economic growth has not been to identify expansive interests overseas that require new capabilities for offensive operations and long-range combat power projection for their protection. Instead, it has reinforced China's interest in external stability as an important factor in its development and in its domestic stability, both to avoid a costly conflict and to ensure the ability to access resources in other countries and the free flow of trade on which China's economy relies.

The relationship between regime insecurity and other foreign policy outcomes in China since the end of the Cold War strengthens the plausibility of the argument in this article. Throughout the 1990s, for example, China compromised in numerous territorial disputes to enhance regime security, especially in its large ethnic-minority frontier regions (Fravel 2005; Fravel 2008b). Similarly, a key goal in the 2006 Foreign Affairs Work Conference was to ensure that foreign policy would serve China's domestic priorities linked with growth and stability (Glaser 2007). Because the CCP's legitimacy depends heavily on continued economic growth, concerns about political instability among China's leaders are likely to persist and should continue to influence China's military strategy.

Whether China's rise will continue to be peaceful is a question that animates scholars and policy makers alike. The growing role for noncombat operations in China's evolving military strategy provides cautious ground for limited optimism. These operations are manpower intensive and, moreover, require specialized training and organization. Although they may enhance the ability to conduct traditional combat operations, especially in the areas of logistics and communications, they draw resources away from other aspects of military modernization and may help dampen heightened security competition, especially in areas far from China. In particular, the rise of noncombat operations suggests that the PLA is devoting fewer resources to long-range power projection than it otherwise might and that such capabilities will grow at a slower rate than they otherwise would. The emphasis on noncombat operations, especially domestic ones, also suggests that China's leaders will continue to maintain an inward orientation and preoccupation with domestic politics, not foreign policy. As long as China's leaders remain wary of potential threats to regime security, the importance of developing noncombat operations is likely to continue.

Notes

For helpful comments, I thank Dennis Blasko, Michael Chase, Michael Glosny, Avery Goldstein, Paul Godwin, Michael Mastanduno, T. J. Pempel, Vipin Narang, Robert Ross, and Etel Solingen. For their generous financial support, I thank the Smith Richardson Foundation, the U.S. Institute of Peace, and the National Bureau of Asian Research. An earlier version of this chapter appeared as "Economic Growth, Regime Insecurity, and Military Strategy: Explaining the Rise of Non-combat Operations in China," in *Asian Security* 7, no. 3 (2011), and is reprinted here by permission of Taylor & Francis Ltd.

1. A complete and literal translation of the Chinese is "nonwar military operations." China's armed forces have three components: the People's Liberation Army (PLA), the People's Armed Police (PAP), and the militia. In this article, I focus on the PLA and PAP. The PLA's principal mission is external defense, but, as argued in this article, it also plays an important role in domestic noncombat operations, especially disaster relief. The PAP is a paramilitary force whose principal mission is maintaining public order. On these distinctions, see Blasko (2006: 18–19).

2. China's labor force consists of 1.06 billion people, of which 780 million are employed (*jiuye*).

3. For two overviews the PLA's new historic mission concept, see Hartnett (2009) and Mulvenon (2009: 1–20). Unlike Hartnett and Mulvenon, I translate *shiming* (使命) as "mission," to mean "purpose," and not "missions" as in specific military tasks or objectives, which is the common usage in the U.S. military. In other words, the party has identified a new purpose for the army of historical importance. Hu Jintao makes clear that there is one mission that requires the "correct grasp" of four tasks. English-language PLA publications such as the *Jiefangjun Bao* also translate *lishi shiming* as "historic mission."

4. Hartnett identified this and another online reference to Hu's speech, which has not been openly published (see Hu Jintao 2004).

5. The figure for 2009 is calculated on the basis of information in Mi (2010).

6. "Magnitude 7.9—Eastern Sichuan, China," U.S. Geological Survey, http://earthquake.usgs.gov/earthquakes/eqinthenews/2008/us2008ryan/#summary.

7. On discussion of the costs of conflict by Chinese military strategists, see Peng Guangqian and Yao Youzhi (2001: 423–425).

8. For a discussion of this concept, see Blasko (2009).

9. The Chinese definition of nonwar military operations includes some operations that would be classified as combat operations, such as sea-lane security.

10. The 2004 white paper notes that 230,000 PAP soldiers were deployed in such operations, but it does not mention the number of PLA soldiers.

11. Also, see Relief Web's database at http://reliefweb.int (accessed December 13, 2010).

12. This figure assumes that each of the seven flotillas includes roughly 880 sailors and marines.

13. See China's white papers on national defense, various years (State Council Information Office 2006, 2009, 2011).

14. According to the 2006 white paper, the PAP "is tasked to perform guard duties, handle emergencies, combat terrorism, and participate in and support national economic development. In wartime, it assists the PLA in defensive operations."

15. For a detailed analysis of related organizational changes, see Blasko (2010).

16. On the debate in China over carriers, see Li and Weuve (2010) and Ross (2009).

Works Cited

2009. *Zhixing duoyanghua junshi renwu zhong de zhengzhi gongzuo* [Political Work in the Implementation of Diversified Military Tasks]. N.p.: Benshu bianxiezu.

2011. "China's 'Floating Population' Exceeds 221 Million." *Xinhua*. February 27.

Bao Bin and Wang Guifang. 2006. "Tigao duifu feichuantong anquan weixie nengli: Quanjun feichuantong anquan lilun yantao hui shuyao" [Raise the Capability to Deal with Nontraditional Security Threats: Summary of an Army-wide Symposium on Nontraditional Security Theory]. *Jiefangjun bao*. November 16.

Blasko, Dennis. 2006. *The Chinese Army Today: Tradition and Transformation for the 21st Century*. New York: Routledge.

———. 2007. "PLA Ground Force Modernization and Mission Diversification: Underway in All Military Regions." In *Right Sizing the People's Liberation Army: Exploring the Contours of China's Military*, edited by Andrew Scobell and Roy Kamphausen. Carlisle, PA: Army War College, 281–384.

———. 2009. "Military Parades Demonstrate Chinese Concept of Deterrence." *China Brief* 9 (8): 7–10.

———. 2010. "U.S. and Chinese Approaches to Peacekeeping and Stability Operations." Paper presented at Naval War College conference on Chinese and American Approaches to Non-Traditional Security Challenges: Implications for the Maritime Domain, Newport, RI, May 4–5.

Chase, Michael, and Kristen Gunness. 2010. "The PLA's Multiple Military Tasks: Prioritizing Combat Operations and Developing MOOTW Capabilities." *China Brief* 10 (2): 5–7.

Chen, Jia. 2010. "Country's Wealth Divide Past Warning Level." *China Daily*. May 12.

Chen Yong. 2006. "Quanqiuhua beijing xia de jundui lishi shiming" [The Military's Historic Mission Under the Background of Globalization]. *Zhongguo junshi kexue* (1): 15–27.

Chen Yong, Xu Guocheng, and Geng Weidong, eds. 2003. *Gaoji jishu tiaojian xia de lujun zhanyi xue* [The Science of Army Campaigns Under High-Technology Conditions]. Beijing: Junshi kexue chubanshe.

China Labor Bulletin. 2007. "Unemployment in China." http://www.clb.org.hk/en/node/100060 (accessed November 12, 2010).

Choucri, Nazli, and Robert Carver North. 1975. *Nations in Conflict: National Growth and International Violence*. San Francisco: W. H. Freeman.

Copeland, Dale C. 2000. *Origins of Major War*. Ithaca, NY: Cornell University Press.

David, Steven R. 1991. "Explaining Third World Alignment." *World Politics* 43 (2): 233–256.

Dong Qiang. 2010. "Falu baozhang jiuyuan xingdong youxu gaoxiao" [Orderly and Efficient Legal Protection for Rescue Operations]. *Jiefangjun bao*. April 28.

Fan Yuejiang. 2003. "Lun jingji quanqiuhua dui woguo junshi anquan de yingxiang" [On the Impact of Economic Globalization on China's Military Security]. *Junshi jingji xueyuan xuebao* (3): 40–43.

Fan Zhenjiang and Ma Baoan, eds. 2007. *Junshi zhanlue lun* [On Military Strategy]. Beijing: Guofang daxue chubanshe.

Fewsmith, Joseph. 2009. "Social Order in the Wake of Economic Crisis." *China Leadership Monitor* (28): 1–13.

Fravel, M. Taylor. 2005. "Regime Insecurity and International Cooperation: Explaining China's Compromises in Territorial Disputes." *International Security* 30 (2): 46–83.

———. 2007. "Securing Borders: China's Doctrine and Force Structure for Frontier Defense." *Journal of Strategic Studies* 30 (4–5): 705–737.

————. 2008a. "China's Search for Military Power." *Washington Quarterly* 31 (3): 125–141.

————. 2008b. *Strong Borders, Secure Nation: Cooperation and Conflict in China's Territorial Disputes.* Princeton, NJ: Princeton University Press.

Fu Zhanhe, Zhang Ce, and Yang Jianjun, eds. 2008. *Feichuantong anquan junshi xingdong zhihui yanjiu* [Research on the Command of Nontraditional Security Military Operations]. Beijing: Jiefangjun chubanshe.

Gill, Bates, and James Mulvenon. 2002. "Chinese Military-Related Think Tanks and Research Institutions." *The China Quarterly* (171): 617–624.

Gilpin, Robert. 1981. *War and Change in World Politics.* New York: Cambridge University Press.

Glaser, Bonnie S. 2007. "Ensuring the 'Go Abroad' Policy Serves China's Domestic Priorities." *China Brief* 7 (5): 2–5.

Han Weigong and Yue Shixin, eds. 2008. *Wancheng duoyanghua junshi renwu falu yuyong yanjiu* [Research on Legal Applications for Accomplishing Diversified Military Tasks]. Beijing: Jiefangjun chubanshe.

Hartnett, Daniel M. 2009. *The PLA's Domestic and Foreign Activities and Orientation.* Testimony before the U.S.-China Economic and Security Review Commission.

Holsag, Jonathan. 2009. "Embracing Chinese Global Security Ambitions." *Washington Quarterly* 32 (3): 105–118.

Huang Zaisheng and Zhang Kenan. 2008. "Jingji quanqiuhua beijing xia guojia liyi yu woguo anquan zhanlue xuanze" [National Interests Against the Backdrop of Economic Globalization and Our Country's Security Strategy Choice]. *Junshi jingji yanjiu* (6): 6–8.

Hu Jintao. 2004. "Renqing xinshiji xinjieduan wojun lishi shiming" [Recognize Our Army's Historic Mission in the New Phase of the New Century]. December 24. http://gfjy.jiangxi.gov.cn/yi1.asp?id=11349.htm (accessed June 23, 2009).

Huntington, Samuel P. 1968. *Political Order in Changing Societies.* New Haven, CT: Yale University Press.

Jiang Zemin. 2006. *Jiang Zemin Wenxuan* [Jiang Zemin's Selected Works], vol. 3. Beijing: Renmin chubanshe.

Jiefangjun bao bianjibu. 2006. "Lun xinshiji xinjieduan wojun de lishi shiming" [On Our Army's Historic Mission in the New Period of the New Century]. *Jiefangjun bao.* January 9.

Jundui tufa shijian guanli yanjiu xiaozu, ed. 2008. *Jundui canyu chuzhi difang tufa shijian lingdao shiwu* [Leading Practice for the Military's Participation in Local Sudden Incidents]. Shenyang: Baishan chubanshe.

Kennedy, Paul M. 1987. *The Rise and Fall of the Great Powers: Economic Change and Military Conflict from 1500 to 2000.* New York: Random House.

Kugler, Jacek, and Douglas Lemke, eds. 1996. *Parity and War: Evaluations and Extensions of the War Ledger.* Ann Arbor: University of Michigan Press.

Li Jijun. 2004. "Quanqiuhua shidai de Zhongguo guojia anquan sikao" [Reflections on China's National Security in the Era of Globalization]. *Zhongguo junshi kexue* (2): 38–43.

Li, Nan, and Christopher Weuve. 2010. "China's Aircraft Carrier Ambitions: An Update." *Naval War College Review* 63 (1): 13–32.

Ling Shengyin and Hua Ren. 2005. "Jingji quanqiuhua tiaojian xia jiaqiang jundui jianshe de sikao" [Thoughts on Military Building in the Age of Globalization]. *Junshi jingji xueyuan xuebao* (12): 20–23.

Liu Fengan. 2008. "Goujian xinxihua tiaojianxia junshi xunlian xin tixi" [Establishing a New System for Military Training Under Informationized Conditions]. *Jiefangjun bao*. August 1.

Liu Junjun and Cai Pengcheng. 2010. "Zai suixing duoyanghua junshi renwu zhong chengzhang: fang Zongcan yingjiban zhuren Li Haiyang" [Growth During Implementation of Diversified Military Tasks: Interview with Director Li Haiyang of the General Staff Department's Emergency Response Office]. *Jiefangjun bao*. December 3.

Liu Xiaoli, ed. 2009. *Jundui yingfu zhongda tufa shijian he weiji feizhangzheng junshi xingdong yanjiu* [A Study of Nonwar Military Operations by the Armed Forces to Deal with Major Sudden Incidents or Crises]. Beijing: Guofang daxue chubanshe.

Liu Xingliang. 2004. "Xin anquanguan dui xinshiji guoji anquan de yingxiang" [Impact of the New Security Concept on International Security in the New Century]. *Zhongguo junshi kexue* (1): 90–96.

Liu Yuan, ed. 2009. *Feizhanzheng junshi xingdong zhong de zhengzhi gongzuo* [Political Work in Nonwar Military Operations]. Beijing: Jiefangjun chubanshe.

Lu Desheng. 2009. "Quanjun weihe gongzuo huiyi zaiJing zhaokai" [Armywide Meeting on Peacekeeping Work Held in Beijing]. *Jiefangjun bao*. June 26.

Mearsheimer, John J. 2001. *The Tragedy of Great Power Politics*. New York: Norton.

Mi Aini. 2010. "Weilai 10 nian quntixing shijian cheng zhizheng zuida tiaozhan" [Mass Incidents Will Be the Greatest Challenge to Governance over the Next Ten Years]. *Liaowang dongfang zhoukan* (4): 30–31.

Ministry of Finance. 2010. *Report on the Implementation of the Central and Local Budgets for 2009 and on the Draft Central and Local Budgets for 2010*. Beijing: Ministry of Finance.

Mulvenon, James. 2009. "Chairman Hu and the PLA's 'New Historic Missions.'" *China Leadership Monitor* (27): 1–11.

Naughton, Barry. 2007. *The Chinese Economy: Transition and Growth*. Cambridge, MA: MIT Press.

Nodskov, Kim. 2009. *The Long March to Power: The New Historic Missions of the People's Liberation Army*. Copenhagen: Royal Danish Defence College Publishing House.

Office of the Secretary of Defense. 2010. *Military Power of the People's Republic of China 2010*. Washington, DC: U.S. Department of Defense.

Organski, A. F. K. 1958. *World Politics*. New York: Knopf.

Organski, A. F. K., and Jacek Kugler. 1980. *The War Ledger*. Chicago: University of Chicago Press.

Peng Guangqian and Yao Youzhi, eds. 2001. *Zhanlue xue* [The Science of Military Strategy]. Beijing: Junshi kexue chubanshe.

Posen, Barry. 2003. "Command of the Commons: The Military Foundation of U.S. Hegemony." *International Security* 28 (1): 5–46.

Ran Ali, ed. 2008. *Shiming: Duoyanghua junshi renwu de feizhanzheng xingdong houqin* [Mission: Nonwar Military Operations Logistics for Diversified Military Tasks]. Beijing: Haichao chubanshe.

Ross, Robert S. 2009. "China's Naval Nationalism: Sources, Prospects, and the U.S. Response." *International Security* 34 (2): 46–81.

Shi Hongtao. 2004. "Zhongguo nengyuan anquan zaoyu 'Maliujia kunju'" [China's Energy Security Encounters the "Malacca Predicament"]. *Zhongguo qingnian bao.* June 15.

Shih, Victor. 2010. "China's 8,000 Credit Risks." *Asian Wall Street Journal.* February 8.

Shou Xiaosong, and Xu Jingnian, eds. 2009. *Jundui yingfu feichuantong anquan weixie yanjiu* [Research on the Military's Handling of Nontraditional Security Threats]. Beijing: Jiefangjun chubanshe.

Song Guocai, Shi Limin, and Yang Shu, eds. 2009. *Feizhanzheng junshi xingdong shili yanjiu* [Case Studies of Nonwar Military Operations]. Beijing: Junshi kexue chubanshe.

State Council Information Office. 2006. *China's National Defense in 2006.* Beijing: State Council Information Office.

———. 2009. *China's National Defense in 2008.* Beijing: State Council Information Office.

———. 2010. *China's Human Resources.* Beijing: State Council Information Office.

———. 2011. *China's National Defense in 2010.* Beijing: State Council Information Office.

Sun Huangtian. 2009. "Guoji jingrong weiji dui wojun caijing gongzuo de yingxiang yu duice" [The Impact of the International Financial Crisis on Our Army's Financial Work and Related Countermeasures]. *Junshi jingji yanjiu* (2): 5–8.

Tan Wenhu. 2008. "Duoyanghua junshi renwu qianyin junshi xunlian chuangxin" [Diversified Military Tasks Draw Innovations in Military Training]. *Jiefangjun bao.* July 1.

Tang Fuquan, Ye Xinrong, and Wang Daowei. 2006. "Zhongguo haiyang weiquan zhanlue chutan" [Initial Exploration of the Strategy for Protecting China's Maritime Rights]. *Zhongguo junshi kexue* (6): 56–67.

Tanner, Murray Scot. 2004. "China Rethinks Unrest." *Washington Quarterly* 27 (3): 137–156.

———. 2009. "How China Manages Internal Security Challenges and Its Impact on PLA Missions." In *Beyond the Strait: PLA Missions Other Than Taiwan,* edited by Roy Kamphausen, David Lai, and Andrew Scobell. Carlisle, PA: Strategic Studies Institute, Army War College, 39–98.

Tian Yixing. 2009. "Wojun chuzhi tufa shijian zhihui gaoxiao kuaiti" [Our Army's Speedy Command System for Managing Sudden Incidents]. *Jiefangjun bao.* September 23.

Waltz, Kenneth N. 1979. *Theory of International Politics.* New York: McGraw-Hill.

Wang Guifang. 2006. "Guoji liyi yu Zhongguo anquan zhanlue xuanze" [National Interests and Choosing China's Security Strategy]. *Zhongguo junshi kexue* (1): 76–83.

Wang, Hongjiang. 2009. "President Hu Calls for 'Mighty' Support from Armed Forces for National Interests, Social Stability." *Xinhua*. March 11.

Wang Mingwu, Chang Yongzhi, Xu Ge, and Zhang Nan, eds. 2006. *Feizhanzheng junshi xingdong* [Nonwar Military Operations]. Beijing: Guofang daxue chubanshe.

Wang Nachang. 2009. *Qiangxian jiuzai xingdong yanjiu* [Research on Rescue and Relief Operations]. Beijing: Junshi kexue chubanshe.

Wang Shumei, Shi Jiazhu, and Xu Mingshan. 2007. "Luxing jundui lishi shiming, shuli kexue haiquanguan" [Establish the Scientific Maritime Rights Concept to Fulfill the Military's Historic Mission]. *Zhongguo junshi kexue* (2): 139–146.

Wang Wenrong, ed. 1999. *Zhanlue xue* [The Science of Military Strategy]. Beijing: Guofang daxue chubanshe.

Watson, Cynthia. 2009. "The Chinese Armed Forces and Non-Traditional Missions: A Growing Tool of Statecraft." *China Brief* 9 (4): 9–12.

Wen Jiabao. 2010. *Zhengfu gongzuo baogao* [Report on the Work of the Government]. Beijing: Quanguo renmin daibiao dahui.

World Bank. 2010. World Development Indicators. http://databank.worldbank.org (accessed November 30, 2010).

Wu Chaojin, ed. 2010. *Feichuantong anquan jundui xingdong wenti yanjiu* [Research on Nontraditional Military Operations]. Beijing: Junshi kexue chubanshe.

Xiao Tianliang. 2009. *Junshi liliang de feizhanzheng yunyong* [The Nonwar Use of Military Power]. Beijing: Guofang daxue chubanshe.

Xiao Tianliang and Li Guoting, eds. 2009. *Feizhanzheng junshi xingdong zhishi wenda* [Questions and Answers About Nonwar Military Operations]. Beijing: Junshi kexue chubanshe.

Xinhua. 2011. "China's 'Floating Population' Exceeds 221 Million." February 27.

Xiong Zhengyan and Cao Guochang. 2010. "Zhongguo jundui yingji zhuanye liliang yijin 10 wanren" [Specialized Emergency Forces in the Chinese Military Approaches 100,000]. *Jiefangjun bao*. October 13.

Xu Jingyue. 2011. "Hu Jintao zai shengbuji lingdao ganbu zhuanti yantaoban kaibanshi shang jianghua" [Hu Jintao's Speech at the Opening of a Special Study and Discussion Session for Provincial and Ministerial Leading Cadres]. *Xinhua*. February 19.

Yang Jin, Xu Feng, and Xu Lisheng, eds. 2008. *Feizhanzheng junshi xingdong gailun* [Introduction to Nonwar Military Operations]. Beijing: Junshi yiwen chuban she.

Yang Zhongxu. 2010. "13.7 wan dajun ruhe bushu" [How 137,000 Troops Were Deployed]. *Zhongguo xinwen zhoukan* (20): 38–42.

Zakaria, Fareed. 1998. *From Wealth to Power: The Unusual Origins of America's World Role*. Princeton, NJ: Princeton University Press.

Zhang Aihua, ed. 2004. *Feizhanzheng xingdong* [Nonwar Operations]. Beijing: Jiefangjun chubanshe.

Zhang Wei. 2007. "Guojia haishang anquan lilun" [Discussion of National Maritime Security Theory]. *Zhongguo junshi kexue* (1): 84–91.

Zhang Yuliang. 2006. *Zhanyi xue* [The Science of Campaigns]. Beijing: Guofang daxue chubanshe.

Zhao Zongqi, ed. 2009. *Suixing duoyanghua junshi renwu zuzhi zhihui yanjiu* [Organization and Command for Carrying Out Diversified Military Tasks]. Beijing: Junshi kexue chubanshe.

Zheng Weiping and Liu Mingfu, eds. 2005. *Jundui xin de lishi shiming lun* [On the Military's New Historic Mission]. Beijing: Renmin wuzhuang chubanshe.

Zheng Weiping, Wang Jianwei, and Liu Mingfu, eds. 2005. *Jundui luoshi kexue fazhanguan* [The Military's Implementation of the Scientific Development Concept]. Beijing: Renmin wuzhuang chubanshe.

Zhu Jiashu and Wang Yaobao. 2010. "Wojun jiji canyu qiangxian jiuzai he reda zhuyi jiuyuan" [Our Army Actively Participates in Disaster and Relief and Humanitarian Aid]. *Jiefangjun bao.* July 31.

Zong zhengzhi bu. 2006. *Shuli he luoshi kexue fazhanguan lilun xuexi duben* [A Reader for Establishing and Implementing the Theory of Scientific Development]. Beijing: Jiefangjun chubanshe [internal circulation].

8 Information-Age Economics and the Future of the East Asian Security Environment
Michael C. Horowitz

T HIS CHAPTER FOCUSES ON THE WAY CHANGES IN MODES OF military and economic production in the information age may shape the relationship between economics and security in East Asia. The global spread of commercial information technology, especially electronics and computer systems, potentially presents a double-edged sword for the East Asian security environment. This chapter argues that the globalization of production and spread of civilian information technology throughout East Asia may cause spillovers into the military realm in the medium term in a way that makes it easier for many East Asian states to become cutting-edge defense manufacturers. The result of such a shift, while making wars of conquest more difficult, would be increased instability throughout the region.

Even for the United States, the production of big-ticket defense items like carriers, fighters, and tanks currently requires components drawn from subcontractors in countries around the world. Stephen Brooks argues that this globalization of the production of military technology is stabilizing for the international security environment because it generates dependencies that encourage actors to cooperate with one another (Brooks 2005).

What about a future world in which military power comes in large part from unmanned aerial vehicles (UAVs), cybercapabilities, and advanced robotics, whose core technologies are commercially available, rather than from traditional big-ticket weapons? Given America's preexisting conventional military edge, it would be extremely difficult for a country to challenge the

United States in the area of manned fighters, manned tanks, or aircraft carriers. For example, even if the Chinese Navy does push to develop fleet aircraft carriers, something that is still uncertain at this point, the organizational challenges associated with operating them, if history holds, will guarantee a long learning period.

In the medium term, the current globalization of commercial production and the spread of information technologies could introduce a shift in the production of military power in East Asia. As the basis of defense production shifts from technologies whose underlying basis is more exclusively military to those more based on commercial software, it could decentralize the capacity to produce important military hardware. As a region with several developed and rapidly industrializing economies, many countries in East Asia, including but not limited to China, Japan, and South Korea, could take advantage of these spillovers in the production of military power toward software rather than hardware. The result is that more countries will have very similar advanced military technologies than at present, although the pattern of diffusion is likely to be halting and asymmetric. This trend could be especially important in light of China's rapid economic development, which is already increasing its capacity to integrate new military technologies.

The chapter begins by outlining the role of globalization in driving East Asian economic development and how that process has resulted in many East Asian nations now leading the way in information-age production. A discussion follows of how the commercial spread of advanced information technologies could spill over into the military realm and, were this to occur, the potential consequences for the international security arena. The basis of growing multipolarity in defense production in East Asia could have several consequences. For example, if more countries in East Asia produce their own advanced weapons, it could potentially destabilize traditional alliance patterns, as it would remove a major capabilities-based reason for some alliances. Such changes, especially given the prevalence of territorial disputes in East Asia, could make it harder for the region to avoid arms-race dynamics, although economic interdependence would certainly have a dampening effect. As scholars dating back to Deutch and Singer have shown, controlling arms race dynamics becomes difficult in multipolar military systems since each state has to worry about the balance of power with so many different potential actors (Deutch and Singer 1964: 403). In East Asia, the combination of existing territorial conflicts and nationalism means regional stability in a world of multipolar defense production would likely rest on a knife's edge rather than on a stable foundation (Friedberg 1994). Although these scenarios are certainly speculative and far from certain, the evidence presented below shows that economic trends already under way in East Asia could make this more unstable future a potential reality.

The Information Age and Economic Leadership in East Asia

Despite the economic turmoil of the past several years, as Chapter 1 of this volume shows, the interconnections among the economies of East Asia have increased, as have their ties to the United States. Thus far, East Asian governments have mostly refrained from enacting significant trade restrictions. Most multinational corporations are still heavily invested in global supply chains running through East Asia. The number of regional trade agreements and level of trade between countries has grown throughout this decade and regional interdependence reached levels not seen since before World War II by 2004 (Petri 2006: 386–387). Even China and Japan, which have experienced nationalistic flare-ups during the past several years, experienced eleven consecutive years of higher bilateral trade before a brief decline in 2009 due to the financial crisis. China, not the United States, is now Japan's largest trading partner (Japan External Trade Organization 2010).

Globalization processes have combined with several other trends to accelerate East Asian leadership in new technological areas. Although they already occupy critical roles in global supply chains, several East Asian countries are also at the forefront of commercial information-age technologies. This means that the preexisting spread of commercial information technologies and advanced production practices are increasing the baseline advanced industrial capacities of many East Asian countries. China's rising economic power, combined with the economies of Japan, Singapore, South Korea, and Taiwan, make East Asia perhaps the most vibrant economic region in the world. These countries lead the world in several emerging technological areas, including Japan in robotics, South Korea and Taiwan in substrate glass production for LCDs, and China and Taiwan in semiconductors. Asian countries feature the highest rate of high-technology exports in the world (International Bank for Reconstruction and Development and World Bank 2009: chap. 5). It is progress in the adoption of advanced information technology, combined with access to transportation hubs, which allows East Asian countries to link themselves into new global supply chains (Arvis et al. 2007). East Asian leadership in burgeoning information technology arenas has grown to the point that some experts predict that "the second Internet revolution won't be North American-centric" (Newman, Hook, and Moothart 2006: 51).

Many East Asian states have also used innovative public-private partnerships to nurture key emerging technological markets. For example, investments in research parks to create interindustry synergies; government support for links between key industries and Korean universities; and governmental research-and-development spending on nanotechnology, biotechnology, and other areas characterize South Korea's successful efforts to stay at the forefront of high-technology industries (World Bank 2008: 145).

Another indicator of future development prospects is the number of people in a given country who are receiving advanced degrees in the hard sciences and other areas relevant to the information economy. On this metric, the nations of East Asia do extremely well, even considering students who earn advanced degrees in the United States, which should stack the deck against East Asian countries, as they have to travel to the United States for school.[1] For example, for the first time in 2006, two Chinese universities passed the University of California, Berkeley, as the universities producing the largest number of people with bachelor's degrees who went on to receive hard science or engineering doctorates in the United States. Of the top-twenty feeder universities for U.S. science and engineering doctoral programs, half came from countries in Asia (Mervis 2008). In 2007, American-born students were more likely to receive doctorates than foreign-born students in fields like the humanities and social sciences, but foreign-born students were significantly more likely than U.S.-born students to receive doctorates in engineering (30 percent to 8 percent) or the physical sciences (24.2 percent to 12.6 percent) (National Opinion Research Center 2008).

In addition to shifts driven by the educational environment, the growth of many foreign firms means the United States is no longer the only location for those interested in working in cutting-edge scientific fields. As David Heenan writes, "Thousands of New Americans have begun boomeranging back to their native countries. What's more, although the exodus is taking place across a wide spectrum, it is especially strong in leading-edge professions in science, technology, and business—the 'high-end' sectors so much in demand in today's Innovation Economy" (Heenan 2005: xi–xii).[2] In addition, although these trends will be most powerful for the stronger economic actors in the region, especially China, they will also have important implications for other regional actors. It is also important to note that the United States is not standing still while these developments are occurring. Despite continuing economic struggles, the United States remains the engine of the global economy, particularly when it comes to technological innovation.

Globalization, Defense Production, and Regional Stability

For most of modern history, most countries with similar levels of economic sophistication could produce relatively similar weapons.[3] What separated the military technologies possessed by countries were small differences in quality and especially the ability of states to ramp up production in times of need. Advantages were often quantitative or based on superior training and organization, not due to significant qualitative differences in technology.

For example, in the age of sail, every navy had ships of the line based on similar, if not exactly the same, technologies. Smaller powers had navies that in function and form looked almost exactly like those of the great powers, only they were smaller (Horowitz 2010). This began to change during the steel battleship era because of the escalating costs of production, and culminated with the overwhelming costs associated with adopting carrier warfare. When World War II ended, the United States (and Great Britain to a lesser extent) had an enormous surplus of aircraft carriers. These carriers were sold or given to allies around the world. However, as the carriers became obsolete over the following few decades, many navies decided to abandon carrier warfare and increasingly either bandwagoned with the United States or developed alternative capabilities to counter the carrier, like antiship missiles and submarines. The escalating cost of developing carriers combined with the organizational complexities involved in operating them placed carrier warfare out of the reach of nearly every navy around the world (Horowitz 2010). No navy other than that of the United States could afford to spend several billion dollars on an aircraft carrier plus hundreds of millions of dollars a year in maintenance.[4]

In addition to rising costs and operational complexity, since the early Cold War the intense systems integration requirements for fully adopting advanced weapons systems has created incentives for the globalization of military production and has narrowed the number of states that could actually develop modern platforms. Stephen Brooks, in his book, *Producing Security*, argues that this trend, the globalization of production, is generally positive for international stability. He shows that defense production, even in the United States, became internationalized in the late Cold War.[5] His evidence shows that building sensitive military technologies in the United States increasingly requires the help of subcontractors that either have international ties or are based outside of the United States. This trend, writes Brooks, may actually make international conflict less likely. The dispersion of the production of military technologies across borders means countries have to be more cautious in their military actions, since if they anger or offend too many other states, they will no longer have the ability to buy and build key components necessary to fuel their militaries (Brooks 1999, 2005).[6] Moreover, rather than providing resources for future production, the repressive techniques required to govern conquered states will undermine the business environment necessary for success in knowledge-based industries. Both Brooks and Jonathan Caverley argue that the internationalized production of military systems is not just a necessity because of modern global supply chains; it is often preferable. Allowing more firms to compete for contracts leads to more efficiency and lower prices (Brooks 2007: 653–654; Caverley 2007).

Globalized production gave the United States a significant advantage over the Soviet Union in the late Cold War. Because the Soviet Union still restricted production to domestic companies, it could not take advantage of lower prices and higher efficiencies, thus helping the American military leap ahead of the Soviet Union in the 1980s. Extremely capital-intensive platforms like fighters, bombers, and aircraft carriers dominated the arsenals of late Cold War militaries. The United States possessed superior systems integration skills to go along with its general economic and political advantages, thereby allowing American defense contractors to integrate components made in a dozen countries into tanks and other equipment that far outstripped the capabilities of any other country. This created a barrier to entry in the production of conventional military power that still exists today in East Asia. Indeed, as Kirshner points out, most of the actors that violently oppose the United States attempt to do so either through terrorism or the acquisition of weapons of mass destruction—and sometimes both (Kirshner 2008).[7] In short, because of the globalization of military production and America's lead in tacit knowledge concerning the construction of the big weapons platforms relevant for producing military power today, the United States has maintained an enormous military edge in East Asia (and throughout the world).

Information-Age Spillovers and Asia's Military Future

What do these two things—the spread of information-age commercial knowledge and the globalized character of defense production—have to do with each other? Critical is the possibility of spillover effects between existing information-age commercial technologies and future military applications. Although in the past it was military research that led to civilian spinoffs, with the Internet being a prime example, today the possibilities go in the other direction as well. As information-age technologies become further embedded in military hardware, this naturally causes changes in the way defense companies produce equipment and even in the types of equipment that national governments want for their militaries. Globalization processes are accelerating the integration of information technologies into military hardware and the capacity of defense and commercial firms around the world to leverage those technologies.

Preexisting commercial developments in East Asia could spill over into the military realm in several ways. First, dual-use technologies utilized by commercial firms could form the basis for those firms to shift toward military production in the future. Barry Watts, of the Center for Strategic and Budgetary Assessments, argues that the critical importance of nondefense research and development for future military technologies means many more nations will be able to leverage their commercial capabilities to build a relevant level of military power, if they choose to do so (Watts 2008: 56–57). A report written in 2006 by an international nongovernmental organization describes the growing linkage between commercial and military technologies:

> As one analyst put it, the technologies that are transforming modern weapons are often the same as those "revolutionising aspects of everyday life, from the supermarket checkout to personal communications." Arms companies and national militaries frequently borrow technology from civilian products and applications. In many cases they use commercially available components sourced from highly globalised civilian industries. For example, digital signal processors used in the latest DVD players can also be found in guidance/target acquisition systems for fighter jet missile systems, and microwave chip technology used in

Hellfire missiles and Apache Longbow attack helicopters is also found in satellite TV dishes and mobile phones. (Control Arms Campaign 2006: 13)

Second, most sales of advanced weapons now involve some sort of licensing or coproduction agreement with defense firms in recipient countries. These agreements are designed, to various extents, to help indigenous defense contractors learn from the expertise of the exporting defense contractors. For example, when South Korea purchased F-16 C/D fighters from Lockheed Martin, the deal included a licensing agreement with Korea Aerospace Industries for coproduction and maintenance (*Defense Industry Daily* 2009).[8] Globalized defense production and licensing agreements can even more directly lead to the spread of dual-use, information-age technologies that may be especially helpful for next-generation weapons platforms. A study of U.S. defense production by Lieutenant Colonel Mark A. McLean, U.S. Air Force, describes how arms exports can lead to the transfer of advanced production knowledge. McLean shows how the exchange of information about producing entire systems or subcomponents then enters the corporate memory of the recipient firm, thereby increasing its tacit knowledge for future production. In addition, recipient firms engaged in trade with third parties can indirectly transfer advanced knowledge about production processes. For example, the Blue Lamp program run by the U.S. State Department monitors the way recipients of U.S. defense exports use the technologies. It has found that "unfavorable" technology transfers, meaning transfers to third parties, happened 18 percent of the time in 2003 (McLean 2005: 7; also see U.S. Department of State 2008).

Third, the spread of today's commercial technologies, if they become the dual-use technologies of the future, could enhance the military capabilities of recipient nations. For example, the diffusion of GPS systems that are accurate within meters or even feet means that even those nations without access to U.S. military satellites may soon have the ability to deploy precision or near-precision weapons. The GPS tail kits placed on joint direct-attack munitions in the U.S. military, according to one estimate, cost only about $1,200 each (U.S. Air Force 2006). Moreover, as more states begin launching satellites into orbit, at least some are likely to gain the ability to control more elements of the system themselves.

These mechanisms through which the spread of commercial technologies today could lead to changes in the ability of East Asian countries, as well as the United States, to produce military power tomorrow could be accentuated by underlying developments in the very platforms countries use to produce military power. The developments growing out of the information age are already generating two areas that seem the most likely to allow East Asian countries to convert their growing expertise in the economics of the information age into the ability to become major defense producers. The fields of cyberwarfare and robotics, in particular, represent the new technologies most likely to have a far-reaching impact on the overall security environment.

First cyberwarfare represents a potentially new field of warfare, like air power or submarine warfare. However, unlike those areas, circuit boards will provide the terminal punch at both the front and the back ends. Even low-powered personal computers, when connected to the Internet, can serve as the base for potentially devastating denial of service attacks, intrusions designed to steal classified information, or attacks designed to take down power grids or other critical services (Arquilla 2003: 219). Many East Asian countries are working to develop cybercapabilities. For example, Taiwan has heavily invested in information warfare, possibly including the development of dangerous computer viruses designed to disrupt the systems of potential adversaries. One variation of the Taiwanese-created CIH virus (named after its creator Chen Ing Hau and also known as the Chernobyl virus) reportedly disabled 360,000 computers on the Chinese mainland in the late 1990s (Mulvenon 2004: 157).

Taiwan's efforts may pale in comparison to what many think is the pace of cyberwarfare-related research in the PRC. Chinese hackers launch daily attacks against the Department of Defense and have had some successes, including the electronic theft of unclassified materials. The Chinese-based GhostNet operation uncovered by the Canadian cybersecurity specialist Rafal A. Rohozinski in 2009 reportedly infiltrated 1,200 computer systems in 103 countries, including both governments and nongovernmental organizations (Markoff 2009). Given the secret and anonymous nature of the attacks, these revelations suggest that the real extent of Chinese operations is probably much more significant than those uncovered.[9]

The technologies at the root of these information-warfare capabilities are fundamentally commercial and off-the-shelf, although militaries may have particular specialized systems. This means that any country can master them, and even countries that lack widespread Internet access can theoretically develop robust information-attack capabilities. Although defenders of classified networks have to win every battle—repel every threat to their systems—adversaries have to punch through only once to steal classified material, input dangerous viruses, or take systems offline. There is some tendency to down-play the importance of information attacks, as they are generally nonkinetic. However, the recent Stuxnet (Markoff 2010) virus, released in multiple locations around the world and apparently designed to disable Iran's nuclear reactor at Busheur, demonstrates that the capabilities are no longer just academic theory. The U.S. military edge and system for producing military power relies in no small part on satellites, real-time information, UAVs, handheld GPS, and other linked components. Attacks that took down U.S. information systems in a crisis could therefore make U.S. military forces particularly vulnerable.[10] In East Asia, information attacks could play a critical role in conflicts likely to be decided primarily in the air and on the oceans. Disabling information networks could cut off forces from their home bases or shut down some types of weapons systems, thus shifting the deciding factor in a battle from the qualitative superiority of networked forces to whichever side has quantitative superiority and the greatest ability to operate off the grid. This is not to say that such an outcome is inevitable just that the spread of advanced computing technologies could have serious implications for the security environment.

Second, just as commercial technologies are turning cyberwarfare into a reality, the field of robotics represents one of the most important new areas of warfare. Just a decade ago, UAVs were still the stuff of Terminator movies to the general public. Now, however, Global Hawk and Predator UAVs have played an enormous role on the battlefields of Afghanistan and Iraq, helping the United States track and sometimes even eliminate insurgent bases and leaders. The United States leads the world in the development of unmanned military systems, from UAVs to battlefield robots designed to seek out and disable improvised explosive devices. However, the United States is far from the only country applying developments in robotics to warfare. In 2008, Unmanned Vehicle Systems International, an international nongovernmental organization that serves as a clearinghouse for those interested in UAVs, boasted more than 250 corporate and government members from thirty-five different countries (van Blyenbrugh 2008).

East Asian countries are among the global leaders in robotics, beginning with Japan, which hosts the International Robotics Exhibition every year. Japan's edge stems from a combination of governmental support and private sector interest. Although Japan has not yet committed massive resources to building explicitly military UAVs, a research report on the Japanese UAV market produced by the U.S. Department of Commerce in 2006 cited the huge potential of Japanese companies if and when they decide to pursue indigenous UAVs for military purposes (U.S. Department of Commerce 2006). South Korea, like in many other high-technology sectors, is also at the forefront of robotics. With more than 80 percent of homes possessing broadband Internet access and a growth rate of more than 40 percent for its robotics industry since 2003, South Korean corporations could become global industry leaders (Singer 2009: 243). The United States rejected an attempt by South Korea to purchase a Global Hawk system in 2005, before reversing course a few years later. It is not yet clear whether South Korea will purchase the systems, given its own domestic plans and the global financial crisis (Global Security 2009).

The Chinese People's Liberation Army and Chinese universities are also spending a great deal on robotics. Commercial Chinese robotics, such as robot waiters produced by the Chinese Academy of Sciences and the "bionic fish" produced by Beijing University, show a clear aptitude for further developments. The Chinese military is also experimenting with UAVs (Office of the Secretary of Defense 2009). A particularly interesting story suggests that China may be working on how to turn its retired older fighter aircraft into UAVs that could flood the battle space in a future conflict and overwhelm an opponent through the sheer power of numbers (Singer 2009: 245–246).[11]

There is a close linkage between the production of civilian and military equipment in the area of UAVs. A great number of UAVs already exist for nonmilitary purposes, including border surveillance, crop spraying on large farms, and other tasks. Converting commercial UAVs to military purposes, in the simplest case, can involve little other than adding more surveillance equipment.

In addition, UAVs have a much lower unit cost than manned fighters, which makes them more affordable and means that losses in training or in battle will likely be more acceptable.[12] For example, a MQ-1 Predator drone reportedly costs about $5 million per unit, compared to more than $200 million per F-22. Robotic systems like the MQ-1 Predator are also functionally simpler than their manned equivalents. They involve fewer subcomponents and simpler production tasks, presuming that a company has mastered the core technologies (which is admittedly a large question). This suggests a very different production future from that for systems such as the F-22 or F-35 in the United States.

Whether a country builds viable air forces or any particular system is a function of cost, desire, and capacity, among other things. A shift in air power toward UAVs will change the cost and capacity parts of the equation, especially for countries in East Asia with vibrant commercial high-technology sectors. Many more countries could build larger air forces at the prices they spend on inferior capabilities if the unit cost of production were closer to $5 million than the hundreds of millions it costs to buy and maintain modern manned fighters. Those East Asian countries with strong robotics industries could be poised to produce new military technologies that can compete with the best the traditional powers can develop. The United States is also placed extremely well to benefit from these developments, as its extensive use of UAVs up to this point demonstrates. This shift could also help the United States ride out the upcoming period of greater fiscal constraints on its military. The lower unit costs associated with UAVs could enable more efficient military spending by the United States, actually helping it maintain its relative military power.

A word of caution is also in order here. Although it might become easier to acquire specific technologies and use them for military purposes, that is a far cry from full integration into a national military. Such integration requires an adaptive military willing to shift its core competences, something that is often beyond even the most capable militaries. In addition, the advanced communications systems, computers, and surveillance technologies such as satellites (C4ISR) needed to fully utilize these technologies might remain accessible mainly to the wealthiest states, such as China and Japan, but even in that case the diffusion of commercial technologies could ease these challenges.

The Political-Military Consequences for East Asia

A world in which cyber capabilities and robotics, with key commercial software at their core, replace industrial-age mainstays like the manned tank is one that would change the military power equation in several ways.[13] Most generally, if it becomes feasible and cost effective for East Asian countries to produce relevant amounts of military power themselves, countries will be more likely to do so.[14] Just having the capability to build more of their militaries themselves, even if some countries do not avail themselves of that option, could change security dynamics.

An implication of more countries being able to produce advanced weaponry is that it will change the decision-making calculus for the members of many traditional East Asian alliances. As the ability to produce advanced military technology at relatively lower cost spreads, it will decrease the current incentives for East Asian countries to bandwagon with the United States or otherwise ally with one another. At present, many Asian countries rely on the U.S. military to protect the commons and/or have some form of military alliance with the United States. The United States maintains the ability to project power in East Asia partly because of its edge in big-ticket conventional platforms. Engineering and systems integration challenges alone could overwhelm a state that tried to compete with the U.S. military. Even the Chinese military, whose level of technological sophistication has skyrocketed in the past decade, just recently operated a single aircraft carrier on a training voyage.[15]

One reason many countries have chosen to bandwagon with the United States and spend less on their militaries than they would in the absence of an alliance is because they lack the ability to effectively produce military power at a reasonable cost. Essentially, the requirements for being able to produce enough advanced military power make choosing an alliance not just a preference but a necessity. Of course, there are other incentives for countries to join alliances as well, ranging from political affinity to an active desire to spend less on their militaries and instead invest that money in their economies (Lai and Reiter 2000; Morrow 1991; Jervis 1985). However, if the relative cost of producing a relevant level of military power declined, it would remove one incentive for the current pattern. Even though the United States is likely to be at the forefront of these new areas of military technologies, the lower unit costs could make it more possible for East Asian countries to field their own forces.

Alternatively, the spread of the ability to produce military power at a relatively lower cost throughout East Asia could lead to a pattern of more robust, but different, alliances. With the pure capabilities reason for forming an alliance lessened, those alliances that emerged might be much more resilient and based on genuinely shared interests. For example, the United States and Japan would probably still ally because they have a great number of shared interests Yet East Asia could also end up with a series of overlapping alliances and agreements much more similar to Europe before World War I than the East Asian alliance structure of the past sixty years.

In addition to potentially shifting alliances patterns, if this change in defense production in East Asia occurs, it could also lead to a more basic change in the military balance. Although the security environment in East Asia has not been bipolar since the end of the Cold War, it has not been multipolar either. In contrast to the present situation, where the United States maintains a lead in conventional military technologies so overwhelming that most states do not even bother to build competitive capabilities, military technology in East Asia could become increasingly "lootable," as militaries build even closer ties to emerging civilian industries and quickly reverse engineer systems built by other countries. Stayne Hoff, who works for A.V. Inc. in California, stated in an interview with Peter Singer in 2007 that countries are already attempting to clone one another's UAVs and that a good signal of the desire to build a clone is when a buyer wishes to purchase only one model of a UAV (Singer 2009: 250).

The implication of these developments, in the most extreme scenario, would be to shift the balance of power toward a more multipolar environment. There are many reasons this might not occur, including but not limited to the failures of some of these advanced information-age technologies to pan out and the ability of larger powers such as the United States and China to persuade others in the region not to arm themselves to the greatest possible extent.

These changes could also be accompanied by what might look to external observers more like traditional European balance of power politics than anything else. Rather than just focusing on niche capabilities or bandwagoning with a great power, countries will potentially have the ability to produce military technologies that are much more comparable than those they can produce today. Information-age militaries might look, in a relative sense, like the armies and navies from early modern Europe until World War I—very similar in form and function, with quantity and very specific technical advantages serving to differentiate forces. This outcome would likely not depend on anything in particular the United States does; the United States would still have the ability, through its own defense investments, to stay ahead of other actors. It is just that America's relative edge might decline as a result of these potential shifts in the means of warfare.

More specifically, the power dynamics in East Asia, especially given the prevalence of territorial disputes and the possibility for competition over energy resources,[16] could begin to resemble the European land and naval balance of power in the late nineteenth and early twentieth century. What separated national militaries were small differences in quality, and especially the ability of states to ramp up production in times of need. Advantages were often quantitative or based on superior training and organization, not due to significant qualitative differences in technology. In that case, although some countries occasionally produced technological breakthroughs, like the British with the HMS *Dreadnought*, other countries had the production capabilities to mimic leading military capabilities in a relatively short period of time (Horowitz 2010). The British maintained a relative military edge at sea and the Germans maintained a relative military edge on land, but those advantages had as much to do with preexisting interests, budget prioritization, and rapid production capacity as with technological prowess. And the size of those advantages was always at risk (for more on this period, see Herrmann 1996). Even countries with alliance relationships, such as the United Kingdom and France, and Germany and Austro-Hungary, kept a wary eye on one another as they carefully monitored the military capabilities of any and all potential adversaries. These dynamics led to a classic arms race, as the weapons each country acquired to enhance its own stability just made its neighbors feel less secure, thus leading them to acquire more advanced weapons in turn.

In East Asia, more multipolar defense production capabilities could produce similar dynamics. There are many ongoing territorial disputes, such as China and Japan over the Senkaku Islands, Russia and Japan over the Kurile Islands, Japan and South Korea over islets currently controlled by South Korea, and China and many of the Association of Southeast Asian Nation countries over the South China Sea (see Chapter 1). These disputes have already engendered low-level military conflicts and ongoing tension, such as the recent dispute between China and Japan over a Chinese fishing boat that collided with a Japanese naval patrol (Jacobs 2010). China's centrality in these disputes reflects its large size and growing military power. Although other actors will have the ability to influence the security environment, especially South Korea and Japan, China will loom large.

A renewed capacity on the part of many East Asian countries to produce advanced military capabilities on their own could therefore engender new incentives for security competition. This could create classic arms-race dynamics because the relevant technologies, whether precision guided munitions, UAVs, or cyber technologies, may create standoffs if symmetrically possessed, but offensive capabilities if possessed asymmetrically (Huntington 1958; Glaser 2000). Thus, the medium term could produce a period of instability during which many more countries produce new types of military equipment, and, as in the interwar period, there is a great deal of uncertainty about how the technologies will perform on the battlefield. This does not necessarily depend on whether the technologies are inherently offensive or defensive (Van Evera 1999). Whether information-age military technologies spread in an asymmetric or symmetric pattern will therefore have a significant impact on the way they influence the probability of arms races and conflict. Then again, even a reasonably symmetric spread of military technologies through an arms race is no guarantee of peace.[17] Uncertainties about the specific applications of many of these technologies could heighten insecurity, unlike a situation in which the utility of a weapon, regardless of whether it is possessed asymmetrically or symmetrically, for either attack or defense, is relatively well known.

If all these developments happen slowly and symmetrically, there is the possibility that these trends could lead to stability.[18] For example, the spread of antiaccess weapons, technologies such as antiship missiles designed to make it harder for a country like the United States to deploy its aircraft carriers close to the coast of a potential adversary, could make it more difficult for the United States to exercise coercive power. Yet the spread of those technologies, if they occurred symmetrically, could constrain all actors. If all countries can independently produce advanced weaponry, no country will have a substantial relative edge. However, it is much more likely that these developments will happen in fits and starts with an uneven pattern of development, thus creating windows of opportunities for military action. For example, an East Asian country that figures out how to create an unmanned fighter replacement and stable communications for their unmanned fighters could potentially have a significant advantage in projecting power against an adversary with manned fighters. The issue is not just that the technology might spread unevenly. The organizational capacity of East Asian militaries to integrate the technologies will also vary. The impact of such a shift might also vary depending on which country makes such a transition. A change by China, for example, would have a much greater impact on the security environment than a similar move by Singapore. Even a shift towards UAVs by Singapore, however, might serve as a role model that triggers other shifts in East Asia.

That being said, rather than making conquest less profitable, as they have done in the current environment, multicountry supply chains in a world where many East Asian countries have greater military power might increase the incentives for conquest. Brooks argues that the enforcement of conquest would almost necessarily involve the destruction of knowledge-based productive capacity (Brooks 2005). Yet if all countries have the necessary knowledge to produce equipment, but not all have the relevant physical production fa-

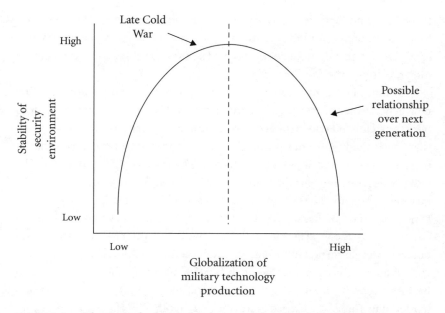

FIGURE 8.1 Theoretical relationship between globalization and security

cilities, conquest could allow a country to take over larger chunks of critical supply chains, thereby increasing its relative power.

Figure 8.1 depicts how this relationship might work, showing how it is consistent with much prior work on globalization and military power but how it also moves beyond it on the basis of some educated conjecture about potential developments in East Asia.

This figure, while suggesting the changes that could come about in the coming generation, is also slightly misleading. At high levels of globalization in the production of military technology, the shift to systems based more on commercial technologies will actually allow more countries to produce military power independently than could before. Production itself may flip, in the end, back to a situation where more local production is possible, but that production will be based on globalized knowledge.

As the leading power in East Asia at present, the United States will not be immune to this trend, as it will become harder for the United States to project power using traditional means such as carriers. There are both risks and opportunities for the United States in this scenario. As analysts like Max Boot

(2006: 455) and Peter Singer (2009: 238–239) point out, more often than not, first movers in new military technological areas end up falling behind as others figure out how to produce equipment less expensively and more effectively integrate it into their militaries.[19]

As Gilpin points out, sometimes leading powers actually end up leading new generations of development instead of falling by the wayside (Gilpin 1981). The United States also has a great number of strengths. However, given that the United States has unmatched conventional military capabilities at present, any sort of change is likely to present risks to the United States. The best possible outcome for the United States is to lead a new generation of military developments. The current American lead in UAVs demonstrates that the United States is not just sitting idly by, although some worry that the focus on counterinsurgency warfare may distract the U.S. military from focusing on potential developments in the Pacific (Mahnken 2010). Moreover, because the United States is geographically much further from probable battle spaces in East Asia than its potential adversaries, technologies that make intervention harder may hinder the United States more than others.[20] If these technologies spread in an asymmetric fashion and the United States military withdraws from the Pacific, they could provide a military advantage for states such as China over potential regional adversaries, thus increasing their coercive capacity. However, presuming that the United States stays engaged in the region, the most likely outcome of this technological diffusion is that it will raise the costs of military action for all actors.

Finally, the description here of changing security dynamics focuses on defense production and the implications for state-on-state conflict. The effects of globalization and the information age might have different, and exogenous, implications for East Asian stability when considering the ability of nonstate actors or minor powers to disrupt economic flows and generate instability. As described above, production in advanced economies is shifting to a just-in-time model by which contractors specialize in making unique components and produce only enough parts to satisfy existing orders. Technologies such as semiconductors and glass substrate for liquid crystal displays (LCDs) sometimes change so quickly that maintaining large stockpiles of products would lead only to obsolescence. The just-in-time model has spread because it is very efficient, helping companies produce high-quality products. Beginning with its genesis in the production plants of Toyota, a Japanese auto manufacturer, many Asian companies at the forefront of industrial production use just-in-time methods.

In theory, just-in-time methods diversify production risks, because there is no one location that, if destroyed, will prevent production. However, if sub-component production for new technologies becomes too specialized, diversified production could magnify the number of targets. Essentially, instead of diversified production making the system more resilient, it could make every link critical to production. In that case, all an adversary has to do to disrupt production is target the least protected aspect of a production line, which might include a dozen countries and rely on pinpoint timing in terms of delivery. To some extent, redundancy in production lines could solve this vulnerability, making sure that there are multiple suppliers for every subcomponent. However, the more complicated the production system and the more different steps required to build a completed product, the more chances an adversary might have to disrupt operations.[21]

Unfortunately, the military capabilities necessary to do this sort of disruption are already widespread in East Asia. There are multiple ways to knock industrial sites out of commission or to disrupt shipments of specialized components. The diffusion of light weaponry around the world, like AK-47s and antitank missiles, can give even small groups of nonstate actors the ability to cause physical destruction. Cyberattacks are another avenue that is not limited to nation-states at present and that are likely to diffuse even further in the future. At the other end of the destructive scale, countries like North Korea, with just a small number of nuclear weapons, have unique coercive power today compared to similarly situated states in previous generations. The destructive power of nuclear weapons means that having just one—or appearing to have just one—can give a nation significant coercive power in some situations. Only during the present period would North Korea, a minor actor according to traditional metrics, have such a great influence on international politics in its region. The further diffusion of weapons of mass destruction is likely to introduce much more instability into the international system. Minor powers, even while lacking the ability to generate significant conventional military capabilities, may increasingly have the option to build some form of weapon of mass destruction (Rosen 2006).

Conclusion

This chapter describes the potential security implications of a particular trend—the relevance of currently commercial information technologies to the future of warfare—and the way this could reshape defense production in East Asia. The information age and already-existing globalization could lead to the diffusion of technologies that allow a greater number of East Asian countries, because of their commercial expertise, to produce critical elements of military power independently. The continuation of these trends and the spillover into the military realm is far from a certainty, however.

In addition, the consequences are also uncertain. Even with the traditional (but imperfect) link between economics and military power, it should not surprise anyone if those countries that lead in new areas of technological development apply those advantages to the production of military power, but other factors might block such a shift. It is possible, for example, that the United States will be able to persuade countries to continue relying on the U.S. military for protection, even after countries gain the ability to provide for their own protection at lower cost than today. There are potential economic incentives for such behavior, especially if countries can free ride off the U.S. military presence and simultaneously build their advanced industrial base by doing vital subcontracting work for the U.S. military.

However, if the shifts described in this chapter occur, they could change the security environment in East Asia. If commercial high-technology components gain greater relevance in the military realm, the arguments in this chapter suggest that it could transform the relationship between economics and security in East Asia, thus broadening the set of countries that can produce innovative military technologies and introducing more instability into the region. Whether robotics and cybertechnologies spread symmetrically or asymmetrically, uncertainties about their potential uses in a conflict could exacerbate the security dilemma and potentially lead to arms races. Such a scenario would be far from certain, but it demonstrates that even if close economic ties in East Asia have enhanced stability over the past generation, there is no guarantee that they will do so in the future.

Finally, these trends, if played out, would also have implications for U.S.-China relations. As the largest economic power in the region, China could benefit from shifts in key military technologies toward new areas in which the United States does not already possess a seemingly insurmountable edge. Such a development could further increase China's sense of its own relative power, something already on the rise in the wake of the financial crisis in the developed world. Although such developments could make it even harder for the United States to influence Chinese behavior, it could also lead to more stability in the U.S.-China relationship if the result is a clearer picture of the future military balance of power. Much will depend, however, on how the United States reacts to the changes described in this chapter and whether it can maintain its lead in nascent technological areas such as cyberwarfare and robotics, even as the American economy continues to sputter.

Notes

The author thanks Rosella Cappella and James B. Sharp for their research assistance.

1. Ironically, nations that are not experiencing information-age development actually face a risk of brain drain: their students go to the United States or other countries in the West to get advanced degrees and then stay there.

2. These concerns have existed for decades, with modern variants of arguments about the decline in U.S. science and engineering talent, along with the potential consequences, dating back to the 1980s (McCulloch 1988). This does not mean the United States is in decline or that the United States cannot stay on the cutting edge of the next generation of science and engineering. It does mean that science and engineering capabilities in East Asia, especially, are improving rapidly.

3. Moreover, when exceptions occurred and an actor mastered a new technology well before other states, it gave them a significant advantage, like the Mongols with the composite bow.

4. The Soviet case is instructive as one example of the difficulties faced by potential adopters of carrier warfare. Despite billions of dollars invested over a few decades, the Soviets failed to build fleet carriers or sufficient carrier air forces to represent more than a minor nuisance to the U.S. Navy (Horowitz 2010).

5. My focus here is just on this one piece of his argument.

6. Among other responses to Brooks, see Kirshner (2007), Caverley (2007), and Gholz (2007). Also see Brooks' response (2007).

7. Although globalization, and especially its identification with the United States, makes the United States a target and will make it harder over time for other states to cooperate with the United States, Kirshner concludes that globalization is likely to accentuate the U.S. economic and military advantages rather than erode them (Kirshner 2006, 2008).

8. Although these sorts of agreements would likely not be the first preference of defense firms, those joint production or licensing agreements are often necessary for the recipient country to agree to the purchase.

9. The Chinese government has denied any involvement in GhostNet or other cyber operations, suggesting they result from the behavior of rogue hackers.

10. The point is not the probability of this sort of attack but the consequences for a networked military, whether it is the United States or another country.

11. This paragraph is only a snapshot of research by militaries in East Asia concerning UAVs. As far as their importance for future warfare, Shawn Brimley, a senior aide to Michèle Flournoy, U.S. undersecretary of defense for policy, writes that

unmanned combat air vehicles clearly represent the future of warfare in the air, and potentially in other areas as well (Brimley 2008–2009: 36–38).

12. It could therefore make forces more usable, potentially increasing the risk of conflict in some situations.

13. Although technologies such as the tank might still be important for land warfare, as most warfare in East Asia would likely take place in the air and on the oceans, these new technologies would be especially important.

14. A key assumption here is that, all other things being equal, countries would rather produce military power themselves than rely on other countries.

15. For more on the relationship between China's economic development and its military strategy, see Fravel (Chapter 7)

16. For a more optimistic take on the possibility for energy competition, see Cohen and Kirshner (Chapter 6).

17. Another factor not addressed here is nuclear proliferation and how that shapes the probability of conflict (Sagan and Waltz 1995).

18. Slow, symmetric military developments could produce mutual deterrence.

19. Singer (2009: 240) also cites sources from U.S. Marines analysts to science-fiction writers to Pakistani generals who argue that the United States may face a challenge to its conventional military superiority sooner than most people suspect. Andrew Krepinevich (2009) makes an even stronger claim, writing that wasteful investments could squander the United States' conventional military advantage.

20. At present, the costs to a potential American intervention in any plausible scenario are likely increasing because of the spread of antiaccess weapons.

21. One thing that could hedge against this possibility is actually the dual-use and off-the-shelf nature of technology in the coming generation, which could make it easier to build rapid substitutes even when supply disruptions occur.

Works Cited

Arquilla, John. 2003. "Patterns of Commercial Diffusion." In *The Diffusion of Military Technology and Ideas*, edited by E. O. Goldman and L. C. Eliason. Stanford, CA: Stanford University Press, 348–369.

Arvis, Jean-François, Monica Alina Mustra, John Panzer, Lauri Ojala, and Tapia Naula. 2007. *Connecting to Compete: Trade Logistics in the Global Economy*. Washington, DC: World Bank.

Boot, Max. 2006. *War Made New: Technology, Warfare, and the Course of History, 1500 to Today*. New York: Gotham Books.

Brimley, Shawn. 2008–2009. "Crafting Strategy in an Age of Transition." *Parameters* 38 (4): 27–42.

Brooks, Stephen G. 1999. "The Globalization of Production and the Changing Benefits of Conquest." *Journal of Conflict Resolution* 43 (5): 646–670.

———. 2005. *Producing Security: Multinational Corporations, Globalization, and the Changing Calculus of Conflict*. Princeton, NJ: Princeton University Press.

———. 2007. "Reflections on Producing Security." *Security Studies* 16 (4): 637–678.

Caverley, Jonathan D. 2007. "United States Hegemony and the New Economics of Defense." *Security Studies* 16 (4): 598–614.

Control Arms Campaign. 2006. *Arms Without Borders: Why a Globalised Trade Needs Global Controls*. October. Washington, DC: Control Arms Campaign: Oxfam International, Amnesty International, and International Action Network on Small Arms.

Defense Industry Daily. 2009. "South Korea Looking to Upgrade Its F-16s." *Defense Industry Daily*. May 31.

Deutch, Karl, and J. David Singer. 1964. "Multipolar Power Systems and International Stability." *World Politics* 16 (3): 390–406.

Friedberg, Aaron L. 1994. *The Political Economy of American "Renewal."* Cambridge, MA: John M. Olin Institute for Strategic Studies, Harvard University.

Gholz, Eugene. 2007. "Globalization, Systems Integration, and the Future of Great Power War." *Security Studies* 16 (4): 615–636.

Gilpin, Robert. 1981. *War and Change in World Politics*. New York: Cambridge University Press.

Glaser, Charles L. 2000. "The Causes and Consequences of Arms Races." *Annual Review of Political Science* 3: 251–276.

Global Security. 2009. "Air Force: South Korea." GlobalSecurity.org. http://www .globalsecurity.org/military/world/rok/airforce.htm (accessed January 13, 2011).

Heenan, David A. 2005. *Flight Capital: The Alarming Exodus of America's Best and Brightest*. Mountain View, CA: Davies-Black.

Herrmann, David G. 1996. *The Arming of Europe and the Making of the First World War*. Princeton, NJ: Princeton University Press.

Horowitz, Michael C. 2010. *The Diffusion of Military Power: Causes and Consequences for International Politics*. Princeton, NJ: Princeton University Press.

Huntington, Samuel P. 1958. "Arms Races: Prerequisites and Results." In *Public Policy*, edited by C. J. Friedrich and S. E. Harries. Cambridge, MA: Harvard University Press, 41–83.

International Bank for Reconstruction and Development, and World Bank. 2009. *World Development Indicators: 2009*. Washington, DC: World Bank.

Jacobs, Andrew. 2010. "China Softens Tone in Japan Dispute." *New York Times*. September 29.

Japan External Trade Organization. 2010. *Japan-China Trade in 2009 Declines for the First Time in 11 Years*. February 16. Tokyo: Japan External Trade Organization. http://www.jetro.go.jp/en/news/releases/20100217809-news (accessed January 13, 2011).

Jervis, Robert. 1985. "From Balance to Concert: A Study of International Security Cooperation." *World Politics* 38 (1): 58–79.

Kirshner, Jonathan. 2006. "Globalization and National Security." In *Globalization and National Security*, edited by Jonathan Kirshner. New York: Routledge, 1–34.

———. 2007. "The Changing Calculus of Conflict?" *Security Studies* 16 (4): 583–597.

————. 2008. "Globalization, American Power, and International Security." *Political Science Quarterly* 123 (3): 363–389.

Krepinevich, Andrew F. 2009. "The Pentagon's Wasting Assets: Washington's Fading Ability to Project Power—And What to Do About It." *Foreign Affairs* 88 (4): 18–34.

Lai, Brian, and Dan Reiter. 2000. "Democracy, Political Similarity, and International Alliances, 1816–1992." *Journal of Conflict Resolution* 44 (2): 203–227.

Mahnken, Thomas G. 2010. "Striving for Balance in Defense." *Proceedings of the United States Naval Institute* 136 (6). http://www.usni.org/magazines/proceedings/2010-06/striving-balance-defense (accessed January 27, 2012).

Markoff, John. 2009. "Vast Spy System Loots Computers in 103 Countries." *New York Times*. March 29.

————. 2010. "A Silent Attack, but Not a Subtle One." *New York Times*. September 27.

McCulloch, Rachel. 1988. "The Challenge to U.S. Leadership in High-Technology Industries (Can the United States Maintain Its Lead? Should It Try?)." NBER Working Paper W2513. http://ssrn.com/abstract=425547 (accessed January 13, 2011).

McLean, Mark. A. 2005. *Defense Procurement Strategy for a Globalized Industry*. March 18. Carlisle Barracks, PA: Army War College.

Mervis, Jeffrey. 2008. "Top Ph.D. Feeder Schools Are Now Chinese." *Science* 321 (5886): 185.

Morrow, James D. 1991. "Alliances and Asymmetry: An Alternative to the Capability Aggregation Model of Alliances." *American Journal of Political Science* 35 (4): 904–933.

Mulvenon, James C. 2004. "Taiwan and the Revolution in Military Affairs." In *The Information Revolution in Military Affairs*, edited by E. O. Goldman and T. G. Mahnken. New York: Palgrave Macmillan, 139–166.

National Opinion Research Center. 2008. *Survey of Earned Doctorates Fact Sheet*. Chicago: University of Chicago.

Newman, Richard J., Carol S. Hook, and Allegra Moothart. 2006. "Can America Keep Up? Why So Many Smart Folks Fear That the United States Is Falling Behind in the Race for Global Economic Leadership." *U.S. News and World Report*. 140 (11): 48–56.

Office of the Secretary of Defense. 2009. *Military Power of the People's Republic of China 2009: Annual Report to Congress*. Washington, DC: Office of the Secretary of Defense, U.S. Department of Defense.

Petri, Peter A. 2006. "Is East Asia Becoming More Interdependent?" *Journal of Asian Economics* 17 (3): 381–394.

Rosen, Stephen P. 2006. "After Proliferation: What to Do If More States Go Nuclear." *Foreign Affairs* 85 (5): 9–14.

Sagan, Scott D., and Kenneth N. Waltz. 1995. *The Spread of Nuclear Weapons: A Debate*. New York: Norton.

Singer, Peter W. 2009. *Wired for War: The Robotics Revolution and Conflict in the Twenty-First Century*. New York: Penguin Books.

U.S. Air Force. 2006. "Joint Direct Attack Munitions GBU 31/32/38." http://www
.af.mil/information/factsheets/factsheet.asp?id=108 (accessed January 13, 2011).

U.S. Department of Commerce. 2006. "CS Market Research: Unmanned Aerial Vehicles (UAVs)." Washington, DC: U.S. Department of Commerce and U.S. Com-
merical Service.

U.S. Department of State. 2008. *End-Use Monitoring of Defense Articles and Defense
Services: Commercial Exports FY07.* Washington, DC: U.S. State Department Di-
rectorate of Defense Trade Controls.

van Blyenbrugh, Peter. 2008. *Unmanned Aircraft Systems: The Current Situation.* May
8. Brussels: UAS ATM Integration Workshop, EUROCONTROL. http://www
.acrtucson.com/Presentations_n_Publications/pdf/6_UVS_International.pdf
(accessed January 13, 2011).

Van Evera, Stephen. 1999. *Causes of War: Power and the Roots of Conflict.* Ithaca, NY:
Cornell University Press.

Watts, Barry D. 2008. *The US Defense Industrial Base: Past, Present, and Future.* Washington, DC: Center for Strategic and Budgetary Assessments.

World Bank. 2008. *Global Economic Prospects: Technology Diffusion in the Developing
World.* Washington, DC: World Bank.

9 The China-U.S. Handshake in Northeast Asia

The Key to Dual Stability in Bilateral Ties and Regional Equilibrium

Yuan Peng

THIS CHAPTER ANALYZES THE PROSPECTS FOR COOPERATION between China and the United States, the two most influential states in East Asia. Simultaneous disruptions to both China-U.S. relations and the Northeast Asian balance of power stalled the promising six-party talks (among China, the United States, North Korea, South Korea, Japan, and Russia) that might have fostered a regional security framework based on partnerships among the great powers. The problems stemmed from the impasse over the North Korean nuclear issue; the controversial sinking of the South Korean patrol ship *Cheonan*, off the western coast of the Korean Peninsula; and the territorial dispute between China and Japan over the Diaoyu Islands (or the Senkakus, in Japanese) in the East China Sea.

With these developments, the possibility of a new Cold War is looming large, and opportunities for regional peace and stability seem increasingly unattainable. On top of this, the stable China-U.S. relationship that had lasted for nearly a decade since the September 11 terrorist attacks experienced a sudden reversal, with fissures erupting over U.S weapons sales to Taiwan, President Obama's meeting with the Dalai Lama, Google's spat with China, the renminbi (RMB) revaluations, and disagreements over sovereignty rights in the South China Sea.

This chapter argues that China-U.S. collaboration in Northeast Asia is a requisite for bilateral and regional stability. Indeed, the two forms of stability are akin to a paradoxical chicken-and-egg situation. Genuine regional peace and stability require long-term China-U.S. strategic stability; such stability, in turn, requires bilateral regional collaboration. Achieving the condition of dual stability promises to break the strategic regional impasse, thereby ushering in genuine peace and stability and expediting cooperation in the broader Asia-Pacific region.

Clashing Chinese Academic Viewpoints

Throughout contemporary history, Northeast Asia has been closely linked with China's development and core interests. It is therefore small wonder that the regional security environment and China's appropriate strategic response to that environment have long been hotly debated topics among Chinese scholars. Their assessments of who China's main opponent is in Northeast Asia can be broken into five contending schools of thought.

The first school considers Washington to be China's primary rival. A global hegemon, the United States has consistently placed a premium on maintaining a position of predominance in Northeast Asia as part of its grand strategy, with the containment of China a chief priority (Shi 2003). Tensions in the region will surely mount as China rises. Therefore, closer ties with other regional powers—South Korea, North Korea, and especially Japan – are of the utmost importance. This approach is based on the principle of "strategic focus," which calls for a new orientation toward Tokyo by moving past historical grievances (Sun et al. 2003). "Of the two evils, choose the lesser," as the saying goes.

The second school views Japan, not the United States, as China's main adversary. These scholars argue that for at least the coming decade, China will remain a regional power in the Asia-Pacific realm, not strong enough to challenge U.S. global hegemony, but certainly powerful enough to exert real strategic pressure on Japan. For more than a century, Tokyo has considered itself a regional leader and an agent for Washington. A rising China challenges Japan's core interests rather than those of the United States. As an outsider to the region, the United States is primarily interested in regional peace and stability. Therefore, a more appropriate policy option is to adopt closer ties with Washington in order to constrain Tokyo.

Scholars from the third school view the relationship between Washington and Tokyo as that between a master and a client. It is therefore nothing short of wishful thinking to believe that it is possible to drive a wedge between the two.

A more effective option for coping with the U.S.-Japan alliance is to close ranks with Moscow and Pyongyang while winning over Seoul (*Globe Weekly* 2005).

The fourth school views Pyongyang as the region's troublemaker. Its belligerence, nuclear ambition, and failure to keep pace with the times are responsible for the current volte-face in regional relations (*China.com* 2009). Thus, China should work together with the United States, Japan, South Korea, and other countries to persuade and even force North Korea to abandon its nuclear weapons program and introduce political reform. This would not only result in the denuclearization of the Korean Peninsula but also help normalize Beijing-Pyongyang relations and bring about strategic collaboration among China, the United States, Japan, and South Korea, thus ushering in a new power configuration on the Korean Peninsula (Phoenix TV 2010).

Finally, the last school proposes discarding the traditional security approaches of distinguishing friend and foe. Instead, it recommends adopting a more neutral and open viewpoint. These scholars argue that China should seek omnidimensional, multitiered cooperation in the region without identifying a specific country as a fixed threat (Liu 2010).

Meanwhile, divergent views also exist among Chinese scholars regarding the future of China-U.S. relations. Some assert that the two countries are strategic rivals, more foes than friends. These observers call for discarding the illusion of partnership and preparing for eventual competition with Washington by building up strength and convincing other countries to pressure the United States into accepting the reality of a rising China (Yan 2010). Others believe that the two powers are destined to cooperate with each other, a fate predetermined by their national attributes and by the forces of globalization, multipolarity, and the information revolution (Tao 2004). They point to the record of the past thirty years, which has proved that trans-Pacific cooperation is in the common interests of both parties. Therefore, these scholars advocate, building a community of values in addition to the current community of interests will serve as the foundation for a stable new type of strategic relationship. Still others point to the dichotomy of rivalry-containment and cooperation-engagement in U.S. policy toward China. Accordingly, they argue, China's policy toward the United States should be one of neither enemy, nor friend, and should instead rely on the two-pronged tactics of confrontation and collaboration. They insist that the question of whether the United States is friend or foe can be settled only through China's own policy initiative and bilateral interactions (Zhen 2007).

Anticlimax in Northeast Asia

A dynamic region at the turn of the twenty-first century, Northeast Asia has recently witnessed rapid progress in economic relations and increased regional economic interactions between China and Japan and between China and South Korea. Political changes have also occurred in the region. These included warming relations between Beijing and Seoul, with the latter edging toward the former and away from Washington, as well as the growing preference for Asian regionalism over the kind of subordination to the United States reflected in the foreign policies of Premiers Yasuo Fukuda and Yukio Hatoyama. Summits involving leaders of the three East Asian countries were further symbols of a positive shift in regional relations.

Unfortunately, these relations soured in 2010 as tensions heightened between China and Japan over the disputed the Diaoyu Islands and the territorial waters in the East China Sea. The illegal detention of a Chinese fishing boat nearly escalated into a much larger confrontation, with public anger in both countries expressed through protests and demonstrations. In the case of South Korea, official attitudes toward China have likewise sunk to their lowest point in nearly a decade. In contrast, South Korea's disposition toward the United States has been exceedingly positive, with repeated joint air and naval exercises turning Northeast Asia into the world's most active region in military maneuvers. As if all of these developments were not enough, the anointing of the once-mysterious Kim Jong-un, the youngest son of North Korean leader Kim Jong-il, as heir apparent added uncertainties to the already-bewildering regional scene.

Three factors are responsible for the deterioration of the regional environment. First, China's emergence as the world's second-largest economy has ended the strong-Japan-versus-weak-China dynamic that existed over the past century and caused a historical imbalance in the regional power architecture. At the same time that this shift has caused strategic frustration and even fear in Japan, it has fueled unprecedented self-confidence in China; both attitudes have been manifest in the countries' respective foreign policies. Nuclear weapons in the hands of Pyongyang, the economically weaker of the two Koreas, have also turned the tables on Seoul. The result is a drama of "diamond cutting diamond" unfolding in the Korean Peninsula.

Second, a key component in President Obama's global strategy, the renewed focus on East Asia, includes an increase in the forward deployment of U.S. military forces in Northeast Asia. This is evidenced by the efforts to transform Guam into a key military base and plans to build the Trans-Pacific Partnership. This has effectively reinvigorated the previously deteriorating U.S. alliance with Tokyo and Seoul. As a result, the schedule to transfer the wartime command of U.S. troops in Korea to the Korean military leadership has been postponed from 2012 to 2015. Japan, per Washington's insistence, also decided that the Futenma U.S. air base should remain inside Okinawa. The strategy of turning away from America and toward Asia has also been replaced by one of embracing America to constrain China, which indicates yet another shift to the right in the Japanese regime. In addition, Pyongyang recently began orchestrating small-scale reforms and an orderly leadership succession. All these developments have resulted in shocks to the power configuration in Northeast Asia.

Finally, untimely accidents added fuel to the flames. The sinking of the *Cheonan* warship tightened the Washington-Seoul alliance, impaired trust between Beijing and Seoul, and precipitated a tense standoff between the two Koreas. Similarly, disputes over the Diaoyu Islands have also brought about mutual resentment among the Chinese and Japanese publics, thus leading to deepening confusion over future bilateral relations.

In essence, these three destabilizing factors are the outcome of the unique security situation in the region. Northeast Asia is still shrouded in the shadows of the Cold War, where the U.S.-Japan and U.S.-South Korea alliance, the Korean Peninsula partition, territorial disputes, and military confrontation remain as salient as ever. Historical legacies continue to impede progress in relations between China and Japan, South Korea and Japan, and Russia and Japan. Geopolitics are also relevant. The most dynamic region in the world happens to be a focal point at which the interests of China, Russia, the United States, Japan, and the two Koreas converge into a landscape that underlies the halting progress of a promising process of economic integration. Understandably, this process failed to break the political stalemate. Instead, the divide between political and economic matters deteriorated into a minefield featuring a mixture of rivalry and restraint.

Moreover, the three outcomes capable of dampening the flashpoints— the denuclearization of the Korean Peninsula, China-Japan-U.S. dialogue, and regional security cooperation—all remain unrealistic objectives, hanging over the region like the sword of Damocles. An emboldened nuclear North Korea may further explore the road of entrenched nuclear armament and adventurism, thus making denuclearization even more unattainable and triggering a domino proliferation effect involving Japan, South Korea, and even Taiwan. The current bilateral U.S. alliances with Japan and South Korea may evolve into a multilateral troika, triggering a Beijing-Moscow-Pyongyang reaction and creating an ominous quasi-bipolar structure in Northeast Asia. Territorial and maritime disputes over the Diaoyu Islands, the Northern Islands between Russia and Japan, and the maritime borders in the East China Sea and South China Sea are all in delicate situations that may erupt into hostilities at any time. All these nightmarish scenarios require urgent breakthroughs.

A Cloudy Future in China-U.S. Ties

China-U.S. relations have also encountered difficulty more recently with the stable bilateral relationship of the past eight years grinding to a halt. Obama's initial efforts to warm relations with China turned out to be short lived with the outbreak of disputes across a spectrum of issues: quarrels over climate change, the Google dispute, the weapons sale to Taiwan, Obama's meeting with the Dalai Lama, disagreements over the exchange rate, and disputes over the Yellow and South China seas.

There are three notable features in the current China-U.S. strategic rivalry. First, the scope of the rivalry is fairly broad. Though not as sensational as the bombing of the Chinese embassy in Belgrade in 1999 and the collision of a U.S. spy plane and a Chinese fighter plane in 2001, the current conflict involves several of China's core interests, including sovereignty, security, development, and dignity, and reflects the overall strategic significance of bilateral relations. Second, the nature of the rivalry is expansive. If the previous conflicts between China and the United States were characterized as power versus superpower, the current rivalry is now more precisely characterized as one between emerging power (as China may be the world's second most powerful state) and global hegemonic power (as the United States remains the sole global superpower), a situation reminiscent of the rise and fall of great powers in modern world history. Third, the implications of the rivalry are wide ranging. The rivalry closely affects not only China's relations with its neighboring countries but also the broader diplomatic landscape as a whole. Any mishandling of the bilateral relationship is likely to have far-reaching implications for China's modernization.

These three salient features have heightened the risks in the latest rivalry between the two giants. Sparks from the Yellow Sea and the South China Sea dispute could cause the rivalry to erupt into even more severe conflicts. In the case of the RMB exchange-rate dispute, the possibility of a currency war cannot be entirely ruled out, let alone a political conflict due to clashing ideologies. The maritime disputes, the currency battle, and the ideological tussles are all intertwined, thus making the costs all the more prohibitive for the both sides and detrimental to the interests of all countries in the Asia-Pacific region.

There are four principle reasons underlying this sea change in bilateral relations between the United States and China. First, changes in the regional balance of power have caused subtle discomfort in the strategic psyche of the United States. Although China's gross domestic product (GDP) was only a tenth that of the United States a decade ago, the ratio of the former to the latter is now more than a third. Moreover, Beijing has overtaken Tokyo as the world's second-largest economy, five years ahead of the most optimistic U.S. predictions. More important is the sharp contrast in the rates of growth of the two countries. This is reflected, on the one hand, by the spectacular Beijing Olympics, the Shanghai World Expo extravaganza, the grand ceremony of the sixtieth anniversary of the founding of the People's Republic of China, and the high rate of growth amid the global financial crisis. On the other hand, the United States has been struck by the catastrophic September 11 terrorist attacks, the financial crisis, the sluggish U.S. economy, high rates of unemployment, a demoralized populace, and a once-vaunted but now under-fire Washington Consensus. Collectively, this has led to ballooning self-confidence in the case of the former versus dwindling strategic morale in the latter. In a sense, the current dynamic between the two countries is almost an exact opposite of their previous relationship, thus leading to divergent perceptions on various issues. For instance, although Washington perceives Beijing's reaction to its habitual weapons sales to Taiwan over the past thirty years as hard line, Beijing views the sales as continuous violations of Washington's own promise. Thus comes the trial of strength and exchanges of anger.

Second, as part of its so-called return to Asia, the United States has shifted its strategic focus away from antiterrorism and toward coping with emerging powers, particularly China. Since Barack Obama became president, the previous U.S. policies of modest strategic retrenchment and restraint have been replaced by excessive overseas expansion. And with U.S. domestic politics focused exclusively on the economy, rapidly growing China has become a convenient scapegoat for the U.S. economy's downturn, especially in the 2010 midterm elections.

Third, accidents and the role of third parties have precipitated an outburst of tensions. The sinking of the *Cheonan*, for instance, resulted in the U.S.–South Korea joint military exercises that occurred at China's doorstep in the Yellow Sea, infuriating Beijing. Likewise, Vietnam and Malaysia have facilitated the U.S. return to Asia, enabling it to battle China by proxy through its exercise of smart power.

Last, rising nationalism in China has added a new, pluralistic dimension to its diplomacy, which must take into account the diversity of interest groups. This has made it increasingly difficult for the Chinese leadership to formulate and implement a top-down, relatively unified, and consistent policy toward the United States.

All this indicates that the current tensions may persist for some time. Even if interactions between the militaries and leaders of the two countries temper occasional outbreaks, the bilateral strategic rivalry may persist and present considerable risks. Similarly, military conflicts may occur across the domains of maritime, outer space, and cyberspace. Given the profound transformations in the domestic political and social conditions in the two countries, disputes, once ignited, will be difficult to control. Moreover, the financial standoff centered on the exchange rate of the RMB and the opening of China's capital market, which, if unchecked, could spark a currency war having adverse effects on Asian finance from the euro and the yen. In addition, the deep suspicions of one another as strategic competitors and even adversaries that are advanced in Chinese and American think tanks, if not defused in time, may result in a self-fulfilling prophesy. As such, overcoming the current bottleneck in search of a path toward long-term strategic stability is of utmost importance.

Dual Stability: Necessity versus Feasibility

The current challenges in Northeast Asia are inherently related to the sudden chill in China-U.S. relations. The continuing tensions between the two capitals have resulted in diverging perspectives in assessing regional developments. Although Washington unequivocally believed Seoul's allegations regarding the sinking of the *Cheonan*, charges that Pyongyang refuted as trumped up, Beijing stood in favor of further authoritative investigations by other countries. From the view of the Chinese leadership, it was ill advised for the White House to jump to hasty conclusions and, worse still, to resort to twisting Pyongyang's arm. Given a relatively stable China-U.S. relationship before and after the accident, a turnaround should have been possible. Instead, a tit-for-tat ensued, beginning with joint U.S.–South Korea air and naval exercises directed against North Korea and media hype regarding the deployment of the USS *George Washington* aircraft carrier to participate in the military exercises in the Yellow Sea. This, in turn, sparked strong resentment in the Chinese military, which perceived the exercises as a U.S. effort to block the Chinese Navy under the pretext of the *Cheonan* accident. It then prompted a chain reaction with an even closer Washington-Seoul alliance and a revival of Beijing-Pyongyang relations. As another example, the dispute between the United States and China over the South China Sea led to a divergence over the East China Sea with Washington's pronounced partiality toward Tokyo and the resulting standoff between the United States and Japan on one side and China on the other.

Incidentally, were China and Japan to emulate the precedent of bilateral cooperative agreements established by the disputants in the North Sea, they could jointly develop the hydrocarbon deposits around the disputed Diaoyu Islands, which have become a symbol of surging nationalism. The joint development of the fields where the China-Japan maritime boundary claims overlap could help bridge the dispute. The disputes over sovereignty in the South China Sea could be similarly resolved. Yet intervention by the United States, despite its status as an outsider to the conflict, has aggravated the problems and stoked the smoldering flames.

Indeed, outside interference has not benefited any of the Northeast Asian countries. The following ifs substantiate this argument. If the *Cheonan* accident had not occurred, China-U.S. détente would have persisted; if the quarrel over the Diaoyu Islands had not occurred, China-U.S.-Japan interactions would have been smoother; if Kim Jong-il had not visited China twice in a span of two months, there would have been less concern in the Pentagon over the recent Hu-Kim embrace. You see wheels within wheels! In all of this, we can clearly perceive the logic of dual stability in China-U.S. ties and in Northeast Asia. The key to cracking the dual catch-22 of synchronized deteriorations in China-U.S. relationship and in the Northeast Asia landscape lies in cutting the Gordian knot by fostering genuine regional collaboration between the two great powers.

China-U.S. collaboration in Northeast Asia, a handshake between the two powers, is in fact within easy reach. In Central Asia, there is already the Shanghai Cooperation Organization, a relatively mature institution targeting terrorism, separatism, and religious extremism. Even if the United States were to participate in some capacity in the future, a China-U.S. agreement in this region would be unthinkable. In Southeast Asia, there are the even more mature ASEAN+1 (the ten ASEAN countries plus China, Japan, or South Korea), the ASEAN+3 (ASEAN plus China, Japan, and South Korea), and the China-ASEAN Free Trade Agreement. A China-U.S. agreement here would have to usurp ASEAN leadership and confound the already-complicated territorial and maritime disputes in the South China Sea. In Northeast Asia, however, the flashpoint awaits a China-U.S.-led multilateral security mechanism that could complement the alliances between the United States and Japan, and between the United States and South Korea. Such a framework could break the Cold War straitjacket that has long prevented regional growth. Furthermore, both sides share extensive common interests in the region: the denuclearization of the Korean Peninsula, the establishment of a multilateral cooperation mechanism that addresses the interests of both parties, and the economic integration of Northeast Asia as an avenue for a windfall of reciprocal benefits.

Moreover, both sides possess respective strengths and interests that provide the groundwork needed for regional teamwork. Although far ahead of China in absolute strength, the core interests of the United States lay not in the Asia-Pacific region but elsewhere. Historically, the country has never exercised real control over this region with the exception of indirect leverage through its alliances with Tokyo and Seoul. Therefore, when possible, it seeks to avoid an excessive input of resources and energy here at the expense of strategic deployments in the Middle East, Central Asia, South Asia, and Southeast Asia. This explains the consistent U.S. interest in maintaining regional order. By contrast, despite its inferior position, the same region is the apple of China's eye, affecting the country's core interests of survival, security, and prosperity. Beijing has therefore been willing to invest heavily in the region because of its relevance to its surrounding security environment and the resurgence of Northeast China. Thus, such asymmetry in strength, interests, and strategic inputs may actually function as a starting point for bilateral strategic collaboration.

In addition, the groundwork for such an agreement already exists. Mutual political trust has been built up during the course of the several rounds of six-party talks concerning the North Korean nuclear issue. Repeated efforts to explore the possibility of a Northeast Asia security cooperation mechanism and the feasibility of a trilateral China-U.S.-Japan strategic dialogue have also been undertaken. Further, it is especially noteworthy that none of the other regional players—Japan, Russia, and the two Koreas—desires a continuation of the ongoing tensions. This provides the proposed China-U.S. nexus with the requisite external environment in which to move forward.

Road Map for Collaboration

A novel framework for strategic stability in Northeast Asia is needed. Neither the experience of the West nor existing international relations theories can explain China's rise or prevent the fatal rise and fall of great powers in modern history. Unlike the former Soviet Union, China does not possess the comprehensive national strength to militarily confront the United States and is unable to achieve a Cold War–like bipolar stability based on nuclear threats. Similarly, China is unable to have a relationship with the United States like that of the European Union or Japan, easily acquiescing to U.S. leadership, because of its ideology, values, and domestic system. Thus, both China and the United States will need to blaze a trail by fostering long-term strategic stability. Unlike the rise of previous great powers in modern history, China's ascendance is characterized by the following special features.

Rather than an isolated phenomenon, China's resurgence comprises a part of the collective rise of the non-Western world. This synchronic ascendance of various regional blocs also includes India, Russia, Brazil, Turkey, and South Africa. Thus, rather than respond with a hysterical outcry regarding the supposed structural threat emanating from a rising China, the United States and the West should accept the reality of such a collective rise. Indeed, the only way forward is through consultation and cooperation. China has adopted an independent path of peaceful socialist development with Chinese characteristics, a path that results in integration into rather than separation from the world system. China's successful experience over the past three decades will certainly guide its handling of its relations with the outside world through cooperation and not conflicts.

China's rapid rise has not been accompanied by a steep decline of the United States. The latter's current economic, financial, and security predicament

The China-U.S. Handshake in Northeast Asia   247

does not spell the loss of its supremacy in military, cultural, educational, scientific, and technological fields—advantages not to be replaced for a considerable period of time to come. Rather, the current U.S. decline results from the setbacks to its hegemonic behavior and the weakening of its capabilities to dominate the world through brawn rather than brains. This, however, does not mean a loss of its absolute power. Indeed the rise of China and the decline of the United States is not a zero-sum game. On the contrary, a win-win outcome is entirely possible, especially in a world undergoing globalization, multipolarity, and the information revolution.

All of this indicates that China and the United States can avoid the seemingly cyclical pattern of history, which predicts that military conflicts herald the rise and fall of great powers. A new opportunity presently exists for China and the United States to collaborate fully in the transition of the international system, including on matters such as the reform of the United Nations, the restructuring of the international financial system, the reshaping of international security under a banner of denuclearization, and the fostering of world governance characterized by the climate-change summits.

China's revitalization represents the arrival of a regional power in the Asia-Pacific realm. To reverse its decline and preserve its strategic initiative, the United States is pursuing a strategic retrenchment on its own by shifting its strategic center of gravity eastward toward the Asia-Pacific region. In other words, the two countries are facing a strategic task of managing their peaceful coexistence over the coming five to ten years, the success of which bears directly on the long-term strategic stability between them. In this sense, their collaboration in Northeast Asia represents a historical logic.

Yet Northeast Asia remains burdened by its history during the Cold War, and successfully moving beyond this legacy is a significant precondition for genuine cooperation. The U.S.-Japan military alliance, along with the forward deployment of the U.S. military, is the hallmark of this Cold War legacy. Therefore, promoting trilateral strategic dialogue between China and the U.S.-Japan alliance is of vital significance in preventing the continued rivalry, just as the ties between NATO and Russia presaged the end of the Cold War in Europe. This has certainly been recognized by scholars and officials from the three countries who have been exploring its possibility in recent years through track-one and track-two diplomacy, and have even sought to test the idea with the press. Unfortunately, domestic politics and accidents have nipped this initial venture in the bud. In the wake of the China-U.S. disagreement over the Yellow Sea, however, and the turmoil over the Diaoyu Islands, the need for trilateral dialogue has taken on additional importance and urgency. Such a dialogue not only could enable Northeast Asia to step out from underneath the shadow of the Cold War but also could allow the three countries to hedge against unanticipated disputes in the future. And, building on this precedent, other strands of dialogue, such as among China, the United States, and South Korea, or among China, the United States, and Australia, may follow.

The other obvious issue requiring China-U.S. collaboration is the denuclearization of the Korean Peninsula and the broader region of Northeast Asia. The six-party talks have proved the most successful and effective mechanism for dialogue. Premised on Pyongyang's readiness to return to the negotiating table, China and the United States should seize the opportunity to reinvigorate the six-party talks by moving beyond the *Cheonan* accident and temporarily setting aside the abductions of Japanese hostages by North Korea. Gaining control of the North Korean nuclear issue is the first step toward encouraging Pyongyang to abandon nuclear weapons altogether. At the same time, China and the United States should try to prevent Japan and South Korea's statements of possibly "going nuclear" from becoming policy. Indeed, only denuclearization can genuinely safeguard peace, stability, and development in the region.

Although the original source of the faltering progress of the proposed regional security mechanism is Pyongyang's unwillingness to abandon its nuclear ambitions, the situation has since become far more complicated. The regional security landscape has expanded beyond the North Korean nuclear issue to include strategic disputes among nearly all the members of the region. Such a complex environment requires that China and the United States depart from the legacies of the Cold War and embrace an innovative mechanism for security cooperation in Northeast Asia that considers the security concerns and interests of all the regional parties. Such a mechanism would usher in a future-oriented political atmosphere of enduring peace and prosperity. In light of this, it is perhaps worth concluding with an ancient Chinese verse that captures both the current challenges and opportunities for Northeast Asia: "The hills and mountains have no end, there seems to be no road beyond; but dim with willows, bright with flowers, another village appears: one has a sudden glimpse of hope in the midst of bewilderment."

Works Cited

China.com. 2009. "DPRK's Intransigence Will Only Aggravate the Situation." http://english.china.com/.

Globe Weekly. 2005. "China-Russia Joint Military Exercises Drawing Worldwide Attention as Reflecting Great Power Politics, Interview with Yan Yuetong, an International Affairs Expert." August 31.

Liu, Jiayong. 2010. "Discarding the Unscientific US Security Model for a Sustainable Security Concept." http://www.chinanews.com.

Phoenix TV. 2010. "China Feels Hidden Risks from US-Japan Pressures on the DPRK."

Shi, Yinhong. 2003. "The Principle of Strategic Concentration and Its Significance." *Journal of World Economics and Politics* 7: 1–3.

Sun, Shulin, Ma Licheng, Shi Yinghong, and Lu Shiwei. 2003. "China-Japan Interaction Calls for a New Thinking." *Current Affairs Report* 7: 13–23.

Tao, Wenzhao. 2004. "China and America: Dilute Contradictions for Enhanced Cooperation." *Current Affairs Report* 4: 39–41.

Yan, Xuetong. 2010. "China and America: For More Than Friend." *National Herald Leader.* March 23.

Zheng, Bijian. 2007. "China's Path of Peaceful Development and the Future of China-U.S. Relations." In *Thoughts in the New Century,* edited by Bai Yan. Beijing: Research Press.

Index

Italic page numbers indicate material in tables or figures.

SOMTC+3 Consultations, APT, 100
South America, 163
South China Sea: ASEAN Regional
    Forum on, 29; cooperation on seis-
    mic soundings, 106; Hillary Clinton
    on, 32n6; overall relations, 137,
    244; sovereignty disputes, 105–107,
    126–129, 241
Southern Common Market, 83
Southern Kuril Islands (Northern
    Territory), 134–137
South Korea. See Korea, South
South Vietnam. See Vietnam
sovereignty: bargaining, 49–50, 55,
    56–58; claims of, 10–12, 108; mean-
    ing of, 50; pooled, 49, 79
Soviet Cartography Line, 121
Soviet Union. See Russia/Soviet Union
spillover effect, 96–99; of information
    technology, 212, 217, 230; on non-
    traditional security cooperation,
    99–104, 114; policy maker resistance
    to, 68
SRPA (self-managed reserve pooling ar-
    rangement), 45
stability-instability paradox, 32n9
statist-nationalist coalitions, 71
steel battleship era, 215
stock indexes, international effect of,
    34n15
Strait of Hormuz, 151, 161
Strait of Malacca, 153, 157–158, 161–162,
    192
"strategic focus" principle, 237
Stuxnet virus, 220
submarines, 166, 215
Sudan, 157, 165
Summers, Robert, 32n10
Sunda Strait, 159
supply chains, internationalization of,
    216, 226–227
surveillance mechanisms, 43–44

systems integration, 215–216, 226

TAC (Treaty of Amity and Cooperation
    in Southeast Asia), 105
Taishet, 164
Taiwan (Republic of China): 1995–1996
    crisis, 129, 166; Chinese concerns
    about energy blockades over, 153,
    158–159; cyberwarfare-related re-
    search, 219; ECFA, 77–78; effect on
    China-Japan relations, 132; exclu-
    sion from regional organizations,
    86; growth rate, 18; intraregional
    trade, 46; leader in semiconductors,
    213; leader in substrate glass pro-
    duction, 213; relations with United
    States, 11, 24, 236, 241–242; relations
    with Vietnam, 124. See also China-
    Taiwan relations
Taiwan Relations Act (1979, U.S.), 11,
    34n16
Tajikistan, 139, 198
Takeshima (Dokdo) dispute, 132–134
Taliban, 198
tank warfare, 229, 232n13
Tanner, Scott, 198
tax rebates, 167n1
technology transfer, 218–219
territorial sea baseline claims, 106
terrorism, 100–101, 103, 161, 182, 216
Thailand: annual growth rate, 18; APT
    Health Ministers Meeting in, 101;
    "Asian Panama Canal," 161; partici-
    pation in CMIM, 44; Preah Vihear
    conflict with Cambodia, 9, 67, 84,
    139; relations with United States, 17,
    34n16. See also ASEAN
theoretical perspectives on political
    economy of national security, 14–17
"thin gruel" of Asian regional organiza-
    tions, 4
Tibet, 189, 199

trade: benefits of, 14–15; China sur-
passing United States in trade with
Japan, 21; intraregional, 75–76; key
conditions conducive to, 49–50; political impediments to, 47–50
traditional and nontraditional security,
187–189
transformation by economic interdependence, 73
transgovernmental elite networks, 58
transnational crime, 98–101, 106
Transneft, 157
Trans-Pacific Partnership, 240
Treaty Line (China/Soviet Union), 121
Treaty of Amity and Cooperation in
Southeast Asia (TAC), 105
Treaty of Peace and Friendship (China/
Japan), 129
Treaty of Portsmouth, 135
trust: affective, 58; momentary, 58;
reputational, 58
tsunami (Indian Ocean, 2004), 102,
103–104

UAVs (unmanned aerial vehicles), 211,
220–222, 224
UN Commission on the Limits of the
Continental Shelf, 127
UN Convention on the Law of the Sea,
106, 130
unequal treaties, 121
unipolarity after Cold War, 17
United Kingdom, 215, 225
United Nations, role of, 75
United States: 2010 midterm elections,
243; administration of Diaoyu
Islands, 129; administration of
Dokdo, 132; aircraft carriers, 32n8,
212, 215, 223, 226; annual trade with
East Asia, 6–7, 7; command of the
commons, 193; consumption of oil
in, 152; during crisis of 1997–1998,

41; dependence on oil, 152; effects of
2008 global recession, 242; energy
strategy, 149–153; and future military balance of power, 228, 231n7,
232n19; internationalization of
defense production, 216, 226–227;
intervention in South China Sea disputes, 127; naval presence in Persian
Gulf, 151; preference for bilateral
ties, 51–52; relations with East Asia,
51, 97, 217; relations within sphere
of influence of, 133; relations with
South Korea, 22, 239, 240, 243,
244–245; relations with Taiwan,
11, 24, 236, 241–242; relations with
Vietnam, 11, 34n16, 141n5, 243; as
sole superpower, 2, 17, 217, 224, 241;
still the largest economy, 20–22, 215;
strategic petroleum reserve, 151; as
"ultimate security guarantor," 108,
112; use of UAVs, 222; U.S. Seventh
Fleet, 166. See also U.S.-China relations; U.S.-Japan relations
University of California, Berkeley, 214
unmanned aerial vehicles (UAVs), 211,
220–222, 224
Unmanned Vehicle Systems
International, 220
urbanization, 181
Urumqi, 189, 199
U.S.-China relations, 17–23; during
and after Soviet breakup, 2–3; both
opposed to AMF, 52; and China
bilateral economic ties, 22–23;
China holding U.S. debt, 23; China
national security zone incidents, 12;
Chinese academic viewpoints on,
237–238; collision of spy plane and
Chinese fighter, 241; first consultation over Asia-Pacific affairs, 127;
future of, 230–231, 236, 241–246;
possibility of U.S. blockade over